Thomas Wallace Knox

The Siberian Exiles

A Novel

Thomas Wallace Knox

The Siberian Exiles
A Novel

ISBN/EAN: 9783337041533

Printed in Europe, USA, Canada, Australia, Japan

Cover: Foto ©ninafisch / pixelio.de

More available books at **www.hansebooks.com**

CARL PUSHKIN'S ARRIVAL AT THE PRISON.—See *Page* 14

A Novel.

BY

COL. THOMAS W. KNOX,

*Author of "Overland Through Asia," "The Boy Travellers,"
etc., etc.*

WITH ILLUSTRATIONS BY VICTOR PERARD.

NEW YORK:
ROBERT BONNER'S SONS,
1893.

THE SIBERIAN EXILES.

CHAPTER I.

A MIDNIGHT ARREST IN RUSSIA.

"OPEN the door! Open in the name of the Czar!"

This summons was accompanied by a loud knocking, which was audible at a considerable distance. It was at the door of Carl Pushkin, known among his neighbors and friends, as Carl Pavloff, or Carl, the son of Paul.

There was a momentary pause, but the door was not opened. Again the summons was shouted and the knocking was resumed. The first knocking was with a clenched hand and the second with the hilt of a sword. One, two, three, half a dozen blows were given, and then the door was opened from within. By the light of a candle in his left hand, a half-dressed man of middle age, was revealed just inside the door-way, his face blanched with fright at the midnight summons, which might be of terrible import.

With the opening of the door, the one who had uttered the summons, stepped inside.

His uniform showed him to be an officer of the Imperial Police, in whose hands are supposed to repose the safety and well-being of the Russian Empire. Several decorations were displayed on the breast of his closely-buttoned coat, indicating that he had performed services at different times or possessed sufficient influence to secure these marks of distinction. Two gendarmes or soldiers, who carried rifles with fixed bayonets, were close at his heels, and a little distance from the house, were four mounted Cossacks, one of whom was holding the horse of their commander.

Evidently, the party was prepared for resistance, if any were offered, as the four Cossacks kept their hands on their weapons, as though awaiting a signal.

"What is wanted, Your Excellency?" said the man with the candle, as the other entered the door.

"Carl Pushkin," said the officer, "I arrest you, in the name of the Czar. It is the order of His Imperial Majesty."

The man bowed his head and made no reply. Useless to ask for what reason he had been thus aroused at midnight, and placed under arrest. The will of the Emperor is supreme, and whatever he commands must be obeyed, at least, such is the belief of his loyal and devoted subjects. But not all who live beneath the shadow of the wings of the Two-headed Eagle can be counted as loyal and devoted, and sometimes they venture to deny the autocratic power of the "Great White Czar."

In which category should the prisoner be considered? We shall see at a later period in our story.

His hand trembled as it clutched the candle and his face grew whiter than it had been before. From the room beyond the hall-way where he stood came the sound of wailing, and it did not require a practised ear to discern that the grief-stricken one was a woman.

The officer paused until Carl could sufficiently control himself to ask if he must go at once.

"Yes, see chass," (immediately) was the reply.

Without a word, Carl turned towards the inner room and was followed by the officer. The soldiers remained where they had been standing. Carl embraced his wife and children, who had been roused by the knocking at the door and the voice of the officer, and the air was filled with lamentations. The leave-taking was so long that the officer grew impatient; he was accustomed to scenes of this kind and remained quite unmoved by the grief that surrounded him.

"Poshol! Poshol! (Hurry up! hurry up!)" he exclaimed, "we cannot be waiting here all night. Hurry up!"

The farewells were cut short. Carl donned his coat and cap, took his overcoat from a peg, where it had been hanging in the hall, tightened his waist-belt, slipped on his boots, and otherwise completed his toilet, which had been partially and hastily made before he opened the door. Then, after another quick embrace of his family, he signified his readiness to follow his captor. The latter led the way to the door, gave his prisoner into the custody of the soldiers, ordered that no one should come out of the house until morning, and then closed the door and joined the waiting Cossacks.

The incident just described, occurred in the "gubernium " or province, of Tambov, in Russia, in the year 18—. Tamboy is in that part of the empire known as Great Russia, and is almost wholly devoted to agriculture and the raising of cattle and horses for the markets of Moscow and Nijni Novgorod. In some of the larger towns there are factories for the production of cloth, and there are distilleries, forges, and a few other establishments where manufacturing is carried on. Of all the manufacturing industries of Tambov, that of distilling is the most important ; and the same may be said of many other provinces of Russia. Distilling is encouraged, because it brings a high revenue to the government ; the consumption of the product of the distilleries is encouraged for the reason that a people sunk in drunkenness is more easily controlled than a temperate, thoughtful and ambitious one. The man who leads a riotous, idle and besotted life, is rarely suspected of disloyalty ; suspicion falls only on him who is abstemious, industrious and upright in his ways of life.

Carl Pushkin was a thrifty and prosperous farmer or small landholder of Tambov, about twenty miles from the provincial capital, which is of the same name as that of the province. He was a careful and intelligent cultivator and, furthermore, derived a good revenue from a mill, which he built, for grinding the grain produced in the neighborhood. He had a fair education, in fact, a good one for a Russian of his class, and his advice was often sought by his neighbors and the peasants in the nearest villages.

In the opinion of all who knew him, he was so much occupied with his farming and the work of his mill, that he had little time for anything else. He subscribed for the weekly newspaper, published at Tambov, and also for the Moscow *Gazette*, but the sum of all the intelligence received from these publications was not great. A Russian newspaper can only publish what is permitted by the censor, and sometimes it is restricted to little else than advertisements, essays upon agriculture and manufacturing, and the movements of court officials. The rigor of the censorship varies from time to time, publication being permitted in one year of what is prohibited in another. At the time of which we write, the censorship was severe, as revolutionary movements were in progress and many persons were under suspicion. Consequently, the news which reached Carl Pushkin's house was not of an exciting character, especially as the two papers for which he subscribed were known as devoted servants of the Imperial Government.

Carl's father was a landed proprietor at Tambov at the time of the emancipation of the serfs, in 1861, and, like many others of his class, he was ruined by the liberation of the men who had formerly been obliged to give a considerable portion of their time to the cultivation of his estate, with very little reward for their labor. Probably his intemperate habits and his fondness for the gaming table, had more to do with his financial ruin than the Emancipation Act of Alexander II., but the latter served as an excuse for all kinds of misfortunes.

At the death of the elder Pushkin, Carl came into possession of the estate, which was heavily burdened with debt, and evinced to the most casual observer the bad way in which it had been managed. Carl sold a part of the estate to pay the most pressing of the debts and settle the claims of his brothers and sisters, and by the time he had put his affairs into a manageable shape, there was not a great deal to manage. But his industry and intelligence were rewarded as the years went on, so that he was, as already stated, in prosperous circumstances at the time when our story opened with his summary arrest.

Near where the four Cossacks were standing, there was a tarantass or travelling carriage, to which two horses were attached. At a word from the officer, Carl stepped inside the vehicle ; one of the soldiers took the place at his side and the other mounted the box with the driver. Two of the Cossacks took their position in front of the tarantass, and the other two in the rear with the officer; then the order to march was given, and at a brisk trot the party quickly disappeared in the direction of the town of Tambov.

A brisk trot over the ordinary road of Russia means a great deal of jolting. The tarantass is a large, roomy carriage, bearing a general resemblance to a victoria of rude construction. It has a hood that can be lowered or raised according to the condition of the weather and the desire of the occupants to have the air admitted or excluded ; an apron is usually attached to the front of the hood, so that the occupants can shut themselves in as completely as in a brougham or a landau. Instead of being supported on steel or leather springs, it rests on two poles, which extend from one axle to the other, and these poles are sometimes ten or twelve feet in length. There is a fair amount of elasticity to these poles, but when compared with the steel springs of English or American vehicles, they leave much to be desired.

Despite the jolting, which often threw him violently against his companion and guard, Carl Pushkin was very busy with his thoughts during that night's ride to the provincial capital. He ran over every act of his life, especially during the past few years, and endeavored to settle upon the cause of his arrest. It was evident that some one had denounced him and brought him into his present trouble.

"I cannot remember that I've wronged any of my neighbors or anybody else; at any rate, I've tried to deal justly by all. Of course, I may have harmed somebody without intending it, and so caused myself to be denounced.

"I've submitted to every extortion of the officials without a complaint; it was the easiest way out of the difficulty and the cheapest. Every time one of them has wished to 'borrow' of me, he has found me ready to 'lend,' and not one of the loans has ever been repaid, nor have I asked that it should be.

"Well, it may be that—but, no, that can hardly be possible; I'll try to think of something else."

In due time the tarantass stopped in front of the provincial prison of Tambov. Day was just breaking, or rather, the first streaks of dawn were visible in the East, but there was hardly sufficient light to discern more than the outlines of the grim walls that rose against the sky. Sentinels were pacing up and down the pathway in front of the doors of the prison; the night was chilly and each soldier wore a long, gray overcoat, which forms a part of the military uniform from one end of the empire to the other. Like ghosts, the gray forms came and went, as the men moved along the space marked out for their ceaseless tramp, until the hour for their relief. Like a silhouette against the sky, another sentinel was visible, pacing his round upon the top of the prison wall. So much vigilance betokened that every precaution was taken against the escape of the unwilling dwellers inside these walls of stone.

The Cossacks closed around the tarantass and the order to descend was given. The two soldiers stepped to the ground and Carl followed their example; then, with a soldier at each side, and preceded by the officer, who had dismounted and given his horse once more to the care of the Cossacks, Carl reached the door of the prison. As he halted and waited for the opening of the portal, Carl Pushkin shuddered as the question rose in his mind:

"How long shall I remain in these walls, and where shall I go when I leave them behind?"

CHAPTER II.

SCENE AFTER PUSHKIN'S ARREST.

There was little sleep in the house of the Puskins for the rest of the night of Carl's arrest. Mother and children were wakeful with grief at the calamity which had come so suddenly upon them. The elder children tried to console their mother with hopeful words, and partially succeeded at intervals, but whenever she gave play to her thoughts her sorrow broke out afresh.

"Don't cry, mother," said Ivan, the eldest, a robust young man of twenty, as he twined his arms about her neck. "Don't cry, I'm sure there's a great mistake somewhere, and it will soon be found out. Father will be back here with us in a day or two."

Nadia, a rosy-cheeked girl of nineteen, added her efforts to those of her brother, and gave utterance to hopes like those we have just heard from his lips.

"Yes, yes," was the reply, "there has been a mistake, of course, there has been a mistake. But mistakes are not easily corrected in this country, and your poor father may be years in prison before the blunder that sent him there is found out."

"No, mother, it can't be as bad as that, indeed it can't," said Ivan. "I'm sure we'll see dear father at home in a day or two, I'm sure of it."

The mother was about to speak, but prudence restrained her and she was silent. It is dangerous for a Russian to talk about politics, even to the members of his own household, lest they, innocently, reveal to the ears of a prying spy, something that has been said in an unguarded moment.

The woman's despondency and silence were construed by Ivan to mean that possibly his mother might know of something that had compromised his father with the authorities. He was an intelligent youth, had a good idea of the political condition of the country for one of his years, and knew quite well that a very trivial circumstance is sufficient to bring the police about a household. And when the officers of the Imperial police make their appearance, they do pretty much as they like.

His faith in his father's loyalty and integrity were as firm as a rock, and the most positive evidence would have been required to shake it in the smallest degree. When his mother remained silent, and showed so much trepidation, he felt that she was needlessly alarmed, and redoubled his efforts to comfort her.

"Don't feel so badly, dear mother," he said pleadingly. "Father knows all the officials at Tombov and I've heard him speak of them as his friends. Just as soon as they find he has been arrested, they will help him out of his trouble and we shall be out of ours. I'm as certain as I am of anything in the world, that he will be back at home before the week is out."

Madame Pushkin shook her head and made no reply.

She could not share in her son's hopefulness, but did not wish to say so in words.

"I will go to Tambov to-morrow, and see the governor," said Ivan, "and I know he will set this matter right."

"Yes, you and I will go with Ivan," said Nadia, "and I am sure the governor will send father home with us when he sees how much we miss him and how we are distressed at what has happened."

In spite of her grief, the mother smiled at Nadia's suggestion, which evinced complete ignorance of Russian official ways. That the governor of the province would be influenced by the tears and pleadings of women might be a very natural thought for a young girl, but it was quite contrary to practical experience.

The typical official of Russia is not a man of tender heart; rather is he cast in the mould of the tiger or the crocodile, and the emotions of pity or sympathy are quite unknown to him. He is a worthy disciple of Peter the Great, whose name is famous in history for what he accomplished in bringing his country out of barbarism and making it one of the nations of Europe. Was Peter cast in a tender mould? All the world knows how he worked as a common laborer in shipyards, that he might instruct his people in maritime ways; but does all the world know that he sent his own son to be executed? And does it know that he personally assisted on the scaffold and wielded the sword when the soldiers who rebelled against his authority were beheaded? The official for whom the great Peter stood as a model, is unlikely to heed the tears or the supplications of women, especially when he remembers that his illustrious prototype imprisoned his own sister in a convent until her death.

The younger children clung to their mother's side and joined their tears with hers. Though too young to comprehend the trouble that had come upon the household, they realized that something terrible had happened, they saw their father taken away by the soldiers after he had embraced and kissed them, and when they saw their mother and Ivan and Nadia weeping, they joined in the general lamentation. The sorrow spread to all the servants of the household, and to none was it more poignant than to the old nurse, Francesca.

She had been with the family since her birth. She was a serf on the estate before the Emancipation; she had held Carl in her arms when he was an infant, had seen him reach manhood, saw the evil ways into which his father fell, was present at his death, and saw the young master take possession of the remnant of the property and build it up to its present condition of prosperity. She had cared for his children, one by one, had loved him as an old servant loves a kind master, and knew that as long as he lived she would never be turned away.

Francesca cried as did the rest, and for a while her grief was uncontrolled. But at length her sense of responsibility occurred to her, and she dried her tears as quickly as possible.

"Come away, my dears," she said to the younger children, as they clung to their mother's side. "Come away and go with me."

"Go with Francesca, children," said the mother. "Go with her and leave me with Ivan and Nadia."

They obeyed, though reluctantly. Russian children are trained to obedience far more than those of England or America. The "spoiled child," so common in

American households, is not easy to find in the land of the Czar; and as for the "*enfant terrible*" he is practically unknown.

Francesca led away her charges after each had kissed their mother and tenderly embraced her. Soon as they were alone with the nurse, the eldest said:

"What is all the trouble about, Matiushka, (Little Mother) and why does mamma cry so? Why did the soldiers take papa away?"

"That's what I don't know, my darlings," was the reply, "but I am sure he will be back again very soon."

"Is mother as sure as you are, Matiushka, and is Ivan and Nadia?"

"Certainly, my darlings; didn't you hear Ivan say so?"

"Yes, I know he said so, but if papa is coming back soon, why does mother cry so hard?"

"That I cannot tell you, darling, but I suppose it's because it all came so suddenly. Now go to sleep, like good children, and don't think any more about it. Your grandpapa was taken away just like this, two or three times that I remember, and he came back the next day."

"Oh! if that's so, I'll go to sleep. Good-night!" And in a few minutes the child was sleeping peacefully.

Francesca was not altogether truthful in comparing the arrest of Carl Pushkin to the arrests, by no means unfrequent, of his father, as the latter were the result of his performances while grossly intoxicated or in consequence of the persistence of creditors, who were obliged to resort to the stern measures of the law to secure the adjustment of their claims. But, under the circumstances, her deception was pardonable and no one will censure her for it. She may have had no familiarity with the pernicious adage, "All's fair in love and war," but she regarded everything as perfectly proper, when it came to putting children to sleep. Many a mother and many a nurse, outside of Russia, will fully agree with her.

But though the children slumbered, Francesca was wakeful, in fact, she did not close her eyes in sleep for the rest of the night. Several times she crept to the door of the room where Madame Pushkin remained with Ivan and Nadia, to ascertain if they had yet retired; as long as she heard their voices, she kept about and puzzled her brain in thinking what she could do to comfort them. Her son, Joseph, slept in a distant part of the house; he was the "man-of-all-work" about the place, a sturdy fellow of some twenty-five years, and ready to give his life, if needed, in the service of his master or mistress.

Joseph had slept through all the tumult of the arrest, no one having thought to call him, and his room being so far away that no ordinary sounds were likely to reach him. When Francesca was at her wit's end in regard to the unusual occurrence of the night, she decided to awaken her son and tell him the news.

"Joseph! Joseph!" she called softly at his door.

There was no response, and after waiting a few seconds, she called out again.

Joseph slept soundly; he had spent the evening with some of his friends at the nearest lafka (drinking shop), and was, therefore, in a slumberous condition. Francesca found it necessary to enter the room and shake him before she could make him understand, and even then his intellect was somewhat clouded. He listened in a dazed way to her account of the arrest, but when he fully realized that his master had been carried away to prison, he was fully awake and ready for anything desperate.

But desperation was of no account, as the prisoner was then far on his road to Tambov, if not already there and inside the walls of the prison. Joseph was of such pugnacious mould, that he might have ventured, single-handed, upon an attempt at rescue, if the arresting party had been in front of the house at the time he was fully roused from sleep and heard his mother's story.

He proposed to take one of the horses and go in pursuit of the party, but Francesca reminded him that no one was to leave the house until morning. Then he wanted to go to his mistress and ask if she wished him to start at daybreak for Tambov, and if so, he would have everything in readiness, but from this he was dissuaded. A hundred other schemes entered his head, but all were set aside by his mother, who at length concluded that her son would be all the better in the morning, if he could sleep through the rest of the night. So she left him, and as the voices were no longer audible in the room whose door she had so often visited, there was nothing more to be done. She went to bed, but only a little while before the dawn.

Joseph was an excellent specimen of a Russian peasant. He had the courage of a lion with the simplicity of a child, the fidelity and strength of the mastiff with the gentleness of the dove. To serve his master, there was nothing he would not undertake, but, if left to himself, he was without resource; he had the courage and daring to execute anything he was commanded to do, but he had not the skill to plan. This characteristic is noticeable among the Russian peasants more than with any other people of the world. It is this that makes them such a sturdy reliance when trained as soldiers;

this is the quality that carried them up the heights of Inkermann, over the walls of Plevna, and through the Shipka Pass, to the astonishment and admiration of their foes. It is this element in their nature that has enabled them to conquer Northern and Central Asia, and may yet carry them to the shores of the Indian Sea.

Madame Pushkin had listened to the entreaties of Ivan and Nadia, and gone to bed, and they did likewise as soon as she had retired. But sleep did not come easily to anyone of the three and least of all, to the mother. Several times she fell into a troubled slumber, accompanied by frightful dreams, from which she waked with a start and found beads of perspiration covering her forehead, although the night was far from warm. Ivan and Nadia suffered in the same way, but to much less extent; in times of trouble, sleep is more kindly to the young than to those whose years are far beyond the teens.

Ivan had spent a year or more in the University of Moscow, and returned thence for his vacation only two weeks before the incident with which our story opens.

Throughout Russia the University students have been the cause of much trouble to the government. Not infrequently a University may be closed and the students sent to their homes, because of suspicions of liberal tendencies; arrests of students on suspicion of connection with plots to overthrow the government are of frequent occurrence, and not a few who have begun their careers in the great schools of instruction, have ended them in prison or in Siberian exile. A close watch is kept upon all the professors and teachers, lest they inculcate sentiments of disloyalty in the minds of the youths under their care. In order to hold their places, these men must give proof of unbounded and undeviating loyalty and a readiness to support with enthusiasm all acts of the government, no matter how repugnant they may be to fair-minded men. But, in spite of all care, the students do not always follow the lines of thought laid out for them ; they persist in thinking for themselves and in making their own deductions from the events of the day or of other times.

CHAPTER III.

VISITING A PRISONER.

The arrest of Carl Pushkin became known among his neighbors on the day that followed it. In any other country it would have been the subject of a great deal of gossip, but that is not the case in Russia. Comment upon official action is not encouraged, and if persisted in, is apt to lead to unpleasant consequences. The discovery of a bear in the forest, or the abduction of a sheep by a wolf, would have led to far more local talk than did the arrest and imprisonment of Carl Pavloff.

As an illustration of the way in which the government exercised its power of exiling its subjects without trial, the following story will prove interesting.

When the Grand Duke Alexis of Russia visited the United States, he had upon his staff a young naval officer named Staniukovitch, who was very popular with those who met him in New York and other American cities. His father was a Russian admiral and the young man was considered one of the most promising men of his age. He had special fondness for literature, and after his return home from the tour with the Grand Duke, he resigned his official position and turned his attention to authorship.

He wrote several novels and plays which were successful, and afterwards he bought a Russian magazine, called the "Diello," and published it in St. Petersburg. He became editor and proprietor of the "Diello" and, in 1884, went abroad to arrange about foreign contributions to his publication. In the autumn of that year he started back to St. Petersburg, leaving his wife and children in Germany.

As soon as he crossed the Russian frontier he was arrested and taken to prison in St. Petersburg, the famous prison of Petropavlovsk, where so many political and other victims of Russian authority have been incarcerated. He was not allowed to inform his wife of his arrest or to communicate with any of his friends in the capital city. His wife continued writing regularly to him, but became alarmed when she received no replies to her letters. She telegraphed to the managing editor of the magazine, who answered that Mr. Staniukovitch had not been in St. Petersburg, and they supposed he was still in Germany. Then she hurried, with her children, to Russia, and after some weeks, was able to learn that her husband was in prison. She could not then ascertain upon what charge, but it was afterwards found out that he had been in correspondence with a well known Russian writer, who was then in Switzerland. The correspondence related entirely to literary matters, but this was sufficient for the government to arrest the editor of the magazine in the manner described. He was sent to Siberia for three years, his magazine was suspended, and the gentleman was financially ruined. There was no trial or even the shadow of one; everything was done upon somebody's order and in the most secret manner.

In his trouble, Ivan went to one of their neighbors, who was an especial friend of his father, and sought his aid and counsel. This neighbor, Mr. Hartmann, was descended from one of the German emigrants who settled in Russia during the time of Catherine the Great. Though German in blood, Mr. Hartmann was a native-born Russian. His father and grandfather were also born in the Empire of the Czar, and he was so far Russianized that he was unable to speak the language of Berlin.

Mr. Hartmann had already heard of the arrest, and his greeting of the youth was full of sympathy. The Hartmann and Pushkin families were intimately acquainted; Mr. Hartmann's son, Alexei, was engaged to Nadia Pushkin and the wedding was to take place in the coming year.

"What can have been the cause of my father's arrest, do you think?" was the first question addressed by Ivan to his older friend.

"I cannot possibly guess," was the reply, "but never mind the cause of it, the thing to consider is, how to obtain your father's release as soon as possible."

"That's true," said Ivan, "and now tell me what I shall do?"

"Has your father any ready money or any property that can be converted into cash?"

"I don't know," answered Ivan, "but why do you ask?"

Mr. Hartmann smiled, and then his face assumed a serious aspect.

"Of course, you are too young yet to know much about it," he said, "but you will soon learn that in this country of ours, very little can be done except by the use of money. Officials may be bribed to do anything, provided the bribery will not lead to their detection by a higher authority, except where they receive enough money in hand to divide with the one who might bring them into trouble. Very often they require bribes to induce them to do their duty; and altogether, the system of government rests upon the payment of money through nearly every grade of official life."

"I wonder the Czar allows such a system to continue," said Ivan.

"The Czar is responsible for it," replied Mr. Hartmann.

"How can that be possible?"

"Because the pay of all officers is so miserably small, that they cannot support their families or even support themselves as single men upon their salaries. They must add to their revenues in some way or starve, unless they have private fortunes of their own, and the easiest way of increasing their revenues is by the system of bribery I have mentioned."

"I think, too," continued Mr. Hartmann, "that the Czar could not put a stop to it, if he wished to."

"He might issue an imperial ukase forbidding it," pleaded Ivan.

"That was what a distinguished foreigner once said to the Emperor Nicholas," Mr. Hartmann responded, "and the Emperor's answer was, that in order to have such a ukase carried out he would have to bribe his prime minister to enforce it."

"Now, in regard to your father's case, I ask about ready money, because I know that somebody will have to be bribed."

"Isn't it possible that he was arrested so that somebody would be able to get money in just that way?"

"That is quite possible and even probable. Such things have happened before and a great many times; as for the matter of that, they are not confined to

Russia, though we have far more than our share in consequence of the greater ease with which a blackmailing arrest may be concealed. The large cities of the countries that boast the greatest freedom, England and the United States, have had instances of this sort, and if they can have them, how much more should we expect them in an autocracy where exile by administrative process prevails."

Returning to the immediate subject before them, Mr. Hartmann said it might be necessary to bribe the officials to find that the arrest was a mistake, and that Carl Pavloff Pushkin was apprehended in place of some other Carl Pavloff, for whom the police were looking. If there were any difficulties about this plan, it might be arranged to bribe the jailer to allow Pushkin to escape in the night. The escape might be discovered in the morning and the pursuit would be carefully turned in the direction opposite to that taken by the man who was running away. This is done more frequently than the general public is aware, and though there is a great show of zeal in following an escaped prisoner, he runs very little risk of being actually retaken.

As a preliminary, it was necessary to have an interview with the prisoner, and this would require that the jailer should receive a suitable present from whoever visited him. Before calling upon the prison-keeper, it would be necessary to have a permit from the Chief of Police in Tambov; of course, it would facilitate matters if the Chief received in some manner a substantial token of respect and esteem in the shape of cash.

Ivan thanked Mr. Hartmann for his advice and suggested that he would go at once to his mother and see what could be done about raising the needed money.

"Do nothing of the kind," said Mr. Hartmann, "but go with me to Tambov to-morrow and see your father."

"But how about the money for the Chief of Police and the keeper of the prison?"

"Oh! I'll attend to that," was the reply, "as it will not be a serious matter. A hundred rubles to the Chief and twenty-five to the jailer; that's a mere trifle to what will have to be paid when we talk of release or escape."

It was arranged that they would start early the next morning so as to be in Tambov in time to have the day before them. Mr. Hartmann would take Ivan in his own tarantass, and they would easily get over the thirty versts, or twenty miles, inside of three hours. By setting out at four o'clock, they would be in Tambov by seven, and this would be ample season to arrange for the interview.

Ivan was about to hurry away to tell his mother the plan, but Mr. Hartmann stopped him.

"Tell your mother this and nothing more," said the gentleman. "You and I are going to Tambov to see your father; that's all. If she asks you what our plans are, tell her you don't know. Actually, you don't know, nor do I, as the plan must depend very much upon things as we find them. Don't trouble yourself about money, as I will have enough for all present needs."

Ivan comforted his mother with the information that they would go to Tambov on the morrow, and told her that the start would be made very early. He was to be ready at four o'clock, and Mr. Hartmann would be there with his tarantass at that hour or soon after. No time would be lost by this arrangement, as the Pushkin house lay directly on the road from Mr. Hartmann's to Tambov.

Mrs. Pushkin gave her son several verbal messages to deliver to his father, messages of love and affection, which it is unnecessary to repeat. Then she told Ivan that he had better retire early, in order to be up and ready at the hour when Mr. Hartmann was expected. She suggested that the suit of clothes he was to wear would need to be freshly brushed and possibly might require a few stitches. She would attend to this and send the garments to his room by one of the servants, so that he could have them ready for putting on when he rose.

Nadia wished to be of use and asked her mother what she could do.

"Nothing, my child," was the reply. "Yes, you may write a letter to your father and that will comfort him. Ivan can carry it, and it must be left open, so that the prison-keeper can read it before it is delivered."

Nadia hastened to her room to write the letter. Mrs. Pushkin suggested that Ivan could occupy the remaining hours of the day in attending to certain details of the work about the place that ordinarily came under his father's care; and the youth went out to do as his mother advised.

The woman embraced the opportunity given by the absence of Ivan and Nadia to write a letter, which she placed in the skirt of Ivan's overcoat. It was written on the thinnest of paper, and covered both sides of a closely-written half sheet, and then it was wrapped in another piece of paper covered with printed characters. To conceal it, she ripped the lining of the overcoat at the bottom, and then stitched the paper where the material was turned up to meet the lining. Enough o the turned up portion was cut away to make room fo the folded slip, and when the work was completed, would require the most minute inspection to discover that anything was hidden there.

She had just finished the work, when Ivan returned. Then she turned her attention to the buttons of the coat and took a few stitches here and there, where they were apparently needed.

The other garments received due attention, and were sent to Ivan's room before he retired. Nadia's letter was completed and securely placed in the youth's pocket, and everything was ready for the early departure as previously arranged.

On arriving at Tambov, Mr. Hartmann and Ivan went at once to the office of the Chief of Police. Though it was early in the day, that officer was already at his post, and after a little delay, Mr. Hartmann and Ivan were ushered into his presence.

After the customary salutations, Mr. Hartmann explained that they desired to have an interview with Carl Pavloff, surnamed Pushkin, now in prison in Tambov, and the father of the young man who accompanied him.

The man of authority said the rules of the prison were very severe, and he was uncertain whether the desired interview could be granted. As he spoke, he threw away the papiros (cigarette) he was smoking and began to turn over the papers that lay on his desk.

Mr. Hartman drew from his pocket a cigarette case and proffered it to the officer. The latter took the case and as he did so, Mr. Hartman turned to Ivan and called his attention to a picture at the farther end of the room, in a direction quite opposite to where the Chief of Police was sitting.

Naturally Ivan looked at the picture, and naturally too, Mr. Hartmann's eyes were upon it at the same time. The picture interested both of them quite long enough to give an excellent opportunity for the official to take a papiros from Hartman's case, and with it a note of the Imperial Bank of Russia for a hundred rubles, that had been rolled into the shape of a cigarette and placed among the dozen or more cigarettes in the box "for safety." The real cigarette could be lighted at once, and the imitation one could go into the official pocket for future use.

Russian paper money is not like that of the United States and some other countries, printed in a single color. A considerable part of the population is unable to read, and for the convenience of the unlettered inhabitants, the different denominations of the National bank notes are of different colors. It is easy for an uneducated man to know the value of a note by the complexion of the ink with which it is printed, and easy for an educated official to know the denomination of a note offered him as a bribe, when it is rolled in the form of a cigarette, or otherwise left unfolded. Did the designer of the Russian currency "build wiser than he knew," or did he know his constituency and its needs, and take his measures accordingly?

Did the official appropriate the money thus within his reach? Who can tell? No one saw him take it; no one offered it to him; no one traced the money to his possession. There is no proof of bribery, and the fact that Mr. Hartmann afterwards missed the money from the case, would not be taken as evidence in the court.

"I see no reason why the son of the prisoner should not be admitted to see his father," said the Chief, as he swallowed the smoke from the cigarette and emitted it from his nostrils. "He desires to be accompanied by you, an old friend of the family, I understand?"

"Yes," replied Mr. Hartmann, "a friend and neighbor."

Permission to see the prisoner, Pushkin, was granted, and the callers departed with the precious document in their possession.

At the door of the prison there was some delay while the permit was sent to the prison-keeper and returned. The door was opened and the visitors entered within the grim walls. They were taken directly to the keeper's office, where they were questioned concerning the object of their visit, put under oath not to convey to any one in the building articles of a contraband nature, and examined to make sure that nothing forbidden by the rules was in their possession. Ivan handed over to the keeper the letter which Nadia had written. The latter said he would read it and decide upon its disposition before their visit was concluded.

The guard was instructed to take them to cell number thirteen, where they had permission to remain for half an hour.

As they rose to accompany him, Mr. Hartmann said:

"Can't we leave our overcoats here? The day is quite warm and we shall not need them."

"Certainly, gentlemen," replied the keeper, who may have construed the request as a hint that he would find something for his own use in the garments. Accordingly the overcoats were left in the keeper's office and the visitors followed the guard in the direction indicated; Ivan being of course quite in ignorance of the missive that was thus placed in peril.

CHAPTER IV.

A RUSSIAN PRISON.

When they reached the cell where Pushkin was confined, the guard announced that there were visitors for number thirteen, and as he did so, he rapped on a heavy wooden door. Then he opened a panel about twelve inches square in the upper part of the door, and the face of the prisoner speedily appeared there.

The visitors were warmly greeted and as soon as the door was opened by an under-keeper, who had followed at the heels of the party, they entered the apartment. Father and son embraced and kissed; an embrace and kiss were exchanged between Pushkin and Hartmann, and then there were tears in the eyes of all three of the party. It was a joyous meeting and at the same time a sad one.

Here is the room as it was described by Ivan to his mother. It may be taken as the type of the places where political prisoners are confined in the majority of the prisons in the cities of European Russia. In Siberia, the accommodations are much more restricted as the prisons are generally overcrowded, and sometimes to such an extent as to cause great suffering and an unusual percentage of disease and death.

"The room, or cell," said Ivan, "is about twelve feet long by ten in width, and the ceiling is, perhaps, seven feet from the floor. Walls and roof are of stone, and there is nothing under foot but the concrete or plaster, that is spread over the stone in a soft condition and smoothed off before it becomes hard. The door opens into it from a corridor, and at the other end of the cell is a window about one foot high and two feet long, which lets in some air and light, but not much of either. Outside the window there is a blank wall, the outer wall of the prison, and if the window could be reached, so that a prisoner might look out of it, he would see nothing but the wall and a very little of the sky.

"Some light comes in from the corridor," continued Ivan, "but there is not enough to enable one to read without difficulty; in fact, the whole aspect of the place suggested a tomb more than a place for a man to live in. But, in spite of the somberness of his cell, father was cheerful, or tried to be so, and told me that you must bear up just as bravely as you could.

"There was nothing to sit upon but the bed, which was an iron frame fastened to the wall, and very firmly fastened, too. Close by the head of the bed is an iron slab, also fastened to the wall, and serving as a table; and there is a stove in one corner that is fed through a door in the corridor. Each stove warms two cells, as it is partly in one cell and partly in the next.

"We sat on the edge of the bed and talked. The soldier who had come in with us, stood at the door; evidently, he had orders to do so, as he did not move a muscle or say a word when Mr. Hartmann asked him to go outside. Mr. Hartmann slipped a ruble into his hand, and after he received it he paid no attention to what we said, though he could not help hearing all our conversation when we spoke in an ordinary tone. But anything that was not intended for him to hear was said in a whisper, and to this whispering he made no objection. That was probably the effect of the ruble.

"I gave father all the messages you intrusted me with and told him about Nadia's letter. Then he asked what we had done with our overcoats, and I told him they had been left in the keeper's room, because the prison was so warm.

"He said he was afraid I should take cold in this damp place, without my overcoat, and suggested that I ask one of the under-keepers to go with me to bring it. I did so, and the man went with me to the office of the prison. I made a mistake, and got Mr. Hartmann's coat on my arm, but when I found my blunder, I took both of them to the cell, with, of course, the keeper's permission."

The reason of the keeper's readiness to grant the desired permission to remove the coats was more apparent to Mr. Hartmann than to the youth. The former had left, "for safety," twenty-five rubles in Imperial Bank-notes in the pocket of his overcoat, and later on in the day he ascertained that the money had disappeared. Who had taken it or whether it had fallen out by accident he never knew. But it is certain that the prison-keeper was disposed to be civil and to extend the rules as far as possible. The time permitted for the visit expired, but he did not send word to that effect until nearly an hour afterwards.

The soldier on guard looked in every direction save to where the three friends were seated on the side of the little bed. He could not remove from the spot, his orders were altogether too strict for that, but he was not obliged to keep his eyes fixed on his charge, and he did not.

The letter was removed from its place of concealment and so deftly was the operation performed, while Pushkin was toying with the skirt of his son's coat, that Ivan did not know it. The missive was kept out of sight untill the departure of the visitors, and then Pushkin could read it at his leisure.

No, not altogether at his leisure, as the occupant of a Russian prison is under constant surveillance.

In the door of Pushkin's cell, as in the doors of all cells in the political prisons in the empire, there is a hole about four inches long by half an inch in width, and so placed that it commands a view of the interior of the cell. This is called the " Judas " by the prisoners. It is covered with a piece of wood, hung upon a pivot, and the cover can be moved quite noiselessly. The guard can look in whenever he chooses, and the occupant never knows when he is being inspected.

The guards walk along the corridors in felt boots, which are purposely worn in order that their footsteps may not be heard.

The " Judas " in the door made it necessary that all reading should be done with the greatest circumspection, except in the cases where it was permitted. In the present instance, Nadia's letter furnished the reasonable excuse. The letter was given to Pushkin after his visitors had gone, the keeper having read it carefully and found nothing objectionable in it.

The keeper had not contented himself with reading the letter, he had subjected it to various chemical tests to make sure that there was no concealed writing upon it. Russian revolutionists are well versed in chemistry, and the most innocent letter in the world, so far as its ink is concerned, may contain something of great importance. The writing is done with colorless acids that make not the slightest mark upon the paper; afterwards, an apparently innocent letter is written on the sheet with common ink, and it is this letter that enables the document to travel without seizure.

When the party who is in the secret receives such a letter, he finds somewhere in the innocent document a hints as to the proper method for finding the concealed writing. It may be developed before a fire or may require a solution of one acid or another. It is necessary to change the methods frequently, owing to the alertness of the police. Every letter sent or received is examined with the greatest care, and it is a constant battle of wits between the police and the prisoners and their friends.

Further on in our story we will consider some of the secret means by which political prisoners and refugees hold communication, in spite of the vigilance of their guards.

Pushkin apparently read and re-read many times the letter from his daughter, when, in fact, he was holding between its folds the communication from his wife. He had already secreted, with great care, the printed slip, in which the letter was wrapped as the reader will remember. This printed slip was nothing more nor less than an Imperial Bank-note of a high denomination, which might be useful in many of the emergencies that occur in the life of a man under arrest in Russia. We have already seen that money will do many things in the land of despotism. It should not be understood that money can accomplish everything, as many a man has learned to his sorrow after making an unwise experiment.

The letter which the wife sent to the husband and did not care to have her son knowingly carry, was mainly devoted to the subject which had occupied his thoughts during the ride to Tambov, the cause of his arrest. She did not believe that he had compromised himself with revolutionists or with any of those individuals who might be considered " prejudicial to social order," nor did she think he had offended any of their influential neighbors or the officials with whom he had occasion to transact business from time to time. She had thought the subject over carefully, and settled upon what seemed to her the most probable, or rather the least impossible cause, and this she mentioned with the greatest hesitation.

It was not at all that which had come into his mind during the ride to the prison, but something totally different. It gave him food for thought for the rest of the day and though all the hours of the night that followed.

Immediately after leaving the prison, Mr. Hartmann sought a lawyer of Tambov, and engaged him to do all in his power in behalf of Carl Pavloff. Russia is not an encouraging field for a lawyer beyond the ordinary business of drawing legal papers, managing commercial affairs, collecting debts, adjusting disputes, and otherwise employing himself in a civil way.

Down to the time of Alexander II. there was very little law practice outside of the civil courts, as the criminal affairs of the country were in the hands of the government officials. Alexander was a believer in open courts of justice, and established them after great opposition on the part of the Imperial Council. Persons charged with murder, robbery or kindred crimes, great or small, are tried in open court before judges who are paid by the Crown and forbidden to receive fees under any circumstances. There is a formal act of accusation ; the prisoner may confront accusers and witnesses ; he may be defended ; the jury may be chosen from among men of comfortable circumstances, having an income of not less than five hundred rubles ($250) a year ; and a majority of the jury can render a verdict.

Criminal practice in these courts gives the Russian lawyers more business than formerly, and when the accused is a man of wealth, and the case is desperate, heavy fees are paid to counsel, just as in England or the United States.

It was hoped that the establishment of the courts would do away with the old abuses, but injustice dies hard in whatever country it may exist. Though the judges and jurors are forbidden to receive fees, instances have occurred in which they have done so, and we have already seen that exile by administrative process, without a trial or even a hearing, is a common practice in Russia.

The lawyer whom Mr. Hartmann engaged to look after Pushkin's case, went at once to the Chancellerie in search of information. But though he pressed his inquiries in every quarter among the officials of that establishment, he was politely but firmly refused any particulars whatever, and when he left the place, he was no wiser than when he went there. He could not even ascertain whether any charges had been made against the prisoner, and was, therefore, quite unable to plan any course of action. To make a defence, it is necessary to have something to defend.

The prison officials were equally ignorant or uncommunicative or both. All that the keeper of the prison would say, was that Carl Pavloff was in custody under the usual rules and would remain there until further orders. With the permission of the Chief of Police the lawyer might visit the prisoner, subject to the rules of the establishment governing cases of this kind.

The day ended with very little progress in the direction of discovering why Carl Pavloff had been arrested or the probable disposition of his case. Mr. Hartmann and Ivan spent the night at a small gostinitza (hotel), where the former had often lodged before. The accommodations were meagre, but such is the case in all the small hotels of Russia, and nobody thinks of complaining. The room that they occupied contained two broad benches or sofas, on which there was a covering of straw, held in place by coarse cotton cloth, nailed along the edges of the board. These benches served as beds, and each patron was expected to provide his own bed clothing from the rugs and wraps carried in his tarantass. This is the custom through the interior of Russia; it is only in the cities that one can find beds in conformity with Western ideas.

During the evening they were visited by an individual who hesitated a while before saying who he was and only did so on the promise of secrecy. He hinted that he was a personage of much influence with the authorities, and finally came to business.

"How much would it be worth for Carl Pushkin to be able to escape across the frontier?" was the question he propounded.

Mr. Hartmann was unable to answer.

"He can get there for fifty thousand rubles," said the man, "but the money must be ready and in my hands before he starts."

Then he unfolded his plan. He was a power behind the throne with the authorities in Tambov, and could arrange for a hearing in the case of the prisoner. This hearing would take place at the Chancellerie, at the request of Pushkin's lawyer, and could be so protracted that it would be dark before the affair was concluded.

On the way back to the prison Pushkin could escape; a carriage waiting around the corner would receive him, and with a forged passport, describing him under another name, he could easily make his way to the frontier without question. Any pursuit that was undertaken would be directed quite opposite to where he would be found; in fact, the whole affair should be discreetly managed from beginning to end.

"Think it over until to-morrow," said he, as he rose to go, "and you will certainly find it the best way out of the present difficulty. You will have to act soon, as there is no telling when an order will come for him to be taken elsewhere."

After he had gone, there were several minutes of silence, in which Hartmann and Ivan regarded each other thoughtfully. The former was the first to speak.

"That's in accordance with what I told you yesterday," said he to the youth.

"Yes, that's so," was the reply. "And what do you think of his proposal?"

"I can't give an answer without considering several matters that present themselves. In the first place, the man may be an impostor, without the influence he pretends to have, and the whole thing a trick to extort money from us. In the second place, we want your father's opinion, then that of the lawyer, and then, if we conclude to negotiate, we must have some assurance more than his mere word, that the plan will be carried out. We can do nothing about the matter until to-morrow. So now let us try to get some sleep."

Then they separated and each sought the rest he so much needed.

Ivan was an earnest and voluminous reader, but, until he went to the University, his chances for reading were very limited. He greatly enjoyed his opportunities at Moscow, and his experience at the University gave him more information about Russia and the rest of the world, than he had obtained in all the years down to the time when he left home. He read only such works as were "approved," but every book that he perused caused him to think, and thinking is exactly what is undesirable for a loyal subject of the autocracy of the Czar.

One day Ivan took from the law library of the University, a volume containing, among other things, the Imperial regulations concerning exile by administrative process. As he read his face changed color repeatedly. He was in his own room or this circumstance might have brought trouble upon him. And when he finally placed the book on his table, he remarked to himself:

"Can it be possible that such a law really exists to-day? I must have been reading something about the centuries that are gone; but, no, here is the imprint of the book in this very year. I will ask Kanchin about it. Here he comes."

Ivan had glanced from the window as he spoke and saw the form of that individual crossing the street in the direction of the house where our young friend lodged. He rightly judged that he was to be honored with a visit and, sure enough, in just sufficient time for the other to climb the stairs, there was a knock at the door.

"Come in," said Ivan, cheerily. The door opened and the youths met and kissed as affectionately as school-girls.

Men kiss each other in Russia very much as women do in America. It is an odd sight to American and English eyes to witness greetings and farewells between bearded fellows at railway stations and in other public places, but the Russians take it as a matter of course. Sometimes the spectacle is quite comical and the stranger must tax his powers of self-control to avoid smiling. A pair of intoxicated mujiks have been known to prolong their affectionate osculations in the market place, when the thermometer was below zero, to such an extent, that their beards became frozen together from the congelation of their breath; sometimes the mass of beard is so thick on each of the faces brought together for a kiss, that considerable effort is required to bring the pairs of lips in contact.

"Sit down," said Ivan to his friend, and as he said so, he proffered a cigarette.

"You have illustrated the truth of the old adage, that we speak of angels and hear their wings rustle immediately. I was just saying to myself that I wanted to ask you a question, when I espied you crossing the street."

"Complimentary, I'm sure," replied Kanchin, "to be taken for an angel. What was your question about?"

"It was about exile by administrative process."

"Well?"

"I never heard of it before. Nobody that I know of was ever exiled from our neighborhood, and that's probably the reason why I never heard it talked about."

"I was reading yesterday," continued Ivan, "about the system of trials by jury, and how it was conducted, and to-day I read about the process of exiling a person from his home without any trial at all. I wanted to ask you if these systems do not interfere with each other."

"Not at all," replied Kanchin; "trial by jury is one thing and exile without trial is another. Trial by jury is something new; while exile without trial is as old as the time of Peter the Great. The two systems work well together. When there is a clear case against a man, he can be tried by jury and convicted, but when there is nothing to go upon but suspicion, or very slender proof, then he can be exiled by the village Commune where he lives or by order of the Minister of the Interior or upon complaint of any person of respectability."

"Oh, that's the way of it," said Ivan. "I'm much obliged."

Then Kanchin went on to explain that in the old days of serfdom it frequently happened that a land-owner might have on his estate an idle, worthless serf, against whom it was difficult to bring any specific complaint, but whose presence was demoralizing to the rest of the people. The owner could easily rid himself of the man's presence by going to the nearest police bureau and saying that he wished the serf sent to some other part of the empire. Forthwith the man was arrested and sent into exile, generally to Siberia, and the record against him was, that he was thus deported " by the will of his master." He might be required to remain there for a period, not exceeding five years; if, at the expiration of his term, he returned to the estate and incurred his master's displeasure, he could again be sent into exile for the same reason as before.

"I see the reason of it," said Ivan, " but didn't such a regulation sometimes lead to abuses? It is said that there was never a law in the world that was not abused at one time or another."

"That is quite true," said Kanchin, "and the law of which we are talking was no exception to the rule. There is no doubt that it has been outrageously abused. A serf might have money which his master desired, or he might have a pretty wife or daughter on whom the master looked with favor; nothing more natural in the world, than that the man should be sent to Siberia for three or five years ' by the will of his master.'"

"But serfdom exits no longer," said Ivan.

"You are right," was the reply, "but the power formerly possessed by the master is now vested in the local authorities, who can send anybody into exile when they think proper to do so.*

"Furthermore, if any person is obnoxious to the government, or his presence anywhere is considered 'prejudicial to social order,' or it is suspected that he corresponds or associates with anybody who is not in sympathy with the government, he may be sent to Siberia or anywhere else that the Minister of the Interior may designate. There is no need of telling him what charges have been made against him or who has accused him, and he cannot ask for a hearing or a trial or take advantage of the habeas corpus that we read about in other countries. His friends are not allowed to communicate with him, nor he with them, until such time as the government pleases. It may be a day, a month, a year, a decade or a century."

* In the year 1885, 15,766 persons were sent to Siberia. 5,536 of these were women and children, voluntarily accompanying husbands or fathers. Of the remaining 10,230, 4,392 were exiled by sentence of courts, and 5,838 by administrative process. 3,751 of those thus sent to Siberia without trial were exiled by the order of the Communes and not by the general government.

Naturally this conversation occurred to Ivan on the night of his father's arrest, and again while he lay awake after his conversation with Mr. Hartmann. He racked his brain to discover what could possibly have been the cause of the sudden visit of the police and his father's transfer from the delights of his home to the rigors of the prison at Tambov. He could think of absolutely nothing that his father had done to bring suspicion in his direction, and finally gave up the effort in despair.

Next, he turned to measures for his relief and release.

"Here is the terrible character of these administrative arrests," he said to himself. "In the first place, we do not know of what he is accused, and even if we did, we could not call any of his friends to testify to his loyalty without bringing them under suspicion. It is dangerous to be any man's friend in Russia. What a horrible state of affairs."

CHAPTER V.

THE RUSSIAN POLICE SYSTEM.

The man who had called upon Hartmann and Ivan was an attache of the Imperial Police at Tambov and had a brother of much higher position than himself.

While they were at breakfast the next morning, the youth asked Mr. Hartmann to tell him something about the police system of the empire of the Czar.

"Well," said the gentleman, "you must know that Russia is essentially a paternal country, the goverment being the sole authority in everything, and the Czar standing as the father of all his subjects. The citizen, or subject, has no voice in selecting his rulers and is considered incapable of managing anything but his own personal affairs; even his ability to do that is not admitted, and he must refer to the police a great many things that he would decide for himself in other countries, especially in England or the United States.

"You know very well, as a Russian subject, living in Russia, that you cannot travel without a passport; you cannot change your residence from one house to another without notifying the police, and, if you wish to open a cigar shop, a grocery, or a place for the sale of boots and shoes, the permission of the police must first be obtained. If a man has a drug store, he is forbidden to sell medicines of a powerful nature, such as poisons, narcotics and anesthetics, on the prescription of any doctor not named on a list given you by the police. A doctor cannot practice without permission of the police, and when he practices, he must go to every call in the night, unless he has the police permit to refuse to go out at that time. Performances at theatres and shows of all kinds are under police supervision, but to this no valid objection can be made, and the regulation, within certain limits, is a good one. The same thing is done in other countries, but we Russians go a good many steps beyond other nations."

"Suppose," said Ivan, "that I want to get up a concert for the aid of a hospital, asylum or some other charity, what must I do in that case?"

"You must get the permission of the police before you can do anything, and, in applying for it, you must file your entire programme, naming each person who is to appear and exactly what he is to sing, play or recite, and, if you vary the programme on the night of the affair, you may find yourself in serious trouble."

"That would be inconvenient," Ivan remarked, "but as everybody would understand it, the rule wouldn't be serious."

"But the police supervision does not end here," Mr. Hartmann continued, "you must hand over the proceeds of the entertainment to the police, and the money must pass through their hands before reaching the charity for which it was intended. It is liable to great shrinkage during this passage and, in fact, it may disappear altogether. It is very certain that it will not be increased by contact with the hands of the police."

"Why do they make you put the money in their hands?"

"The reason for this regulation is, that evil-disposed persons are in the habit of getting up entertainments, ostensibly for the benefit of well known charities, when in fact they are for supplying funds to revolutionists, at home or abroad, or prisoners in the hands of the government."

"Oh! I understand," said Ivan.

"One of the regulations of the police refers to the censorship of price-lists of goods, notes of invitation to parties and personal visiting cards; also for the censorship of seals, rubber stamps and business cards of individuals or corporations. Another order regulates the sale of soap, starch, tooth-brushes and insect powder, and another controls the printing on the paper used in making cigarettes. The incongruous nature of the orders issued by the police, are illustrated by the circumstance that one order concerning religious instruction in secular schools, and another about measures to prevent horse-stealing, are placed side by side."

Ivan laughed at this and then asked how the police force of the empire was constituted.

"All the police are under the control of the Minister of the Interior," was the reply. "Down to a few years ago the detective and secret police were under independent control, and their business related wholly to political matters, but it was found that crime and politics were so closely allied, that the management would be easier if it were all in one department. The municipal police force is not unlike that of English or American cities; the rural police includes two classes of men, one appointed by the government and the other elected by the peasants; and the detective or secret police are as secret as possible. The outside public does not know much about them, and the little it does know is often wrong."

While talking further on this subject, Ivan asked Mr. Hartmann a question as to the number and extent of the secret police.

"That's something I can't tell you," he replied. "If I could, it wouldn't be a secret. But this I know, that there are not many members of the force outside of the cities, for the very good reason that it is chiefly in the cities that their services are needed. Revolutionists are not found in the country as much as in the cities, and when a man in the country has revolutionary tendencies he is very likely to go to the city to carry on his work. In the days of the Emperor Nicholas it was a common saying that when three persons were together one of them was a spy and the other two were quite liable to be in the same line. Matters improved somewhat under Alexander II. but became worse again after Alexander III. ascended the throne."

"I suppose the secret police are better paid than our rural policemen, are they not?"

"They must be better paid or better bribed," replied the gentleman. "No man can live honestly on a policeman's pay in the rural districts, and it is no wonder that he extorts money from the peasants on which to exist. On a salary of two or three hundred rubles ($100 to $150) a man cannot support a family, keep himself provided with uniform, sword and revolver, make an occasional present to his superior, and otherwise meet the expenses of his position. We are all obliged to make presents to the local police; if we do so quietly, it is much better for us than to resist, as then they will make us pay for all the expense and trouble of making their collections.

"It is a suspicious circumstance," he continued, "when a local police official, of whatever grade, refuses to take bribes. Let me tell you a little story on this point."

Of course Ivan was quite willing to hear it, and his friend continued :

"Some years ago, several young men of liberal views, well-educated and of good families, thought they would benefit the peasants by going into the country and finding situations as bee-sers (district secretaries), where they could teach the people something of their rights and protect them from the swindles of the small traders who were leagued to rob them. Of course they went under assumed names, but they were all discovered because they refused to drink vodka (whiskey) or take bribes. If their habits had been dissolute and they had shown a readiness not only to take all bribes that were offered, but to force payment from those who did offer them, they would not have come under suspicion."

"You mention the small traders who rob the peasants," said Ivan, as Mr. Hartmann paused. "How is that done ?"

"Generally by combination with the stanovoi or chief police officer of a district or village. You will find in nearly every village a kulak, that is, a man with some capital, who makes money out of the peasants by lending at high rates when they are in distress, buying their grain for whatever he chooses to pay, and otherwise taking advantage of their necessities.

"I know one case where several of the peasants had arranged to load their grain on a barge and float it down the river to a market town, where it would bring a good price. They could thus get nearly double what the kaluk had been in the habit of paying them, and would be able to deal directly with the consumers of the grain.

"The kaluk heard of the scheme and went to the stanovoi to propose something to their mutual advantage.

"He told what the peasants were intending to do and then said :

"'These people cannot go more then thirty versts from home without your permission on their passports, and the place where they expect to sell their grain is at least two hundred versts away. Now, you can make various excuses for not giving them their passports, which are in your possession ; they will have to sell the grain to me and we can divide the profits.'

"The stanovoi embraced the opportunity, and when the peasants came for their passports, he said they had been sent to the governor of the province and could not be expected back again for several weeks. He was very sorry it so happened, but there was no way in which he could let the men go more than thirty versts away without their passports, as they would certainly be arrested and imprisoned if found beyond the limits without them.

"The men waited a while and finally grew tired and sold the grain to the kulak for what he would give."

"What an infamous piece of business !" exclaimed Ivan.

"You may well say so," replied Hartmann, "but from one end of Russia to the other, the peasants are oppressed by the police and have no redress. Your father and I have paid a great deal of money to the police just to remain undisturbed and to keep them from interfering with us under one pretext or another. Whenever they want money, they devise ways of raising it and keeping within the requirements of the law at the same time.

"Once, while we were in the midst of the harvest, the local stanovoi gave notice that all the peasants on our estates must be called together to hear the law read to them. It was the busiest time of the year with us, and he intimated that he could not put off the reading without great inconvenience. We had become so accustomed to this kind of thing, that we understood at once what he meant. We asked him how much the inconvenience would be, and he answered, 'fifty rubles.' He received the money and the law was not read until autumn, when the peasants had very little to do."

A traveller, who is well acquainted with Russia and its customs (Mr. George Kennan) says, that one of the most lucrative things that can fall into the hands of a stanovoi, is the body of a man who is supposed to have been murdered. The law requires the stanovoi to go to the place where the body is found and then remove it to the dead-house in the nearest village to await the arrival of the district surgeon. The surgeon is generally in another part of the district and cannot be expected for a day or two, perhaps longer. Few villages have official dead-houses, and, in default of such buildings, the stanovoi can place the corpse in any house he chooses to select.

Under these circumstances, he goes to the richest man in the village and proposes to leave the ghastly object in his dwelling. The man knows that the official has the right to do so and quickly comes to terms by paying anywhere from ten to fifty rubles to be left alone. The same thing will be done at the next house and the next, in fact, the whole village will be "squeezed," and then the body will be deposited in an abandoned shed or, possibly, it may be carried away to exploit another village the same way. Instances have been known of the exploiting of three villages in succession with the same cadaver.

But we are forgetting Carl Pavloff in our talk concerning the Russian police and their crooked ways.

The man who had made the proposal for Carl's "escape" for fifty thousand rubles, called at the hotel in the morning to renew his offer.

"You have thought over what I said, have you not?" he remarked, addressing Mr. Hartmann.

"Yes, I've thought the matter over somewhat," was the reply, "but there are difficulties in the way of accepting your terms."

"What are they?"

"In the first place, I think the figures altogether too high. Carl Pavloff isn't a poor man, but fifty thousand rubles is a great deal of money, and he couldn't raise that amount without considerable negotiation. He would have to sell or mortgage his estate, and that, you know, would attract attention, and might bring you and your friends into trouble. People would connect his escape with the sale of the land, and that wouldn't be agreeable to anybody concerned."

"That need not give any trouble," replied the official. "But it will not be necessary to sell or mortgage the property. I will make it forty thousand rubles or even thirty thousand, and instead of insisting upon all the money being actually in hand, half of it may be paid over and the other half can be secured for future payments. I can bring you the necessary legal papers whenever you name the time."

There was a pause and then the man spoke again.

"I think I understand another of your objections to

closing the negotiation. You are uncertain as to my standing in the matter and think it possible I may be an imposter. That suspicion is the most natural and, under the circumstances, a proper one. I'll satisfy you on that point."

Then he drew from his pocket his commission in the service of His Imperial Majesty, which showed him to be exactly what he said he was. Evidently he had told the truth, and no doubt he would have been ready to take issue with any one who hinted that he was otherwise than irreproachable in character, in spite of his peculiar views touching the question of bribery and connivance at the escape of a prisoner.

After the commission had been inspected, he exhibited two or three letters from his brother, which were equivalent to a full power of authority for the transaction of the business. It was plainly to be seen that these worthy gentlemen were determined to make the most of their opportunity in the uniform of The Great White Czar. They were under the Imperial banner for purposes of revenue, rather than for patriotism.

One important point was thus settled. The discussion of other points was cut short by the arrival of Mr. Kosavitch, the lawyer, who had been engaged to look after Pavloff's case. He came in unannounced and before the officer had time to withdraw. The meeting was a confusing one, especially to Captain ———, but he concealed his annoyance with a cordial greeting and some commonplace comments upon the weather and the general prosperity of the province. Glancing at his watch, he pretended to remember an engagement and speedily withdrew.

"You need not tell me what he was after," said the

lawyer, as the door closed on the retiring form of the official gentleman.

"He proposed an escape on payment of a handsome amount of money?"

Mr. Hartmann made no response, as he felt bound by his promise of secrecy, though he was entirely satisfied that the lawyer should know what had happened. He believed in the idea that a lawyer ought to be informed of everything bearing on a case; and certainly this matter had a very important bearing.

"He can do exactly what he says he can," continued the other. "Stop a moment, I don't know what he has said and, therefore, must particularize."

He then recounted, almost word for word, what the visitor had proposed. It was evident that the lawyer had dealt with him before and knew his man.

But before deciding upon their line of action, the gentlemen went again to the prison to discuss the matter with Pushkin. A new permission was necessary, and this was obtained without difficulty and without any necessity for another cigarette. But the cigarette case had been prepared for the occasion, and if the official had demurred, it would have been presented as before.

At the suggestion of the lawyer, Ivan was not present at the interview. He passed the time strolling about the streets of Tambov, studying the groups in the market-place, and looking in the windows of the shops of the Gostinna Dvor or centre of trade. Every Russian town or city has an establishment of this sort, and the larger the town or city the more extensive is the collection of shops. The finest in Russia are, unquestionably, those of Moscow and St. Petersburg. That of Moscow is the most interesting, as it contains many features of

Oriental life that are not found in the younger capital on the banks of the Neva.

The result of the interview in the prison was, that the lawyer should arrange for a hearing as soon as it could be brought about and, in the meantime, Mr. Hartmann and Ivan were to return home and wait for a message from their legal adviser. They were also to raise thirty thousand rubles and have the money ready whenever it was needed. The lawyer thought this amount of money could be "put where it would do the most good."

He had planned to circumvent the official who proposed the escape and consequent exile of Pushkin, by arranging that he should have a hearing and be liberated under bonds to come before the authorities whenever called. This would enable him to live at home instead of spending his days abroad or dwelling under a fictitious name in some other part of Russia. A part of the money would be paid to the officious gentleman to secure his silence, and the rest would go into the hands of those who controlled the preliminary hearing.

All was progressing favorably, so far as indications could show, and the family of the prisoner were resting in the belief that he would soon be a free man and once more with them. Several days passed, each day bringing a hopeful message from the lawyer, who said the arrangements had been made for a hearing on the following Monday, when the presence of Mr. Hartmann and Ivan would be desirable.

Preparations were made for an early start on Monday morning, so as to bring them in Tambov before the hour fixed for the hearing. The money had been raised and was in notes of a thousand rubles each, the thirty notes being all crisp and new and evidently fresh from the bank. In most countries of the world, coin is preferred to notes in transactions of this kind, for the reason that it cannot be traced. But in Russia they are not so particular and, furthermore, there is no gold coin in circulation, the currency of the country being at a great discount, which has caused the complete disappearance of all coins except those of small denominations.

"I'll bring father home with me to-night," said Ivan to Nadia as he kissed her good-bye. "And, mother, I'll tell him while we're coming from Tambov, how much we've all missed him and how we've prayed every day for his release."

In a few moments the tarantass was rumbling over the road, and in due time it halted in front of the home of the lawyer, who was just at that moment coming out of his door. A glance at his face showed that something had gone wrong, and Mr. Hartmann immediately asked what was the matter.

"Come into the house and I'll tell you," was his abrupt reply. He was unwilling to talk in the presence of the driver of the tarantass and within hearing of anyone who might be passing along the street.

They followed him into the house and to the room which served him as office and reception parlor. Mr. Hartmann repeated his question; the other hesitated a moment and then said he had painful news to communicate.

"Last evening," said he, "an order was received from the Minister of the Interior for the immediate deportation to Siberia of Carl Pavloff, surnamed Pushkin. At midnight he was taken from the prison and sent away. I knew nothing of the matter until early this morning, and thus far I have not been able to find by what road he has gone. I was just on my way to the Chancellerie in the hope of learning something. I have already been there twice this morning, but no one who could tell me anything had then arrived."

"Sent to Siberia!" exclaimed Ivan, his face white with terror. "How can I go back to mother and Nadia with this dreadful news?"

CHAPTER VI.

ON THE ROAD TO EXILE.

Inquiry at the prison and at the Chancellerie availed but little. All that could be learned was what they already knew, that Pushkin had been taken from the prison at midnight by order of the Minister of the Interior and sent away. The prison-keeper did not even know if he had been sent to Siberia; all he could say was that a sergeant of police had brought an order for the prisoner's removal and had taken him away in a telyega (a common wagon) under escort of a soldier. The order was entirely regular in form and in fifteen minutes after delivering it the sergeant departed with his prisoner.

There are several ways out of Tambov, and nobody knew by which one of the roads the prisoner had gone. The railway from Saratov on the banks of the Volga to Koslov and Moscow passes through Tambov, and Pushkin might have been taken in either direction, east or west. Going to the west, he would in all probability be sent to Moscow, while if he was taken eastward, he would reach the terminus of the railway at Saratov, whence he might be sent up the Volga to Kazan on the great road from St. Petersburg and Moscow to Siberia. Or he might be sent from Saratov to the other side of the Volga and thence by one of several wagon roads to the land of exile. A hundred miles or so to the North of the Koslov-Saratov railway is another line almost parallel to it; a wagon-road northeastward from Tambov intersects the railway at Penza, where the train could be taken to Syzran, another landing on the Volga higher up than Saratov. The convicts in Siberia have a saying to the effect that "He who runs away has but one road, he who pursues him has twenty." The same proverb rises painfully to the thoughts of the friends of one who has been spirited away in the night when they seek to discover in what direction he has been taken.

Let us follow the fortunes of Pushkin on his way into exile. As he stepped into the telyega he was handcuffed to the soldier to make sure that he did not escape. The sergeant mounted the box at the side of the driver of the vehicle and then the order was given to go on. As they neared a corner of the street, two or three blocks from the prison gate, the sergeant gave the command:

"*Na Leva* (turn to the left)!"

A little further on the order "*Na Prave* (turn to the right)!" was given, and the driver without checking the speed of his horses obeyed the instruction. In a few minutes they were out of the city and in the open country, as was evident by the change in the condition of the roads. The telyega is at best an uncomfortable vehicle, far worse than the tarantass; the latter is built with some attention to the comfort of its occupants, while the former is made solely for purposes of transportation. Compared with the tarantass, the telyega is like the common farm-wagon of America compared with a family carriage. On a smooth road, and filled with straw and blankets for a passenger to lie upon, it is uncomfortable enough ; on a rough road, with two men chained together to occupy it and a driver urging his horses at their best speed, the telyega is an instrument of torture of no mean order. Especially so, when one of the occupants has been torn from home and friends and is on his way into exile.

But the torture was not to continue long, for the telyega followed a road nearly parallel with the railway and stopped at the first station to the eastward of Tambov. The police had reasons of their own for not taking their prisoner to the station in the city and making their departure from that point, but what those reasons were they did not choose to say. The journey had been so timed that the party had only a short while, less than half an hour, to wait at the station, ere an eastbound train arrived and took them on board. The telyega remained at the station until after the departure of the train and then was driven slowly back to the city. Perhaps we shall again hear of this very telyega and another journey that it made.

The train rolled leisurely along, this is a habit of most railway trains in Russia, and arrived at Saratov only an hour behind its schedule time. During its journey Pushkin had occupied a place in a convict car along with several other men in the same category as himself, prisoners on their way to Siberia ; their guards sat or stood with their weapons ready to prevent any attempt at escape. Escape would have been next to impossible under the circumstances. Pushkin had been freed from the handcuffs which bound him to the soldier, but he was chained to a fellow prisoner, all the gang of prisoners being chained together in couples. Even had the doors been wide open and the guards offering no resistance, it would have been very difficult for two men thus hampered to get away. The windows of the car were strongly grated like those of a prison van.

Pushkin had visited Saratov on previous occasions and always admired it, as it is a very picturesque city. It has a hundred thousand inhabitants and more; it possesses a considerable trade with the country on both sides of the Volga and far into the interior. It can boast a goodly proportion of inhabitants of German origin; its streets are wide, and its houses are generally well built. There is a great deal of wealth at Saratov, and its churches are second only to those of Moscow and St. Petersburg. The prisoner had neither the opportunity nor the mood for looking at Saratov or anything it contained. A covered wagon, like an omnibus, or rather resembling the "Black Maria" as it is known to the denizens of Boston and New York, was at the station waiting for its prey. The exiles were huddled into it and then driven rapidly to the prison, which swung wide its gates when they approached and closed with a clang as they passed within. Here they were to wait until a convoy was ready for Siberia. It might be a day or two, or it might be longer; who could tell?

In the Russian exile system it is the custom to accumulate those who are to form a convoy at certain central points. When a sufficient number has been gathered the convoy is started, and it is expected to keep up a certain rate of march day by day until its destination is reached. In the large towns or cities there are depots or forwarding prisons, and it is here that the convoys are made up. A great deal depends upon the activity of the police, the amount of crime, or the imperative orders of the Minister of the Interior and his satellites; if there is a pressure of business, the convoys are too numerous, and the forwarding prisons become crowded; while, on the other hand, if there is a lull in crime, or in revolutionary movements, the convoys are small and the prisons have space to spare. Unhappily, the latter contingency is rarely known.

There is a story of an Oriental king who one day told his grand vizier that he wanted to behead a hundred men the next morning, and ordered the vizier to take his pen and make out the list.

The king named man after man among those who were at court, but after naming all he could think of he lacked one of the complete hundred. He paused to reflect; his pause lasted several minutes, and then he said to the waiting vizier :

" I can't think of any one else, put down your own name."

The vizier did as he was directed and was duly beheaded with the others on the following morning.

Russians say that the Minister of the Interior orders arrest and exile by administrative process very much as this Eastern king ordered men for execution, solely for his amusement and to keep his jailers in practice ; they intimate that he sometimes does not hesitate to consign his own followers to the hard fate which he so readily decrees to others.

Down to his arrival at Saratov, Pushkin had worn the clothing in which he was arrested. But he was now on the road to Siberia, was associated with convicts, was, in fact, a convict under sentence, although he had been charged with no crime so far as his friends and himself could ascertain, had never been tried and consequently never been convicted. The will of the Minister of the Interior, whom he had never seen, was the law which condemned him to exile in Siberia.

He was required to give up his ordinary clothing and adopt a convict's suit, which consisted of a coarse shirt and trousers of gray material, a gray overcoat and a rimless cap with a broad top. Cap and coat are of the same color, and thus a runaway prisoner can readily be distinguished and his apprehension facilitated.

For his feet he had a pair of boots and a pair of coarse stockings and he was allowed to buy a change of clothing with the little money that he admitted was in his possession; he had managed to secrete the bank-note which his wife conveyed to him, and this he carefully kept for the time when it would be sorely needed. The government generously gave him a linen bag in which his spare clothing was placed, but the bag and clothing were regularly searched to make sure that they contained nothing contraband.

In one respect he was better treated than he had been at the prison in Tambov, as he was not held in solitary confinement. In what may be called the preparatory stage of his exile life, a prisoner is secluded from others, and this seclusion may last for years, but when he starts on the road to Siberia he has the advantage of companionship. True, this companionship may often be repulsive to a sensitive man, as all sorts of people are herded together,—the high-born political offender with the common burglar or other criminal. Formerly the government made a distinction between political prisoners (who are generally spoken of as "politicals") and those condemned for ordinary crimes. They went in separate convoys, and were usually kept apart from each other but in more recent times this distinction has altogether been set aside.

Politicals and criminals are now sent in the same convoys, live together in the same prisons, work at the same benches or in the same gangs, and are not infrequently chained together. They are subject to exactly the same treatment in every way, and this circumstance implies a great deal, as we shall find in one of the sad experiences of Carl Pavloff. For the present we will deal with the practice of isolating prisoners and never allowing them to see each other.

In the great prison of Petropavlovsk at St. Petersburg, which we have already mentioned, the prisoners are confined in separate apartments in the casemates. When they enter the place they are stripped and examined, and after the examination they are supplied with prison suits of coarse shirts and trousers and long wrappers like dressing-gowns. Their guards are forbidden to talk to them, other than to give orders in the fewest possible words, and as soon as the change of clothing is effected and the examination is complete, they are locked in their cells and left to themselves.

One of Pushkin's companions in misfortune (Dubayeff was his name) had been an inmate of the Petropavlovsk prison and thus described his experiences :

" It was about midnight when I was arrested at my lodgings in St. Petersburg and within half an hour I was inside the gloomy fortress. The closed carriage was driven into a court-yard, and I was ordered to step to the ground and follow the officer who arrested me. We were preceded by a soldier carrying a lantern, and I could see nothing except what was immediately around me. Before the carriage stopped, we had been driven around and around through a great many corridors and passages, so that it was utterly impossible for me to know in what part of the great fortress I was locked up.

"The casemates of the fortress were originally intended for cannon, but for a century and more they have been occupied by prisoners and not by artillery. It is fortunate for those of us who are locked up there that the architect of the fortress intended the casemates for the legitimate uses of those places, as they are much larger than the ordinary cells of a prison. The one I was in was about 25 feet x 15 feet and the ceiling was fully 12 feet high; there was a window in one end and a door in the other, but the window was so high up that I could not reach it. It was heavily grated on the outside, and the iron sash could be moved at the bottom so as to admit or keep out the air."

"Were there any evidences that anybody else had been there before you?" Pushkin asked.

"Evidences! plenty of them. A small lamp was burning in the cell, and as soon as I was left alone I took it up to examine the place. On the floor I discovered a path worn in the solid concrete, worn by the steps of others who had paced back and forth thousands and thousands of times from one corner of the cell to the corner diagonally opposite. For years and years the place had been occupied; men and women, perhaps, had come and gone, each one adding to the pathway until it was as easily perceptible as the track of a hundred wagons across a field. And remember, this path is made with felt slippers, as they take away your boots when you enter the prison and give you a pair of soft slippers instead.

"My brain went in a whirl at this discovery. I thought perhaps I might be in the very cell that was occupied by Lieutenant-Colonel Battenkoff and perhaps my fate might be the same as his."

"Who was he?" Pushkin inquired. "I never heard of him."

"He was one of the so-called Decembrists, the men who, in December, 1825, at the time of the death of Alexander I. and the accession of Nicholas, sought to overthrow the existing government and establish one founded upon a constitution. They were unsuccessful in their attempt; five of the leaders were hanged, others were imprisoned in St. Petersburg, and others (about two hundred) were sent to Siberia for life.

"Colonel Battenkoff was kept in solitary confinement in the Petropavlovsk prison for twenty-one years and was then exiled to Siberia. During the time he was in prison he never saw anybody but his guards, never saw a newspaper, and had no communication with his family or any one else. He was practically as dead to the world as a man in his tomb."

"I wonder he did not become insane," remarked Pushkin as the other paused.

"That is the fate of a great many prisoners," was the reply, "and probably would have been that of Colonel Battenkoff if he had not been allowed some occupation. He was permitted to have a Hebrew Bible and a dictionary, and during his imprisonment he translated the Bible from the original Hebrew into Russian. That was all that saved him."

"Did you ever know about the insanity of prisoners in that fortress?"

"Yes, I could name several, yes, many, who became

insane and either died in a state of raving madness or lapsed into the condition of hopeless idiots. There was Midshipman Diboff for one, Lieutenant Zaikin for another, young and promising men when they were shut up in the fortress and deprived of all occupations. They were not allowed anything to read, could have no writing materials, and so could do nothing except walk up and down their solitary cells or sit on their beds and think, think, think. Can you wonder that their minds gave way under this treatment and that their reason fled never to return?

"Many women have gone insane in that dreadful prison. Think what it must be for a woman, reared in the highest circles of society, educated, refined, delicate, unaccustomed to the rough side of the world, to be suddenly torn from home and friends and buried alive in the tomb-like vaults where the Emperor sends so many of his subjects. Days, weeks, months and years s without a word from outside that pile of stone, to comfort her in her captivity. She sees no one but her guards, hears no friendly voice, can look on nothing but the walls dripping with moisture, and cannot even regard the blue dome of the sky above. Reason totters and falls, but the Czar and his minions are without pity; it is their intention to drive the prisoner to madness in the hope that in her raving she may reveal something which will lead to the arrest of others and secure their incarceration where they can no longer be a menace to the security of the Imperial throne.

"O! my brother," Dubayeff continued, "your lot is terrible, but it is happiness supreme compared to that of many victims of Imperial hate who are to-day imprisoned in the fortress of Petropavlovsk. It is better, far

better, to be on the road to Siberia than locked in the casemates of that prison whose very name blanches the face of every liberal-minded Russian from one end to the other of this vast empire. Shout for joy that you have air, sun, sky and companionship, and are not buried in that awful tomb, over whose doorway may well be written the words of Dante in his description of Inferno :
"All hope abandon, ye who enter here."

CHAPTER VII.

A PLOT TO ESCAPE.

Eight days after his arrival at Saratov, Pushkin learned from one of the guards that the convoy would be sent off to Siberia on the following morning. An hour after receiving this information he was summoned to the barber's shop of the prison, where one side of his head was shaved bare, the hair being allowed to remain on the other side. Then he was sent to the blacksmith's shop to be fettered. Ten or twelve others received a similar summons and were similarly treated.

A belt of leather was passed around his waist and buckled in front. From this belt hung two chains which reached to the ankles, where they were secured to the ankle-irons by rivets that could not be loosened except by filing their heads on the opposite ends. Leather straps were passed around the ankles inside the irons so that the flesh should not be chafed; these leathers are supplied to the prisoners as a part of their outfit, and we may be sure that the victims of Russian cruelty take good care of them in order to reduce their personal sufferings as much as possible. The government makes a pretense of mercy by ordering that the irons placed on a prisoner shall not exceed five pounds in weight, but it oftens happens that this regulation is not complied with. Many a prisoner has worn chains weighing six, seven, eight pounds, or more; when he complained of his illegal treatment, he was laughed at by his jailers and very likely punished for "insubordination."

The irons that were placed upon Pushkin were not above the regulation weight, but when placed upon him they seemed to weigh not five pounds but as many hundred. It was not altogether the amount of iron as indicated by the scales that made this great weight, but the sense of humiliation that came with the fastening of the rivets and the thought that the irons must be worn day and night, night and day, for so many long months and for many and many a weary mile. At this hour, as you read these lines, thousands of men are wending their way along the roads of Siberia, clanking their chains at every step, through pools of mud or clouds of dust in summer and in winter through the deep snows that fall in the severe climate of the North. And thousands, many thousands of prisoners, men and women, have walked these roads before them in the same way, driven by that authority which cannot be disputed wherever the Russian flag holds it domination, the despotic authority of the Great White Czar.

Setting aside all question of humiliation and degradation caused by being compelled to wear the chains of his imperial master, Pushkin found that the burden of five pounds of iron was far from light. The movement of his feet were greatly hampered; his steps were slow, and he fully realized the utter impossibility of attempting to escape as long as he was thus fettered. Should he seek to conceal his irons beneath his garments, the clanking of the links would reveal their presence to every one who came near him, and it was quite out of his power to increase his pace to a run.

Dubayeff's turn to be ironed came immediately after that of Pushkin, and as soon as the work was completed they were taken back to the "kamera," or room whence they had been brought to receive the attentions of the blacksmith.

Pushkin threw himself on the floor and wept like a child.

"Cheer up! cheer up! my brother," said Dubayeff, gently. "We are companions in misfortune, and grief will do us no good. Do you suppose your tears will move the Czar's minions to release you from these irons or give you back to your family?"

At the mention of his family, Pushkin's sorrow was greater than before, and his sobs were mingled with lamentations and prayers.

The other did all in his power to comfort the sufferer, but to no effect. Pushkin had borne with bravery his arrest and imprisonment, together with his condemnation to Siberia, but this last blow had broken his spirit, and he said so to his companion as soon as he could bring himself to speak coherently.

"That is one purpose of putting you in chains" said Dubayeff in reply. "Our imperial master wishes to break our spirit, and there is no better way than this. These chains are the decorations that he gives us to make us love him, just as he gives his faithful officers the decorations that they wear on their breasts. It's only a change in the way of wearing our insignia, that is all."

We may well realize that Pushkin was in no mood for jesting, but the ironical remark of Dubayeff had more

eeruh
he
rist
yet.

effect in drying the sufferer's tears than anything that
ad been said before. In a little while he was able to
talk calmly upon their situation.

"I've worn the chains before," said Dubayeff, "and
become accustomed to them. When they were first
placed on me, I felt as you do, and was ready to die
rather than bear those marks of degradation. But I
found that other men by the hundred and thousand, no
worse than I, had worn chains and were wearing them
yet; so I reasoned that they were badges of honor
rather than otherwise, and I would rather stand in fetters as I stand to-day, than be the honored guest of the
emperor who can sit calmly down to his banquets while
so many men and women are dragging out their lives
in poverty and suffering, solely because of his autocratic
will."

The conversation was interrupted by ıd "brodyag,"
or vagabond, who had just been ironed. He crept up to
Pushkin's side, and, at the pause which followed the last
words of Dubayeff, the brodyag said in a low whisper:

"Brother, for a ruble, I'll tell you how to loosen your
irons so that they won't hurt you near as much."

"To tell is one thing, but to do is another," responded
Dubayeff, who overheard the brodyag's words.

"To tell is a good part of it," retorted the criminal,
for such he was, and had seen a great deal of service
under the state. "For a ruble I'll name the man."

"What does he mean?" queried Pushkin, turning to
his friend.

"He means that there is somebody in prison who can
supply a file with which you can loosen the rivets of
your irons. You can make this loosening serve you in
two ways. If you are in a plot to escape, you can get
your irons ready, so that when the time comes they can

be thrown off and you will have full use of your legs for running away. If you escape and are retaken, you will be flogged and sent to the mines, and in escaping you must travel a long way, in constant danger of arrest, as you have no passport. Many prisoners use the file to loosen the rivets of the chains so that they can partly remove them at nights and thus make their sleeping easier. They do this on the great road to Siberia, and for small bribes the guards will connive at this arrangement, though they will not allow the irons removed altogether, lest they might get into trouble.

"Our brodyag friend, whom we will call Nemo, as we will never know his real name, proposes to tell us which one of the guards of the prison will lend us a file for the purpose. Of course, the guard must be well paid for his trouble and the risk of discovery that he runs."

"What would you advise me to do?"

"Frankly, I advise nothing at present. We shall be watched so closely in the early part of our journey that there will be no chance of escaping and a great deal of being discovered. Better wait till we are well on our road, and then there will not be so much vigilance exercised by the officers who have us in charge."

Nemo admitted the force of Dubayeff's advice, and then moved away. But before doing so he intimated that they might find him useful, and he would always be ready to render any service in his power, if they were willing to pay for it.

"You'll see plenty of this kind in Siberia," said Dubayeff, after the fellow was out of ear-shot. "He's an old offender, and has probably been to the mines more than once; he belongs to the Don't-remember family, which is very numerous in Siberia.

"There are brodyags who have been ten or twelve

times to the mines," he continued. "They manage to escape and travel back to European Russia or to the valley of the Obi by paths known only to them and their kindred; they are compelled to keep to these paths, as they would surely be captured if they ventured on the regular roads where a careful watch is maintained. When their paths are discovered, they make new ones, and they have a way of conveying information about these routes that is known only to the initiated. I'll tell you more about the secret roads when I have more time; at present we must think of leaving here for our great march to exile. God grant that we may meet no misfortune greater than we have now!"

At six o'clock the next morning all the prisoners were turned out of the kameras, and ordered to be ready to move. A breakfast of the regular prison fare, black bread and barley soup, was furnished to them, and they ate it hastily. Each man was provided with a wooden spoon, which he was allowed to retain; metal spoons were not allowed, lest they might be shaped into weapons or into implements that might facilitate escape. They were sixty in all, and when the breakfast was over, they were drawn up in line and the roll was called. Every man answered to his name, the blacksmith and a soldier examined the irons to see that the rivets had not been tampered with, and then the jailer turned to an officer and muttered the single word "*gotovey* (ready)!" Each prisoner shouldered the linen bag that contained his scanty belongings, the gates were opened, and escorted by soldiers in front, in rear and at both sides, the column filed into the outer world and moved in the direction of the landing-place of the river steamboats.

At the head of the column of prisoners were four old

men, who had been chosen as recipients for that day of whatever gifts might be made to the "unfortunates," as the exiles are called by the Russian populace. This is an old custom that has prevailed throughout the empire, ever since the exile system was established. When a convoy is in motion along the road, or when a party of prisoners is at work, certain ones among them are appointed to receive gifts on behalf of all. At the end of the day, there is a fair division, if the articles are such that they can be divided; if no division is possible, the donations are utilized for the benefit of all.

Loaves of bread and other edibles were given by the people, and a stranger's attention would have been drawn to the circumstance that by far the greater part of the gifts were from poor peasants, and not from those who had been blessed by birth or fortune or both. The poor of Russia are charitable, but the rich are not so. Of course, there are exceptions on both sides of the rule, as with other rules the world over.

At the landing-place lay a government steamboat, the steam escaping from her pipes and showing that she was ready to start. The sixty prisoners, the majority of them criminals of various grades, were marched on board the boat and into a "cage" that occupied a considerable part of the lower deck. This cage measured about thirty feet by sixty, and the sides and the ends were formed by iron gratings, in which the apertures were four or five inches square. The brodyags spoke of it as the "chicken-coop," and it certainly bore a strong resemblance to a chicken-coop on an enormous scale. It is just such a cage as we might find in New Zealand to-day, if that enormous bird of former times, the moa, were still in existence, or such as the ostrich farmer of South Africa or Arizona, at the present time, would use for enclosing his biped stock.

When all were on board, the order was given to start. The lines were cast off, the boat swung into the stream, the engines were put in motion, and steadily the *Nadeshda* (Hope) stemmed the current of the Volga. Then, and not till then, the prisoners learned from one of the guards that they were to be taken up the Volga to Kasan, whence they would ascend the river Kama to Perm. At the latter city they would be on the great road to Siberia, the route which has been watered by the tears of the many thousand of "unfortunates" who have been condemned to traverse it.

On and on went the steamer. The occupants of the chicken-coop were allowed to do pretty much as they liked, except that they could not leave their quarters; they had light and air and could look upon the landscape that was presented to their view during the progress of their floating prison, and at night they descended to the sleeping cabins below deck, where the guards assigned them to places among a series of benches that served as beds. Scanty rations of bread and soup were supplied to them, and the gifts of the compassionate in their march through the streets of Saratov, added materially to the comfort of their evening meal.

The boat had been only a few hours on her way, before some of the prisoners formed a plan to escape. The plot was hatched among the criminal convicts, who agreed not to include the politicals until the last moment, for fear they might be betrayed. But through the kindly act of the brodyag, Nemo, with whom we have already made acquaintance, the scheme was made known to Dubayeff, under promise of secrecy. Considering it had a possible chance of success, Dubayeff sought an opportunity to talk it over with Pushkin, and get his opinion on the subject.

Pushkin listened with an air of vacancy to what his friend whispered; in fact, he paid very little attention, and heard not more than half of what was said. His thoughts were with his family, and as he pictured the home made desolate by his absence, his eyes filled with tears that he could not retain.

Had he known the occurrences of the last few days, and the new troubles that surrounded his wife and children, he would have been in the depths of despair, and ready for any enterprise that gave him the least hope of rejoining them, however desperate and dangerous it might be.

CHAPTER VIII.

THE DRAG-NET OF THE POLICE.

After two days spent at Tambov in fruitless inquiries, Mr. Hartmann, and Ivan decided to go home and break as gently as possible the sad news that they had for the wife and daughter of the prisoner. Before doing so, they deposited in the government bank the thirty thousand rubles they had brought with them in the expectation of making use of it.

As they approached Pushkin's house, the driver suddenly pulled up his horses and called to Mr. Hartmann.

"What is it!" asked the latter, as he leaned forward.

"There are ten or twelve mounted soldiers and two carriages standing at the corner of the house."

Both gentlemen looked out and saw what the driver indicated.

"There are some soldiers at the door," continued the driver, "and they stand there as though they wouldn't let anybody in or out."

"Well, drive on," said Mr. Hartmann.

The driver's inclination had been to turn around and get away as speedily as possible, but he was too well trained to demur when an order was given by his master.

As the carriage stopped in front of the house, the gentleman alighted and stepped forward to enter the doorway.

"Halt!" said one of the soldiers as he held his rifle across the door. The gentlemen paused.

Then the soldier called to an officer who was inside. The latter came out in a few moments, and proved to be the one who had made the arrest of Carl Pavloff, as described in the opening chapter. He at once recognized Ivan, and evidently knew who Mr. Hartmann was, as he called both of them by name.

"I arrest you in the name of the Czar," said he, without a word of explanation, as soon as they had answered to their names.

"Which one do you arrest?" Mr. Hartmann asked.

"Both of you," was the reply. "You must be ready to go to Tambov in two hours."

"Can I go, under escort of course, to my own house?" queried Mr. Hartmann.

"Yes," was the laconic reply. "You must be back here in the time I've named, and the guard will make sure that you are here."

The officer immediately detailed one of the gendarmes and two of the mounted soldiers to accompany Mr. Hartmann, who at once returned to his tarantass, after shaking Ivan's hand affectionately. Not a word was spoken by either, as they could say nothing without being overhead by the officer. Mr. Hartman went away for the purpose of bidding good-bye to his family, and arranging as best he could the management of his affairs during his absence, and also of being spared the painful scene inside the house of his exiled friend.

"You can go into the house, if you like," said the officer, turning to Ivan, as soon as the tarantass drove away with Mr. Hartmann. The youth need no second bidding, and entered immediately.

His mother was lying on a lounge and just recovering from a swoon, Nadia was standing over and trying to comfort her. Ivan embraced his mother and sister, and as they did so, the latter said :

"We've been arrested and told that we must start for Tambov in two hours. What shall we do?"

"Be a brave girl, just as brave a girl as the world ever saw," replied Ivan ; " there's nothing else you can do."

Nadia promised through her tears that she would remember his words, and then she busied herself with her mother and showed that she was wonderfully self-possessed for a girl of her age.

Ivan talked a few minutes with his mother, when she had recovered from her swoon, and then said he would arrange matters the best way he could for the care of the place during their absence. He did not say in so many words that he was also under arrest, and was to be taken to Tambov, but the mother fully realized that such was the case.

"Don't trouble yourself," he said cheerily, "about the house and the estate. I will give all the directions to our people, while you and Nadia make your preparations. You heard what I said to Nadia, and she'll help you to get together the things you want."

Then he went away, leaving Madame Pushkin and Nadia alone. He confided the care of the younger children to their governess and the nurse Francesca ; the house was left in charge of the old housekeeper, who had been with the family since his childhood and long before, and the affairs of the estate were left in the hands of Joseph, and more particularly in those of the *nadziratel*, or overseer, who had a thorough knowledge of everything connected with the place. He was born on the estate, was a serf in the days of serfdom, and had risen to his present position through his intelligence and ability.

Within the time specified in the arrest, the preparations for departure had been made. Nadia and her mother had each gathered a few extra articles of clothing and some personal comforts, which they wished to carry, the officer warning them that they must take nothing that would be contrary to the rules. Exactly what the rules forbade he did not specify, as he knew that their hand-bags would be carefully searched by the jailers on their arrival at Tambov.

Ivan had also filled a small travelling-bag, and when he came out of the house, at the expiration of the two hours, he found Mr. Hartmann waiting outside.

The two carriages were called up. The women were ordered into one of them, and the men into the other, and in a few minutes the vehicles were on the road to Tambov.

"They are very lenient," whispered Mr. Hartmann to the youth. "Usually, in a case like this, they separate mother and daughter, and put each of them into a carriage by herself. Then, too, they almost always make arrests at night, just as they arrested your father, and they capture one and take her away before informing the other. The government must be growing humane, or perhaps it is because they couldn't spare the necessary number of carriages and soldiers."

"Can you tell why we have been arrested?" Ivan asked.

"That is something known only to the Czar and those who serve him," replied the other. "I suppose we shall know some time, but for the present I am as ignorant as you."

"Perhaps it is because we are the family of Carl Pavloff," said Ivan, "and you are his friend."

"That is very likely the case," said Mr. Hartmann. "Thousands of arrests have been made in Russia for exactly the same reason. A man is under suspicion, orders for his arrest are issued, and he is seized and taken to prison, and then one after another the members of his family are apprehended, and also anybody who is his friend, or has even a casual acquaintance with him. Did you ever see the instructions to the police concerning persons under surveillance?"

Ivan answered in the negative. Then Mr. Hartmann endeavored to give from memory some of the instructions that are issued from the office of the Minister of the Interior, in the shape of blanks, to be filled up monthly and sent to the Department for the Preservation of Order and Public Safety.

"As nearly as I can remember," said the gentleman, "they require the fullest particulars concerning the name, residence, family, habits and occupations, of the individual under consideration. They wish to know if he lives alone or with some one else, and they want all particulars concerning those he lives with. They must know the name of his laundress, and her residence, the restaurant where he takes his meals, what he eats, and what he pays for his food, what library he visits, and what books he reads, how he supports himself, what time he goes out and returns, and where he goes to when not at home. They must know if he is paying attention to any woman, who she is, where she lives, and how often he calls on her; if a woman is the subject of inquiry they ask the name of her lover (if any), when, or how often he calls on her, and how long he remains. They ask for the name of all a man's visitors and what is done during their visits; and they also ask if he plays cards or is ever intoxicated.

"So you see," he continued, "it is dangerous to belong to the family of a suspicious person, and equally dangerous to be his friend."

"And knowing this danger you did not hesitate to do all you could for my poor father," responded Ivan. "Oh, how good and generous you have been!"

"It would have been very dishonorable for me to refuse all the help I could give at such a time," Mr. Hartmann replied. "Your father has been a good friend to me more than once, and at times when his friendship meant a great deal.

"What they will do with us when we get to Tambov I don't know," he continued, "but it is pretty certain that we shall be separated at the door of the prison. I have sent word to our friend Kosavitch, saying what has happened, and he will do whatever he can in our behalf. I specially asked him to look after your mother and sister, and make their imprisonment as little of a hardship as possible. You and I can endure a great deal more than these unhappy women, especially Nadia, who is so young, and has so little knowledge of the world."

The gentleman did not say all that he thought, as he knew it would greatly distress his young companion, without helping matters in the least. We will leave them, and look into the other tarantass, which is rapidly rolling along towards the city.

For some time after starting from their home, mother and daughter were clasped in a close embrace, and each gave way to her grief in a flood of tears. Gradually the tears were dried and the women became more composed. The mother was the first to speak.

"You remember Ivan's words to be a brave girl, do you not?"

"Yes, dear mother," was the reply, "and I will be just as brave as I can, so that Ivan will be proud of me. But, oh, mother, what will they do with us?"

"I cannot tell, my child, but we shall probably be separated when we get to the prison."

"Separated! dear mother! shall I be separated from you?"

"I fear so, fear it very much."

Nadia's tears flowed again, but she soon repressed them with the recollection of her promise to her brother that she would be a brave girl.

"What makes you think we shall be separated, mother?" Nadi asked.

"Because that is the custom when people are arrested, as we have been, without warning, and without any charges so far as we know. Husbands and wives, parents and children, brothers and sisters, are thrown into prison, and though they may be under the same roof, they are never allowed to see or communicate with each other. Did you ever hear the story of Marie Prisedski?"

"I never did," was the reply. "Please tell me about it, dear mother."

"You are nineteen years old, Nadia," said Madame Pushkin; "younger persons than you have been arrested and sent into exile, and so you will have need to be a brave girl.

"Ivan Prisedski was a wealthy land-owner in the province of Pultava. He was never suspected of disloyalty, but all his four children were accused of being 'untrustworthy' and sent to Siberia. Marie was the youngest; she was sixteen years old, and one day she was arrested by order of General Strelnikoff and taken to prison. She was placed in a cell by herself, and not allowed to see anybody but her guards and the prison doctor. Two or three times she tried to speak to the guard, but each time she did so, the soldier answered, '*Prikazano ne gavarit* (talking is forbidden).'

"Her cell was small and gloomy, she had no books or papers of any kind, and all that she could do was to think. At home she had every comfort that her father's wealth could give, and without a moment's warning she had been torn away from these comforts and placed in this living tomb.

"To weep and to think, to think and to weep, she could do nothing more. She was taken to the prison at midnight, and all that night she paced the cell in agony. Day brought no relief, except the blessed light, and when the second night came, she began to feel her mind giving way. Then she determined that she would keep herself from going insane, and occupied her time in going over the lessons she had learned from her teachers, making calculations in arithmetic, and repeating the boundaries of all the provinces of Russia, the length of its rivers, and everything else that she could call to mind. In this way she occupied herself, and the days went on one after another."

"And how long did they keep her there, all alone, in that awful prison?"

"Two weeks, fourteen dreary days, after her arrest, she was taken from prison and into a court-room, where everybody was a stranger to her. General Strelnikoff presided in this court and she was not allowed to have anybody to defend her. He began her examination by saying that she was charged with very serious crimes, and was in danger of being exiled to Siberia for a long term of years."

"And was she really guilty?"

"There was no proof that she had done anything, and the whole object of arresting her was to get evidence, if possible, against her older sister, who was under suspicion. The general told her that the government would consider her youth and inexperience, and if she would make a full confession, show that she was repentant, promise to reform, and answer honestly and truthfully every question he was about to ask, she would be set free at once and allowed to go home.

"She declared that she knew nothing, and when she repeated her declaration after many questions, she was sent to Siberia."

The woman's voice choked as she pronounced these words, and she could not proceed. When she was able to speak, which was not for some minutes, she continued:

"Perhaps you are under suspicion, my child, and perhaps they only seek to make you a witness against your father, just as they tried to make this poor Marie a witness against her sister."

"But I don't know anything, not anything, against him or anybody else in the world. How can they use me as a witness, when I've nothing to tell?"

"I understand all that, and I know your father is innocent of any wrong. But I want to prepare you for what may happen, as I know what has happened many and many a time in Russia. Youth is no protection as I have shown you; children of fourteen have been banished to Siberia as dangerous enemies of the government, who could not be allowed to live in the places of their birth."

Again there came silence and tears. The time was rapidly passing, and the separation which mother and daughter feared was approaching as the tarantass sped on its way.

Nadia had hoped to again see her brother when they reached Tambov, but she was doomed to disappointment. The tarantass containing the women had been the first to start, and consequently was in the lead; it had been driven at a brisk pace, while the one containing the men came much more slowly. It had been purposely planned to have the women at the prison and in their cells before the other vehicle drove into the yard; the driver of the second tarantass had his orders to go slowly, and consequently he was a full half hour behind the other in the time of its arrival.

Mother and daughter were sent to different cells, as the former had predicted. Their parting was one that we will not attempt to describe, further than that it was such as to melt the jailers to something like kindness, and especially so in the case of the younger of the two victims of the imperial will. The warder who had Nadia in charge, brought to her cell some things that were not on the list of what is supplied to prisoners by the government, and he really seemed to take pity on account of her youth and apparent innocence.

Hartmann and Ivan were likewise placed in different cells and forbidden to hold communication. They looked the next day and the next and the next for a visit from the lawyer Kosavitch, but he came not.

"Surely he has not deserted us," said Hartmann to himself, for there was no one else to whom he could speak. "He has not deserted us, I'm certain; but we re under such close surveillance that the safety of the government requires that he should not be permitted to see us.'"

And that was exactly the state of affairs.

Chapter IX

A Forged Confession.

Lest the reader may possibly think that the occurrences narrated in the preceding chapter are not founded upon fact, we will here refer to matters which are well known in Russia.

In 1879, Christina Tritchevitch, seventeen years old, and her brother fourteen years old, of Kiev, in the southern part of the empire, were exiled to Siberia. The charge against them was that their two elder brothers were revolutionists, but no complicity was shown on the part of the two exiled children. They were simply members of a dangerous family, and their presence in European Russia was a menace to the security of the throne of the Czar. They were sent to Kirinsk, in the province of Irkutsk, the very heart of Siberia.

At one time, 116 persons of both sexes, most of them young, were arrested in three days in Odessa, in the same manner as the arrests which have been described. No reasons were given, and it was not even charged that the captured individuals had given cause to suspect them of disloyalty; they were taken into custody and flung into dungeons in the hope that they would give

clews to plots which the police thought might be under way, but of which they had no proof. About the same time there were nearly as many arrests of the same kind in Kiev, and a proportionate number in other cities of Southern Russia. School-boys and girls, fifteen, sixteen, or seventeen years of age, were numerous among the captives, not that they were suspected of conspiracy, but because it was thought they might tell of the conversation and movements of older members of their families.

Four days after her incarceration, Madame Pushkin was informed that an officer of high rank was about to visit her.

She was taken, under guard of course, to the reception room of the prison, and there told to wait. In a few minutes an officer entered and said:

"I am Colonel X——— of his Imperial Majesty's service. I do not come here to-day in my official capacity, but as a friend who wishes to do you a kindness and secure the release of yourself and your daughter."

The woman looked intently at him and listened.

"Your husband has confessed his guilt and it will be useless for you to remain silent any longer. He has acknowledged his faults and is sincerely penitent, and he wishes you to tell all you know and save the family from further trouble."

Then he drew a paper from his pocket and read it to her. It was, or purported to be, a confession by Pushkin, that he had been concerned in plots against the government, and especially a recent plot that had been formed at Tambov and had for its object the destruction of the public buildings and the assassination of the governor of the province. It was signed by Pushkin, and witnessed by the law officer of the crown for that district.

After reading the paper he handed it to her, in order, as he said, that she might make sure he had given it correctly. The signature appeared to be that of her husband, and she was dumb with amazement at the contents of the document.

"Did my husband make this confession?" she asked.

"Yes," was the reply; "I was present when he made and signed it. As I said before, I come as a friend and not as an officer of the government, and my advice is that you send word to the crown officers that you are ready to answer truthfully all questions they shall ask. It is not necessary that I should be known in the matter, as I am acting individually and not officially, and you will not be giving any information, but only telling facts which are already known."

The document was a skillful forgery, and the whole confession was a series of guesses with no facts to go upon. It was devised in the hope that by means of it the woman might be induced to put the police in possession of clews that would be useful in making arrests; her husband was already on his way to Siberia, and therefore nothing more was needed on his account.

"If my husband made this confession," she replied, after a long pause, "he was not in his right mind. Some things in it may or may not be true, I cannot answer for that, but there are things stated here that I know are not true, and that he could not possibly have known anything about."

"Then you decline to act upon my friendly advice?"

"I should be stating a lie if I corroborated this paper," she replied. "There is nothing in it, not a line, that I know to be true, and there are several things, as I have just told you, that I know to be false."

He again urged her to think of her family, and especially of Nadia, who might be saved from Siberia if her mother would confess. "Your happiness and future, as well as hers, are at stake," he added, "and you have the choice for both of you of the mines of Siberia or your own home again."

She wept at the picture he presented, but she had no confession to make and repeated her assertion. The officer saw that the search for information in that quarter was useless, and after another refusal he rose to go.

She was taken back to her cell, and there gave way to her feelings in another flood of tears.

Then Nadia was sent for and subjected to the same ordeal. The same story was told, false from beginning to end: that Colonel X—— came not as an official of the government, but as a personal friend, that he wished to save such a young girl from the horrors of exile to Siberia, and all that she had to do was to say that so far as she knew and believed her father's confession was true, and that she was sorry for anything she had done that might in any way be construed as disloyal to their august master and sovereign, the Czar.

The poor girl could say nothing, for the very simple reason that she knew nothing. This she averred over and over again, and after each averment the result of her persistence in denial was set forth in all its horrors. She would condemn, not only herself, but the mother whom she loved, to exile in Siberia for a long term of years; the family would be broken up and might never again be united, her own life would be blasted, and all might be saved if she would only do what her good friend wished. It grieved him to the heart to see her so obstinate, as he felt sure that it was only the thoughtlessness of youth that controlled her.

Nadia cried and threw herself on the bench where she sat in an agony of despair. Her inquisitor continued to urge her to a confession, and even intimated that she would do well to go beyond the truth, rather than suffer the penalties he had portrayed.

"You would have me swear falsely against my father, would you?" she said, rising to her feet and quickly wiping away her tears. "Have me swear to what I know is not true! I would rather go to Siberia for the rest of my life than be a perjured witness to send my father there. I will tell you all the truth, and have told you everything I knew already."

She dropped again to the bench and was silent. It was evident that no information could be obtained from her, and the interview was brought to an end. The girl swooned and fell to the floor; she was carried to her cell, and for hours lay there unconscious.

The foregoing is one of the methods employed by the Russian police to obtain evidence. Forged confessions are taken to prisoners in the manner described, and not infrequently the victim falls into the trap so skillfully set. Sometimes the feelings of parents are wrought upon by telling them that their sons and daughters are about to be hanged, and the only escape for the young people will be through confession of their wrong; the terror-stricken parents are then brought to the cells where their children are held, and we can readily imagine how their tears and entreaties are exerted to bring about the desired confessions.

And all the time the police have no proof by which

the children can be hanged, or even kept in custody by process of law, and their sole object is to obtain proof through confession. During these interviews, which are painful enough to melt the hardest heart, the imperial prosecutor or one of his representatives stands outside the cell ready to take down the confession when the victim consents to say what is wanted.

Picture to yourself a mother bowed with grief and bathed in tears, imploring her son by all the reverence he holds for her gray hairs, by his love for her and for his father, by his dread of the scaffold or of long exile, pressing her face against his, and even falling at his feet in her despair, and begging, oh! so pleadingly, that he will answer the questions which are to be asked by the officials. Not till he answers them can she smile again, and without his penitence, she would rather the grave would open to receive her.

She is seeing him for the last time, unless he yields to her entreaties. The scaffold or Siberia will claim him for their own, and she will abandon hope as she passes out of the prison gate. Terrible is the ordeal for one who has thus before him the temptation to betray his friends, to save himself, and dry his mother's tears. Terrible, too, is the ordeal when the prisoner is ignorant of all complicity in acts that threaten the safety of the empire, and has simply been thrown into prison in the hope that thereby some information, or a clew to it, may be obtained.

Successively the same forged confession was presented to Mr. Hartmann and to Ivan, and with the same result. Afterwards, in order to terrify them, each of the four prisoners was confined in a darkened cell, or, rather, iron hoods were placed over the windows of the cells they occupied. They were thus deprived of light and air; there was a small crevice at the top of each hood, just enough to admit sufficient air to prevent suffocation, and sufficient light to enable the prisoner to discern indistinctly the extent of the walls, and then only by straining the vision. The cells were thus converted into gloomy caverns like the *oubliettes* of the Bastile, or those subterranean dungeons beneath the palace of the Doge of Venice, where state criminals were confined and perished.

This was similar to the measure adopted by General Strelnikoff at Odessa in 1882, in endeavoring to coerce some political prisoners into supplying him with the evidence he desired. It has been tried in other parts of the empire, but never with any great success. In the case of General Strelnikoff, the erection of hoods over the windows of the cells led indirectly to his assassination; the day after his death the official who succeeded him ordered the removal of the obnoxious coverings of the windows, and the prisoners suggested that the material might be used for the erection of a monument to Strelnikoff's memory.

Through one of the warders of the prison, with whom he had established friendly relations (of a financial character), Mr. Kosavitch was kept informed of what was going on within the walls. He repeatedly asked permission to visit the prisoners; he endeavored to convince the governor that they had a right to see their counsel, but the governor peremptorily refused the desired privilege. Next he sought the aid of the keeper, but though the latter was willing enough to earn an honest penny, he felt that he would be running altogether too great a risk in permitting the lawyer to enter the prison without authority. He would very likely be found out, and discovery would mean the loss of his situation and his liberty at the same time. Instead of watching the departure of others for Siberia, he would very likely be going there himself.

Mr. Kosavitch had adopted a cautious method of obtaining from the warder his daily budget of news. When the warder was relieved from duty, he went home to his family; the lawyer knew the road he would take, and very nearly the time when he would pass, and he managed to be at a convenient spot along the route at the proper time.

As the warder approached and saw the lawyer, the latter would be absorbed in something that had just attracted his attention. At one time he was looking into the window of a shop, at another he was measuring the diameter and height of a lamp-post, at another he was looking for a knife he had just dropped in the street. The warder paused to look at whatever occupied the lawyer's attention, and this naturally brought their heads within whispering distance of each other. Then, in the lowest tones, the warder told what he wished to communicate, but without looking at Mr. Kosavitch or appearing to speak to him. When he finished talking, he had apparently satisfied his curiosity and moved on, while the other man strolled away in the opposite direction.

In this way the lawyer learned of the forged confession and the attempt to extort its approval from each of the four prisoners, and he also learned of the darkening of the cells. The latter information was conveyed as he was looking for his pocket-knife in the dust of the street, and though he indicated no emotion by his outward demeanor, his face flushed with anger, and he restrained himself with difficulty. And every one who is familiar with lawyers is aware that it is no ordinary circumstance which rouses them to anything like emotion.

As he recovered his knife and thanked the warder for helping him to find it, he turned rather quickly on his heel, in fact, a good deal more quickly than usual.

"That is brutal business," he said to himself. "Try to make a woman betray her husband, a daughter and son to betray their father, and when they fail in their effort they darken the windows of the prisoners' cells. I'll go to the governor about it the very first thing to-morrow morning."

With this resolve he went home and spent a part of the evening in making up his mind as to exactly what he would say to that high official. He framed an admirable speech for the occasion, and went to bed in the confident hope that he would be able to turn this cruelty towards the prisoners into something for their advantage.

"I don't believe the governor would permit anything of the kind if he knew it," the lawyer said to himself, as he settled down to rest. "But the trouble is that the matter may be out of his jurisdiction; Colonel X—— may be acting under the direct orders of the Czar, and therefore quite independently, not only of the governor, but of the Minister of the Interior. Such things have happened in more instances than one.

"I won't say to myself what I think about the way things are managed in the empire," was his next thought, "or I might find myself guilty of violating Section 245 of the Penal Code, and be liable to be sent to Siberia." Then he settled a little deeper into his pillow and went to sleep.

Here is the paragraph of the Code that was in his mind :

" Section 245. All persons found guilty of composing and circulating written or printed documents, books, or representations, calculated to create disrespect for the Supreme Authority, or for the personal character of the GOSSUDAR (the Czar) or for the government of his Empire, shall be condemned, as insulters of MAJESTY, to deprivation of all civil rights, and to from ten to twelve years of penal servitude.'

Mr. Kosavitch slept fairly well and was promptly at the door of the governor's office when it opened to visitors the next day. Two or three others were there before him, and he was required to wait a half hour or more till his turn came to have an audience with the representative of Imperial authority.

CHAPTER X.

OVER THE SIBERIAN FRONTIER.

We left Pushkin as the steamboat on which he was a prisoner was ascending the Volga on its way from Saratov to Kasan and Perm.

The plot to escape was discussed by Dubayeff and Pushkin after the former had succeeded in inducing his fellow prisoner to cease thinking of home for a while and consider their immediate circumstances. The plan was to loosen a few of the gratings that formed the cage, and for this purpose some of the prisoners had secured two or three files. A sentinel constantly paced the deck at each side of the cage; the prisoners were to assemble in a group at one side of the cage, some standing and others sitting, for the ostensible purpose of whiling away the time with songs. This would be nothing unusual and unlikely to excite suspicion; every time the sentinel's back was turned those who held the files were to cut at the iron and instantly cease operations when their guard wheeled about at the end of his walk.

The singing would drown the sound of the files and if no inspection should be made of the gratings enough of the rods might be cut away at the bottom to allow room for a man to pass through when they were bent aside. As the work progressed, the notches cut by the files were to be filled with paste made from the rye bread supplied as a part of the rations whenever operations were suspended. Later on, the files would be used to loosen the rivets of the ankle-irons, and all would then be ready for the last act of the plot.

One of the prisoners was to start a fire in their sleeping quarters, and at the flash everybody was to rush on deck in apparent alarm. The attention of the guards would naturally be drawn to the commotion below deck, and this would be the opportunity for throwing off the irons, opening the grating and dropping off into the river. Once in the water each man was to take his own chances and exercise his judgment about making his way to the shore.

All was arranged, and the prisoners assembled for the singing and filing which was to set them free. But the first stroke of the file had not been made before the officer in charge of the convoy ordered the sentinel to cease his walk along the deck and stand where he could keep the group continually in view. Evidently he had dealt with a similar plot on a previous voyage.

Dubayeff and Pushkin had not joined the group, but were in another part of the cage. When the officer gave the order for the sentinel to watch the singers, the former said to his friend:

"I was doubtful at the start of the success of the scheme, but as the rest were willing to try it I made no opposition."

"They'll probably devise something new," Pushkin responded, "now that their first plan has failed."

"Undoubtedly," was the reply. "Within three hours

we shall hear of it, unless this convoy is different from all others I've ever known."

"Ever since I was arrested," said the other "my thoughts have run almost continuously upon how I could get away."

"That is the case with nearly everybody," Dubayeff replied, "and will be as long as prisons and prisoners exist. The prisoner's time is largely occupied with designs for eluding the vigilance of those who have him in charge, and however futile may be his plots, they serve to occupy him and keep him filled with hope. As long as he is planning to escape, he is in little danger of losing his reason; the danger comes when he has abandoned hope and given himself up to despair."

"I suppose there are a hundred plans made for every one that is tried."

"Say a thousand instead of a hundred and you would be nearer the mark. Ninety-nine hundredths of the plots are exactly like those that have been tried before by others; experienced officers know how to provide against them, as you have just seen. Prisoners on board a steamboat as we are, would be very likely to get together to sing the songs that are known to them, and these fellows thought that such an movement would not excite suspicion. Others have thought so before them and done as they did; the officers had reason to suspect a plot of some kind, and forewarned is forearmed.

"Another way of escaping which everybody thinks of is to form a conspiracy among the prisoners to free themselves of their irons at a given signal, the rivets having been previously filed, and then rush upon the guards, using the irons as weapons. It has been tried many times, I could almost say hundreds of them, and was successful in a few instances. But in the great majority of cases the prisoners are shot down and nobody gets away. When an attempt of this kind succeeds, the runaways scatter in every direction, either singly or by twos and threes, and are thrown on their own resources. They are sure to be pursued, and the chances are considerably against them."

" Do the peasantry in Siberia help the police to catch runaways ?"

" As a general thing they do not, but now and then there is a fellow who will do whatever he can in surrendering them in order to get the reward. Most of the peasants are kind to runaways ; they give them food and direct them to outbuildings where they can find shelter. Many of them place loaves of bread on the sills of their windows before going to bed, so that a runaway may obtain food without being seen. They also plant patches of turnips outside the villages, with the special object of affording food to escaped prisoners. When the police or soldiers find these turnip-patches, they trample them and destroy the plants."

Contrary to Dubayeff's prediction, there was no further plot to escape from the steamboat, though their brodyag friend intimated that there would be one. They reached Perm without any incident of consequence ; there the convoy was sent to the forwarding prison, where it remained two days, and was then sent forward by railway along with a hundred and more prisoners that had been brought from Moscow and points beyond that city.

The railway train started in the evening, and the prisoners were crowded closely into convict cars for a full hour before the time of leaving the station. There was just room enough for the occupants of a car to lie on the floor, and each man used his overcoat for a covering and his bag of extra garments for a pillow. The cars were securely locked before starting, and at every station where the train stopped the locks were examined, to make sure they had not been tampered with.

At the end of the railway, the prisoners were taken to a forwarding prison, just as they had been at Perm, to wait for the formation of a convoy. They were now in Siberia, the boundary between Europe and Asia having been passed while they were on the railway train.

"I'm not sure that I've told you this is not my first journey to Siberia," said Dubayeff to Pushkin soon after they had crossed the frontier. "But I'll tell you so now, and later, if we are kept together, I'll let you know more about it.

"There were many things about my first visit that I shall never forget, and one of the most memorable is that of crossing the frontier. We were marching then, as there was no railway, and one afternoon, when the air was keen and frosty and the roads rough from recent rains followed by freezing cold, we came to the boundary.

"We were weary and footsore, and many had broken down and been placed in the string of telyegas that followed the column for the use of the old and infirm. Many were in despair because they were soon to leave Russia behind them and enter another country; although Siberia is a part of the Empire, those who go to it unwillingly look upon it as altogether another land than their own.

"There was the boundary post, a column of brick covered with stucco, indicating that to the west lay Europe, while to the eastward was Asia. The officer who commanded the convoy ordered a halt for the double purpose of allowing us to rest and to bid farewell to Europe.

"I sat down on the ground and cried, cried like a child, to think I was leaving the land of my birth; then I rose and kissed the western side of the boundary-post as I would have kissed the cheek of one to whom I was bidding a long farewell. Others were doing likewise, while some kissed the earth beneath our feet and called the names of friends whom they feared they would never see again. Several tried to write words of farewell on the rough stucco, and others passed the time of the halt in prayer.

"Our officer was kind to us, and for more than an hour we were allowed to stop. Then, at the word of command, we were drawn up in line and carefully counted, to see that none had escaped, and when the count was completed the order to march was given. We were two hundred in that unhappy convoy; out of the two hundred it is not likely that more than twenty have seen or will ever see the soil of Europe again."

As he ceased speaking Dubayeff buried his face in his hands and wept at the recollection of the scene.

There can hardly be in all the empire of Russia a more melancholy spot that the site of the post where the eastbound traveller enters Siberia. How many thousands, yes, how many hundreds of thousands, have dragged their chains along this road, and have here said farewell forever to the land of their birth! Since the days of Peter the Great, the originator of the system of exile to Siberia, a million prisoners have passed this spot, men, women, and children, of all social ranks, from the highest noble to the lowest peasant, from the favorite of the Czar to the outcast of the poorest village. To nearly all of them Siberia has been, in every way, a place of burial.

"We are buried in Siberia," said Dubayeff, when talking of the effect of banishment. "We cease to exist, our names are forgotten, our heirs can claim our property unless, as generally happens, it is confiscated by the crown, and our wives, if we have any, become widows and can marry again if they choose."

"And do many of them do that?" Pushkin asked.

"To the credit of the sex I tell you that the number is small and very largely confined to the criminal classes. There are very few instances in which the wives of political exiles have done otherwise than remain faithful to the love which they gave their husbands at the altar. Thousands of wives have followed their husbands into captivity, though every one of them well knew that by so doing she must share the hardships of exile, and could not return to Europe until he was released by expiration of sentence, pardon or death. Many who have been urged by their husbands to remain in Europe have not complied with the request, and others, while complying with it for the sake of their children, have continued faithful through years and years of waiting, to go to Siberia when their children had reached an adult age, or to welcome the returning husband when his sentence had expired.

"Several of the Decembrists had been married only a short time before the events that sent them to Siberia. They were, without exception, I believe, followed by their young wives, through all the hardships and perils of the long journey. Princess Troubetskoi was the first of them, and for some time the government refused to allow her to go. When finally the favor she asked was granted, she was notified that she would never be permitted to return to Europe."

"And she readily accepted the condition, did she?"

"Yes, she started in midwinter, with her servant maid, and travelled to Nertchinsk, nearly seven thousand versts (5,000 miles) in a sleigh. She had several narrow escapes from death, and on more than one occasion was pursued by wolves; they ran alongside the sleigh, and if the horses had stumbled and fallen there would have been nothing but scattered bones, fragments of clothing and harness, and the abandoned vehicle to tell the story to whoever passed along the route the following day. At one time she was lost in a storm, and when it abated she was nearly famished for want of food. She frequently travelled when the cold was very severe, and sometimes on reaching the stations where the horses were changed, she was so benumbed with the cold as to be unable to stand.

"At the mines of Nertchinsk, her husband, Prince Troubetskoi, was working underground, and when she embraced him, the clanking of the chains told more plainly than words his condition of bondage. She was restricted to prison fare, was not allowed to visit any of the residents of the village, and could only see her husband once a week. A month or two after her arrival two other ladies arrived, and then she had some companionship, but the contrast between the home of the exiles and the life they had led in St. Petersburg was so great that I wonder they survived it."

"And I wonder, too," said Pushkin. "Those women must have been very devoted and very brave."

"No more so than thousands of others," was the reply. "The stories of the heroism of the wives of exiles would fill volumes, and even then all would not have been told. Many of these noble women have never reached the loved ones they followed ; they died of fatigue and exposure while on the journey, and their graves are in many a Siberian cemetery, or along the roadside. Not a few have become insane, hopelessly so, and died in the hospitals, or wandered out into the wilderness, where they perished of hunger and cold. Did you ever hear the story of Dr. Baillie's wife ?"

"I never did," answered Pushkin. "Who was she ?"

"She was married to a young surgeon who was exiled by administrative process, without trial, on the suspicion of the police that he was 'untrustworthy.' His wife was ill and unable to accompany him when he started ; as soon as she was able to travel she set out, and as she could not afford to hire post-horses and a tarantass, she went with an exile party, living on prison fare, walking when they walked, lodging where they lodged, and in every way being treated as a prisoner. She was in the same convoy that I was in from Tiumen to Tomsk, and I heard all about her, but it was months afterwards that I learned the end of her sad story.

"She began to show signs of breaking down some time before she reached Irkutsk, but was held up by the hope that she would soon see her husband, whom she supposed to be in Verkholensk, which is less than 200 miles from Irkutsk ; he was really in Verkhoyansk, 2,500 miles further away. Her mind remained fairly good until she learned that she had still such a long distance to go, and then she became a raving lunatic and died in the hospital at Irkutsk."

Here Dubayeff paused, his voice was so choked that he could not say more, and as for Pushkin, he was unable to speak. When at length they were able to resume their conversation, they changed by silent but mutual consent to a less harrowing subject.

The convoy was allowed to rest two or three days before setting out on the road ; fortunately for Pushkin and Dubayeff, as for all the others, the prison was not crowded, and the food supplied to them was of better quality than they had found while on the railway and before reaching Perm. The worst feature of the establishment was the contracted quarters where they slept, and the foul air they were compelled to breathe at night. There was little ventilation, the advantage of fresh air is a subject that is not studied in Russia, notwithstanding the abundance of that article, and the builders of prisons have little knowledge of sanitary requirements.

And while these unhappy exiles are resting in the forwarding prison we will return for a time to Tambov and to those whom we last saw there.

CHAPTER XI.

THE GOVERNOR AND THE LAWYER.

The governor greeted Mr. Kosavitch courteously as the latter entered the office, and after a few polite phrases the lawyer referred to the object of his visit.

"I have come," said he, "on behalf of four prisoners, two of them women, now detained at Tambov."

"Who are they?"

"Nicolai Hartmann, and the wife, son, and daughter, of Carl Pushkin."

"What do you wish to say concerning them?"

"I respectfully ask that I may be informed of the charges against them. I have been retained as their counsel, and come to you in my professional capacity. I also ask to be permitted to visit them professionally."

"They are detained by order of the Minister of the Interior."

"I understand that," Mr. Kosavitch answered, "but what are the charges against them?"

"They have been arrested under administrative process in the interest of the preservation of social order throughout the empire."

"Certainly, Your Excellency, we are aware of that, and I wish to ask in what way their conduct has been prejudicial to social order."

"It is the custom of the government to arrest those whose conduct is not in accordance with the best interests of the country. You are aware that in recent years there have been many acts of individuals in various parts of the empire that have brought them in a condition to be considered untrustworthy. There have been many violations of the regulations, and especially of Section 245, especially in St. Petersburg and in the south of the empire, at Odessa, Kiev, and other places."

"I am well aware of that," said the lawyer, "and I am also aware that there have been many persons arrested and held in prison for years without trial. The records show that out of more than one thousand persons arrested for alleged untrustworthiness, and held in prison for various periods of from one to four years, only one hundred and ninety-three have ever been brought to trial, and of this number no fewer than ninety were acquitted by the courts, even when the judges were selected by the government."

"You had better confine yourself to the case before you," the governor answered sharply, forgetting, apparently, that in his answers to the lawyer's questions he had himself wandered as far as he could from the subject under consideration.

Mr. Kosavitch was about to add to his remarks that the other eight hundred of the arrested persons had been sent to Siberia without any trial whatever, or were liberated when the government had been convinced, in spite of all its efforts to secure evidence against them, that they were wholly innocent of any wrong-doing.

We will say here, as it is quite pertinent to the subject under consideration, that in the ten years from 1867 to 1876 inclusive, 151,585 persons were sent to Siberia, of whom 51 per cent., or more than half, were exiled by administrative process. In seven years, from 1880 to 1886 inclusive, 120,065 were exiled altogether, and of this number 55,552, or about 46 per cent., went into banishment by administrative process, or without trial. The order of the Minister of the Interior was sufficient for the purpose, as we have already seen in the case of Carl Pavloff.

The intimation of the governor, conveyed so emphatically, was a sufficient warning to Mr. Kosavitch that he had gone beyond the bounds of caution. The speech that he had prepared was not delivered, as he knew that it would be worse than lost upon his audience of one, however select that audience might be considered.

"I will try to confine myself to the case," said the lawyer, "and again beg to ask your Excellency what are the specific acts of insubordination charged against the prisoners."

"That belongs with the Minister of the Interior," was the reply, "and when this bureau is instructed to enlighten you further, I will send for you. Meantime, there is no authority to make public anything more on the subject."

"Your Excellency is a husband and a father," the lawyer continued. "In the name of all your tender feelings for the members of your family I beg that you will consider the case of the two women, mother and daughter, the wife and child of Carl Pushkin, who are now in prison in Tambov and separated from each other. Surely your Excellency will admit that whatever the charges against them may be, the empire can suffer no detriment if they are allowed to occupy the same cell in the prison and have the solace of one another's presence, and of the love which each bears towards the other."

"They are the wife and daughter of Carl Pushkin, you say?" the governor answered, as if he heard this statement for the first time.

"Certainly," was the reply, "the wife and only daughter. The only son is now in prison, and also Nicolai Hartmann, a neighbor and friend."

"Ah, yes, and Carl Pushkin, where is he?"

"I know not, your Excellency, but presume he is on the road to Siberia. He was arrested under administrative process, confined in prison at Tambov for some days, and was then removed in the night. No information has been given as to his whereabouts, but I learn from a friend that he was seen in Saratov in a party of prisoners embarking on the steamer for Perm."

"Ah, yes, Carl Pavloff, surnamed Pushkin, and his wife and daughter are in prison."

The governor turned to look at some papers on his desk as a hint to the lawyer that the interview was ended. The hint was taken and Mr. Kosavitch departed.

He went away disappointed, as he had hoped to accomplish something in behalf of his clients, but the words and manner of the governor had been what we have seen. Not a hint of the charges against any of the prisoners, not a thread on which to hang the least hope! He would be sent for when it was necessary that he should be further enlightened; this was said in a way to imply that until such time as he received a summons to call at the gubernatorial bureau, any applications in behalf of his friends would be not only useless but considered an impertinence.

But that evening, when he met his friend, the warder of the prison, he found that his appeal to the governor had not been without effect.

He was examining an iron plow which had been left at the side of the sparsely travelled street after having been used for turning up the soil of a neighboring garden. The interest he showed in this article of agriculture was such as to indicate that it was quite new to him, and sufficient to attract the attention and rouse the curiosity of the passing warder.

As the latter looked at the plow, he said in an undertone:

"At three o'clock this afternoon, Madame Pushkin and her daughter were placed in one cell, and the smatritel (keeper) said he had orders to allow them to remain together."

"God be praised!" ejaculated the lawyer. "The governor has a heart after all."

The warder did not comment upon Kosavitch's remark, as he considered it more an expression of feeling than something addressed to himself. He went on without emotion, or the least sign of it.

"No orders were issued in the case of Hartmann and young Pushkin, but I overheard something indistinctly that the smatritel was saying to another warder, which makes me think they'll be allowed to see each other every day. *Smotre* (Look)!"

By this time he had finished his examination of the agricultural implement and continued his homeward walk. As he spoke the last word and moved away, he dropped at the lawyer's feet a small wad of paper, which the latter picked up while stooping to see how the clevis was fastened to the beam of the plow.

Very quietly the paper was conveyed to the pocket of its recipient, and it was not removed until he was safe within his house and secure from observation. It could not be a long letter, as the ball was not larger than a pea, and nearly the color of the ground where it fell, but notwithstanding its appearance it was very precious to the recipient.

This mode of communication was long in use in the Petropavlovsk prison at St. Petersburg. The prisoners in solitary confinement were exercised separately for ten minutes daily, in the court-yard. They had a cipher alphabet, known only to themselves, and by writing with the burnt end of a match upon scraps of cigarette paper, which they carefully treasured, they were able to give information which was necessarily very brief. The writer inclosed his communication in a pill, made from the rye bread which forms a part of the prisoner's daily ration, and when the guards came to accompany him in his walk, he would take the pill in his mouth before changing his dress.

In the yard, he watched his chance to drop the pill, and it would subsequently be picked up by a prisoner who stooped under the pretense of arranging his shoe or some other deception. Having obtained the pill, he placed it in his mouth, and retained it until he was left alone again in his cell. In this way important news was often conveyed, such as the names of persons arrested, condemned, escaped, or dead, movements of the revolutionary party, steps that had been taken by the government, or other events. Even should the messages be intercepted, they could not be understood by the guards, as they were always given in cipher.

Mr. Kosavitch was not an adept in cipher writing, and the same was the case with his correspondent in prison, who was none other than Mr. Hartmann. He wrote to advise the lawyer to communicate with a certain individual in St. Petersburg, whose address he gave, and tell him all that had happened. He further advised that his son, Alexei, could be implicitly trusted in everything that pertained to the Pushkin family as well as his own, for reasons that will readily be surmised. The letter was necessarily short, as the scrap of paper on which it was written was less than two inches square; both sides were closely covered with the writing, which was done with a splinter of wood dipped in soot accumulated from a lamp and moistened with saliva. Writing materials are denied to political prisoners in nearly all cases; sometimes those who are held for long terms are permitted a few sheets of coarse paper on which they may compose poems, stories, or anything else that is harmless, but the written sheets must be delivered to the guards without mutilation.

Mr. Hartmann had asked permission to write a letter to his family about certain matters, purely domestic, but this very reasonable request was refused. Ivan asked to be allowed something to read, a history of the country, copies of old magazines, anything that the most exacting censor could not pronounce injurious, but he was told that all reading was strictly forbidden, except by permission of the Minister of the Interior.

"Very well, then," said he to the prison-keeper, "give me pen, ink, and a sheet of paper, and I will write to the minister, asking him to allow me to read books, and if he has any choice he can name the volumes."

"You must first get his permission to have the paper

on which to write," was the reply, "for the use of writing materials is forbidden."

Then he walked away and left the youth to wonder how he could possibly send a petition to the minister, when he was not allowed to have the materials for its preparation.

This reminds us of the case of a Mr. X——, who was sent to Siberia solely because he was an acquaintance of Mr. Y——, who had been suspected of being "untrustworthy," and was therefore arrested. Mr. Y—— remained some months in prison, and was then tried and acquitted, but meantime X——, whose only crime had been that he was acquainted with Y——, was in chains on his way to Siberia, where he was required to serve out his sentence. One can ponder upon the principle of justice on which the Russian government acted in this case, just as Ivan pondered upon the logic that refused him the paper on which to write a petition that would have been an entirely proper one for him to indite.

Ivan asked for the opportunity to keep a journal of the thoughts that occurred to him in his prison life, but, of course, he was unable to do so. And it is very doubtful if the government would have allowed him to preserve a record of what passed through his mind, as it certainly would have been far from flattering to these in whose power he was held.

Of his daily fare he afterwards wrote as follows:

"I had black bread and tea in the morning, and tea and black bread in the evening; for dinner, a little past noon, they gave me cabbage soup, sometimes with karsha (parched barley) and sometimes without. The soup was supposed to have a piece of meat in it, but this was mostly supposition, as I did not find it one time in three. Even when it could be found, the piece was very small.

"They served the soup in a wooden bowl, and I ate it with a wooden spoon, no metal being allowed for fear that it would be converted into weapons. My guard stood over me while I was at dinner, and took away the bowl and spoon as soon as the last mouthful was swallowed; then he gave me five cigarettes and as many matches, and this was my allowance for twenty-four hours. How I treasured those cigarettes and made them last as long as possible!"

It is proper to explain that in Russia nearly the whole population that can afford to do so smokes. Smoking is almost as common with women as among men; unmarried ladies do not, as a rule, smoke in the presence of gentlemen, but married ones are not so particular. Cigarettes (papiros) are generally preferred to cigars, especially by the gentler sex, and the consumption of these articles is enormous. Exactly when Ivan adopted the smoking habit it is difficult to say, but he was certain to acquire it during his student life at Moscow if not a great deal earlier.

"I was constantly watched," said Ivan, "through the 'Judas' in the door, and it seemed at times as though this watching would drive me mad. It was contrary to rules to speak to the guard, except to ask for what was proper, and that was very little, and so there were hours and hours together when I couldn't say a word. I sat down in a corner and talked to myself, but the guard stopped me from that; he said the orders were 'talking is forbidden,' and it made no difference if a man talked to himself or somebody else.

"Day after day went on in this way until once, just after my dinner, the guard came and said there was a visitor for me. Then he went away, not telling who the visitor was or whether he was to see me in my cell or in the reception-room. How my heart throbbed during the minutes that I stood at the door of my cell and waited!"

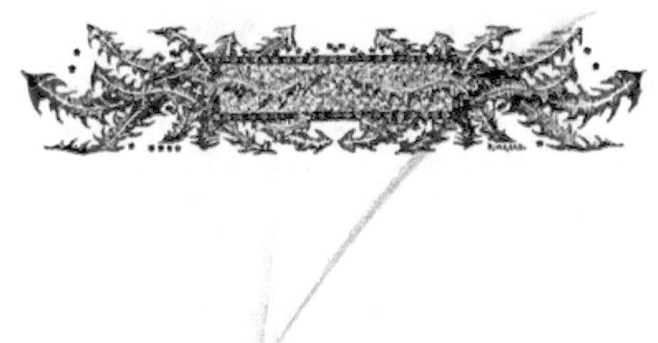

CHAPTER XII.

SPIES AND THEIR WORK.

Ivan waited for the door of his cell to be opened, either for the visitor to be admitted to see him where he was confined, or that the guard should take him to the reception-room of the prison. But in both expectations he was disappointed.

The door was opened, but it was only to admit a soldier, or rather one of the warders. Then the door was closed and locked, and Ivan turned to his companion with the inquiry :

"Are you the visitor that was coming to see me?"

"Talking is forbidden," was the only reply he received.

A moment later the youth's attention was drawn to a noise outside as of some one approaching. The guard opened the wicket in the door and the youth peered outside as far as he could. Soon the visitor for whom he was waiting came within the range of his vision.

Great was his joy to perceive that it was his mother. But his joy was turned to disappointment, when he found that the interview could only take place through the wicket ; he could not clasp her in his arms, feel the pressure of her hand, or smooth the locks on her forehead as he had often done at home. They were required to stand with the door between them, and every word that they spoke was heard by two of their guards.

Not only were their words listened to, but every play of their features, every look and motion, were carefully observed. The guard inside the cell stood directly behind Ivan, his face being just over the latter's shoulder, and the guard outside occupied a similar position behind Madame Pushkin.

The interview between mother and son would have been sad enough had they been allowed to be by themselves, but it was agonizing under the circumstances just narrated. They could only exchange a few commonplaces, and even these were almost incoherent, as the faces of both were bathed in tears, and the woman was barely able to stand on account of her grief. When they met, they were told that they would be allowed no longer than five minutes together, but even this time was more than either cared to endure with the heavy door between them and the spies looking and listening over their shoulders. When the limit had expired, the mother was led away by her custodian, and as she walked along the corridor, her despair was manifested in loud cries that reached her son in his cell and pierced him to the heart. With a refinement of cruelty that would have disgraced the lowest savages, the guards required her to stop for two or three minutes a few yards from his door in order that his sufferings might be prolonged.

"Oh! my dear mother," he wrote in a letter which he tried to send to her by one of the guards, "when your shrieks and lamentations reached me as they rang through the prison, it seemed as though my heart would break. And afterwards, day and night and night and day, they rang through my ears, and I could never drive them out. No matter what I tried to think of, the picture of your face, pale and tear-covered, rose before me and haunted me whether I slept or waked; no matter what I heard or said your sobs and cries filled my ears and drove out every other sound."

A few days later the guard came again to Ivan's cell and announced a visitor.

"Who is it?" the youth asked.

"I am not allowed to tell you," was the reply, "talking is forbidden."

"If it is my mother or sister," said Ivan firmly, "and the interview is to be like the last one, I positively refuse to see her. Say so to the smotretal."

The man went away and soon re-appeared accompanied by the smotretal. The latter assumed a most friendly manner and explained that the former interview was in accordance with the rules and he realized how unsatisfactory it was. The one which he was now to have would be with his sister, and in the reception-room of the prison. They would be allowed to talk freely for ten minutes and the young man must give his word of honor that no contraband articles would be given by either of them to the other.

Ivan gave the required promise without hesitation. There was no reason why he should do otherwise, for he had nothing contraband to give, as he was deprived of everything on entering the prison. He was not an adept in concealing articles, as is the case with old offenders against the law or, what amounts to the same thing, those who have frequently incurred the suspicion of the police, however unjustly it may have been formed.

"Very well, then," said the keeper, "the interview will take place in half an hour."

Ivan did not understand why the interview could not

come off at once, but there were " good and sufficient reasons " in the minds of his custodians for the delay.

There were certain arrangements to be made in order to secure the best possible results from the meeting of brother and sister. The bench they were to occupy during their interview was skillfully placed in a corner of the room ; the walls on each side of the corner were pierced with large holes or windows, which were masked by a sort of lattice-work that extended around the room and was ostensibly intended for ornamental purposes. Behind these holes, which were some eighteen inches square, two spies were stationed, whose duty it was to report all the conversation, or, at any rate, all that was of consequence to the government.

" You must not talk in whispers," said the smotretal, "nor use any language but Russian. That is one of the rules of the government, and it is my duty to inform you."

He did not wait for a reply from Ivan, but turned suddenly to give directions about something to one of his subordinates. Thus it happened that the youth was not under a promise expressly given, and consequently he did not feel himself under restrictions when he entered the reception-room and found himself alone with his sister, or as much alone as one can be when an armed sentinel is pacing the corridor just outside the open door and occasionally looking inside. But the sentinel did not listen to their conversation, and for all practical purposes they were by themselves.

Ivan and Nadia embraced and kissed, and then they sat down with hands clasped in hands to talk over the strange and sad events that had separated them, though all the time they were so near each other. They speculated on the causes that led to their father's arrest, and afterwards that of the rest of the family and of Mr. Hartmann. Ivan told Nadia what he had till then no opportunity of saying, that their father had been taken from prison, but where he had gone the youth was unable to do more than surmise.

At this information Nadia cried, and moved by her sorrow, and its expression, Ivan could only restrain himself with greatest difficulty. In a choked voice he said :

"You must use your discretion in breaking the news to mother."

"I'm afraid it would drive her mad," replied Nadia, as soon as she could speak ; "sometimes she seems to have almost lost her reason, and she spends hours and hours lamenting about something that she will not tell me about."

"Has she given you any hint that will enable you to guess what it is ?" queried Ivan.

"No," answered the girl, "but it is something that distresses her very much. She has promised to tell me some time, but not now."

Down to this time the conversation had been in Russian, but now Nadia said something in French. Ivan reminded her that he had been cautioned that only their native language was to be used, and then she paused.

"But I did not make any promise about it," he added, and then he detailed the circumstances under which the suggestion was made to him.

"In that case," she replied, "we are at liberty to talk just as we like, and can use whatever language we please." But as she said this she pressed his hand by way of caution, a signal that he did not fully understand at the moment.

SPIES AND THEIR WORK.   127

The girl's quick perception had told her that although they were apparently alone, they were likely to be overheard. She thought of this when she entered the room, and it occurred again to her when Ivan mentioned the prohibition of any other language than Russian.

They continued to talk, sometimes in Russian and sometimes in French, until one of the warders came to tell them that their time had expired. Then they kissed and said "good-bye" and were returned to their cells.

When they were out of sight, the two listeners came from their place of concealment and compared notes. They were not much better informed than before the interview, as the only point of possible interest to the government was the allusion to the something that Madame Pushkin had worried about so much and had not yet informed her daughter.

"We must devise a way of finding that out," said one to the other.

"Yes," was the reply; "let them rest a few days and then give them another interview. By that time the mother may have told it, and then we can get at the whole story of the conspiracy."

"They didn't fall into the trap of talking in French so well as we expected."

"No, I thought when the young fellow was cautioned without putting him under a promise, that would be the very thing to give him a hint, but somehow he didn't take it."

"We'll catch them next time, though. We'll have nothing said to them about it, so that they will feel entirely free about their language; then we'll put the sentinel in the doorway, and they'll talk so that he cannot understand their dialogue."

The spies had been selected on account of their knowledge of foreign tongues in addition to their own. It should be remarked that the Russians are the best linguists in the world, or certainly among the best, possibly because their own language is so difficult to acquire. It is no uncommon thing to find men or women who speak French, German and English fluently, in addition to Russian, and it has been said that a stranger in St. Petersburg may address a well-dressed man on the street in French or German, with an even chance that he will be understood. Education begins at a very early age, and every well-to-do Russian puts his children in the hands of a foreign governess or tutor, before most English or American children have conquered the alphabet.

Both the spies understood French perfectly, and felt sure that the young people would put them in possession of the information they so greatly desired, by conversing in that language. The prison-keeper had played his part well in failing to obtain a promise from Ivan, and they were naturally mortified at their failure.

" This will be the way for us to proceed now," said the elder of the two. " Three days from now we will notify the women that they are to be separated the next day at noon, and put into cells by themselves. This will excite them greatly, and especially the mother, who will understand that it may be a long while before she can see her child again. During the night, or the next morning before they are separated, she will tell everything that is on her mind ; then leave the girl to herself for a day or two, and after that let her have an interview with her brother. She will surely tell all she has found out from the old woman, and we'll have the facts to go on."

" I can suggest something better than that," was the reply.

" What is your idea ?"

" Why, let the woman, the old one, have a talk with the lawyer in this very corner. You know a lawyer always wants to have all the facts bearing on a case, and that's the very first thing he'll say to her. She'll be more likely to give him the whole story than she will to tell it to her daughter ; she will have more confidence in his discretion than in that of her child, much as she loves her."

" Not a bad scheme," said the other. " I'll talk with the governor about it, and find out what he thinks, or what he says he thinks. Will meet you at the Chancellerie to-morrow morning."

The spies then separated, and at their meeting on the next day their plans for obtaining information were discussed in all their bearings, and arrangements made for carrying them out.

Atrocious and cold-blooded as these performances may seem to the reader, they are mildness itself compared with some of the schemes in vogue among the Russian police. We have already seen how forged confessions are used for deceiving prisoners into telling what they are suspected of knowing, and how government officials make pretences of personal and unofficial friendship in order to draw victims into traps. Overhearing conversations is a common form of obtaining information, and is not always confined to Russia. The annals of the police in all countries contain instances of convictions obtained in this way, but it is safe to say that none of them are quite as heartless as those in the dominions of the Czar. In playing upon the fears of parents for their children, or those of children for their parents, and taking advantage of the most agonizing circumstances, the Russian police surpass all others.

While the new villainy of the spies upon the Pushkin family is under consideration, we will return to the forwarding prison, where we left the party preparing for the dreary march into the land of exile.

In the afternoon of the third day after their arrival, it became known that on the following morning a marching convoy would be sent away.

There were some preparations to be made, but not many; where one has very little of this world's goods in his possession, he can start on a forced journey at short notice. Each man overhauled the linen bag that contained his change of clothing, took out what he most needed, and laid away what he could spare. Then the bag was closed ready for delivery into the hands of the drivers of the baggage telyegas, and the prisoner was ready for what sleep he could snatch during the night in the close atmosphere of the kamera he occupied along with his companions in misfortune.

While Pushkin was contemplating his scanty belongings, Dubayeff came carelessly to his side, and asked:

"Do you want to communicate with your friends at home?"

"Do I want to? Heaven knows I do, though it is sad news, indeed, that I can give them."

"Well, there's a chance to do so before we go on the road."

"How?"

"From this point we do not have the same guards that we have had thus far. We are turned over to a new escort, and one of the men that was with us will take any letters we have, surreptitiously of course, and deposit them in the post-office after he gets back to Perm. He will do so for half a ruble for each letter."

Pushkin eagerly embraced the opportunity, and having obtained a sheet of paper and an envelope, he wrote in pencil, as pen and ink were not procurable, a short letter, in which he gave a brief account of what had happened to him up to that time. He did not address it to any member of his family, but to Mr. Kosavitch, at Tambov, requesting that gentleman to inform the family as soon as he could. Little did he dream of the actual state of affairs!

Pushkin had changed his large bank-note into smaller ones by paying a liberal commission to one of his keepers who managed the business. He consulted Dubayeff before doing so, and the latter said:

"It won't be safe to let the note go out of your hands before you have the smaller notes for it. The amount is too large to be otherwise than a temptation to the man, and very likely you would never see him or your money again."

"But wouldn't he be in danger of arrest for deserting his post if he staid away from duty?"

"He could easily manage that," was the reply. "He would go to the next man above him and say he wanted sick leave for a few days. He could afford to pay a good bribe, and would get the leave until the convoy was sent away. His superior would ask no questions, but his understanding of the case would be quite correct, that the subordinate had reasons of his own for not wishing to be seen about the prison until the departure of the next convoy."

"How shall I manage it?" Pushkin asked.

"Get one of the warders to bring a money-changer to

you under pretense of wishing to see a friend, or any other ruse that will bring him in. There will be no great difficulty about it, as the money-changer will make it for the interest of everybody to admit him. I saw one here this very day transacting business in a corner with one of the prisoners."

Pushkin acted upon Dubayeff's advice, and found no difficulties in the way, other than the necessity of paying a high commission as already stated. The note he had was for five hundred rubles, and he changed it to four notes of one hundred each, and fifty rubles in small notes. The remaining fifty went in the commission which was retained by the changer.

The transaction was conducted so secretly that none but the two parties to it could know the amount involved unless the information were volunteered. It was the interest of Pushkin that nobody should be aware that he had such an amount in his possession, he would have been liable to extortion by his immediate keepers, and as for the higher officials, they would have forbidden him to have it on the ground that it might be used for bribing his guards to connive at his escape. Then, too, there was further danger from the brodyags and other common criminals in the convoy, to whom robbery is an art they would practice upon a fellow-prisoner as readily as on any one else.

"The money-changer isn't likely," said Dubayeff, "to own up to having changed anything larger than a twenty-five ruble note, or possibly one for fifty. The higher the profits he acknowledges, the greater must be his payments to the prison-keepers, and you can rely upon his lying to the utmost stretch of his conscience, and I very much doubt if he is troubled with any conscience at all."

Pushkin concealed his money where it could not be found except on the most careful search, and no one but Dubayeff knew how much he carried. Even the latter was not intrusted with the secret of its concealment, further than that he knew of a fifty ruble note sewn into a seam of Pushkin's grey overcoat.

Prisoners may carry small amounts of money, not to exceed three or four rubles, but all above the latter figure must be deposited with the chief of the escort or the smotretal of the prison, from whom it may be drawn upon from time to time for the purchase of food or other comforts. Where the holders of the money are honest, and administer their trusts fairly, there is no reasonable ground for complaint, but honest administration is the exception, rather than the rule, in all dealings with prisoners in Russia.

CHAPTER XIII.

SETTING OUT ON THE MARCH.

Early in the morning of the day fixed for the starting of the convoy, the prisoners were supplied with their breakfast of soup, karsha and black bread. Such as had money to pay with were provided with tea by one of the warders; those without money had no tea at all, or depended upon the generosity of more fortunate companions, but few prisoners in Siberia can be generous without great hardship to themselves. The soup was thin and poor, the karsha was badly cooked, and the bread such that no decent baker would think of offering to his customers. But the exiles had no choice other than to eat what was given to them or go hungry.

In groups of ten or twenty the prisoners were called from the kameras into the yard, but before stepping into the open air they were carefully examined to see that their leg-fetters had not been tampered with and their heads were properly shaven. The rule of shaving one side of a convict's head is carefully kept, as it furnishes a means of indentification in case of his escape; the shaving is repeated from time to time in the forwarding prisons, and the hair is not allowed to get a growth of more than two or three weeks between the attentions of the barber.

Formerly the nostrils of all hard labor and life sentence exiles were slit to mark them indelibly, but this practice was abandoned early in the present century. Few, if any, exiles thus disfigured are now living.

Those who are simply banished to Siberia for a short term of years, without any sentence of hard labor, escape the head-shaving, and are not required to wear fetters. It is considered that the brevity of their terms, and the lightness of their punishment, will keep them from running the risk of being placed in the hard-labor class in case of attempting to escape and being recaptured.

Dubayeff and Pushkin were among those sentenced to hard labor, and therefore bore the marks of degradation in the shape of chains and shaven heads. To the casual observer there was no difference between their appearance and that of the criminal convicts in the convoy, and it was evidently the intent of their masters that there should be none. If a political prisoner escapes from custody, the peasants who encounter him have no means of knowing to what class he belongs; all they know is that his dress and the condition of his head indicate that he is a convict and under sentence to hard labor. If they capture him, they obtain the reward that the government offers for the apprehension of runaways from the compulsory service of the Czar.

When the roll was called, all were obliged to answer to their names. Among those included in the convoy, was a young man who protested that he had been arrested and was being sent to Siberia by mistake. His name was Andrew Narishkine, and he claimed that the man who should be in his place was Alexander

Narishkine; Andrew was no relative of his, not even an acquaintance, though he had heard about him from some one who knew him and was sure that a mistake had been made.

"Alexander Narishkine," shouted the convoy officer.

There was no response, and again the name was called.

"This is Narishkine," said one of the warders, pointing to the young man in question.

"Why don't you answer to your name?" said the officer, gruffly. "I called it twice; are you deaf?"

"I'm not deaf," was the reply. "I am not Alexander Narishkine, and won't answer to his name. "I've been arrested and sent here by mistake."

"Is your name Narishkine?"

"Yes, it is Narishkine, but it isn't Alexander."

"Well, then, what is it?"

"Andrew Narishkine."

The officer then took his pencil, erased Alexander and wrote Andrew in its place. "Your name is all right now," said he, "and we won't have any more refusals after this. One Narishkine in Siberia is as good as another."

The young man protested, but to no purpose, as his words were not listened to by the officer, who went on with the roll-call. In all there were some two hundred and fifty persons in the convoy, and sixty or more of them were in chains. Nearly one-third of the whole number were not prisoners at all, but the wives and children of exiles, belonging either to this convoy or to one that had gone before. They were subject to the prison regulations in every way, the only difference in their cases being that they might leave the custody of the government at any of the forwarding stations and settle down to take care of themselves. On the road no distinction was made between them and the rest of the convoy.

As each name was called, and the owner came forward, his linen bag was taken from him and examined by two soldiers to make sure that it contained nothing contraband. If found all right, it was returned to him, and he was told to go on. He went on until he was stopped at the other end of the yard, where his name was checked off on another list and he was ordered to remain in a group that was standing there. Then he placed his bag on the ground and waited.

Twenty or thirty names had been called off and each one had been answered before that of Carl Pushkin was reached.

As he stepped forward with his bag, Carl said to the officer:

"Can I now be told why I have been brought to Siberia?"

"How the d—l do I know?" was the reply. "That's no business of mine. You wouldn't be here if you hadn't been sent." Then turning to the soldier who was examining the bag, he asked if it was all right.

"All right," the soldier answered.

"*Stoopai* (Go on)!" the officer commanded, giving an inclination of his head in the direction that the man should go. Then he called the next name on the list, and there was nothing for the unhappy Pushkin to do but obey orders. With downcast head he joined the group, unmindful of what was occurring around him. He had hoped that he might be heard, and that an explanation could be obtained of the cause of his exile.

Had he been permitted to look at the list, he would

have seen that the offence for which a man is exiled is not mentioned thereon. The convoy officer knew nothing about the right or wrong of the matter, neither did he care, any more than in the case of Andrew Narishkine exiled in place of Alexander.

Pushkin was soon joined by Dubayeff, and both sat down on the ground to await the order to match. Seeing the eyes of Pushkin filled with tears, the other exclaimed:

"Courage, my friend! Courage! Fortune may yet do something good for you, and that when you least expect it. Now that your letter has gone to your friends, they will know where you are, and you will soon hear from them."

Dubayeff's promises were, as he well knew, more hopeful than the circumstances warranted, but he felt justified in using a little kindly deception to his companion in misfortune. They had become much attached during the time they had been together, and each had served to smooth the hardships of the journey for the other.

His words had a good effect, and when Pushkin looked up again, it was with a less despairing look upon his face. The examination and passing of each prisoner took from one to three minutes, and although three convoy officers were busy at the work, three or four hours were consumed in getting the convoy in readiness.

When all was ready the order "*Stroisa* (Form Ranks)!" was given, and the gate of the prison-yard was opened. By the side of the gate stood an officer, who gave each prisoner ten copecks (five cents) in copper coin, which was to supply him with food for the two days of the first stage of the march. This he would buy of peasants along the road, who make their livelihood by supplying the exiles. Of course, the food thus supplied is of the coarsest kind, and the most that can be said in its favor is that it supports life.

Outside the gate were several telyegas, into which the linen bags belonging to the prisoners were piled. Then there were telyegas intended for the infirm, or for those who became footsore on the road. One old woman had been placed in a telyega, and a young woman was pleading with an officer to allow her mother to ride instead of walk.

"Her knee is very bad," said the woman, "and she cannot take a step without limping."

"Then why hasn't she a certificate from the doctor?"

"The doctor said he would give her one, but he didn't. When I spoke to him about it the second time he said he would attend to it immediately, but he hasn't done so."

"Then your mother is a pretender and isn't lame at all. She must walk."

The woman began to cry as the officer turned away. Then she asked him to send for the doctor and ascertain whether her statement was true. Fortunately the doctor happened along at this moment and gave the opportunity for the appeal to be made then and there.

"Bless me!" he exclaimed. "Certainly, this woman is right; I did promise the certificate, but had so much to do that I forgot it."

Then he gave the certificate, filling it out in pencil where he stood. The lame woman was helped into the telyega, and her daughter took her own place in the ranks.

"The doctor is a decent sort of fellow," whispered

Dubayeff to Pushkin, "and he tells the truth when he said he had so much to do that he forgot the certificate he had promised to give. All the officers are overworked, and the doctors the worst of all. When we get to Tomsk, you'll see a fearful state of affairs. The prisons and hospitals are terribly crowded, and the provisions for the care of the sick are not a quarter of what are required. Hundreds die every year of neglect and exposure in the prisons of Tomsk."

"And how is it further on?" Pushkin asked.

"It is bad everywhere," was the reply. "Over and over again the case has been represented to the authorities at St. Petersburg, but they do nothing to remedy the evil."

The telyegas were soon filled with the sick and infirm, and it was evident that there was a considerable number who were unable to walk. The scanty food, the foul air of the prisons, and the general hardships they were forced to undergo, were responsible for this condition of many of the prisoners. It seems strange that when the government goes to the expense of sending men and women to people a thinly inhabited country like Siberia, it does not take better care of them, not from motives of humanity, but out of pure selfishness. A robust colonist is of ten times more value in a new country, than one enfeebled by disease or privations.

The telyegas were common country wagons, entirely open, resting on axles, without springs, and having a little hay or grass inside, on which the occupants were to sit. Four persons were assigned to a telyega; the vehicle was drawn by a single horse, and there was a driver and a soldier on the seat in front.

Pushkin was somewhat surprised to see Nemo

provided with a certificate from the doctor and assigned to a place in a telyega. He mentioned this to Dubayeff, who gave a glance at the fellow, and then said :

" He's a veteran at deception, and for a ruble offered to show me how to get a certificate and be allowed to ride. But I prefer the walking to the horrible jolting of the telyega, and declined his offer.

" How do you suppose he managed it ?"

" He scratched his leg with a splinter of wood day before yesterday, and then applied tobacco to the wound. This caused it to swell and assume an appearance sufficient to deceive a doctor on a hasty examination. The doctor is too busy to give more than a glance at the swelling, and so the brodyag was put on the list of those unable to walk. Some of these scoundrels are able to assume the appearance of serious illness, and sometimes it takes a shrewd surgeon to detect them."

The linen bags of the marching convicts were consigned to the telyegas that followed the ones containing the sick and infirm, and when all was ready, the order to march was given.

Four mounted Cossacks led the column. Then came the marching men and women and then the telyegas, and behind the last of the rumbling wagons was another guard of four Cossacks on horseback.

At each side of the column, scattered at intervals of twenty or thirty feet were soldiers on foot, each of them carrying his rifle ready loaded and with fixed bayonet. Their duty was to keep the column closed, and in case of an attempt of a prisoner to run away, they had orders to shoot, and to kill, if possible.

At the extreme rear of the column was the nachalnik, or commander of the convoy ; he rode in a tarantass and had his pistols ready for use, and on the box at the driver's side was a soldier with loaded rifle and fixed bayonet.

With a confused clanking of chains, and at a pace of about two miles an hour, the column with its head to the eastward soon left the gloomy prison out of sight. The bells on a church chimed one of the prayers of the Russian service, and how like mockery it seemed to Pushkin as side by side with his friend he struggled along the dusty road. "Peace be with you!" the bells said; "Despair be with you!" was the sound as it reached the exile's ears.

As the sound of the bell was lost in the distance, the column reached a "chasovnaya" or shrine, which stood near the road, and displayed a wooden representation of the Crucifixion, sheltered by a roof above it. Men and women crossed themselves in adoration, the men removing their caps and bowing devoutly, but still keeping up their march along the road. Pushkin was a faithful adherent of the church, and was therefore one of the worhippers at the shrine; Dubayeff removed his cap, but did not make the sign of the cross, and it was evident that he was not altogether sound in the tenets of the orthodox faith.

"Did you observe," said he to Pushkin, after they had passed the shrine, "that every robber, murderer or other criminal crossed himself devoutly?"

"No, I did not," was the reply. "But I know that the worst men in my community are the most earnest in observing the rules of the church."

"Probably they think it may help to save them," said Dubayeff. "Here, in Siberia, the worst criminals are the best religionists, at least outwardly. I have known a highway robber to waylay and kill a traveller for the sake of plunder and no other motive. The robber had

ON THE WAY TO THE MINES.—*See Page 142.*

beat it Kid

eaten nothing for nearly two days and was very hungry as you may believe. When he rifled the pockets of his victim, he found a cake and started to eat it, but threw it away instantly, as though it were poison, when he found it contained meat. It was the time of the fast when all good Christians refused to touch flesh; he was a good Christian and kept the fast faithfully, though he had no scruples at committing murder."

"I've no doubt of it," replied Pushkin, "and you can find many people of this sort in all parts of the empire. They say their prayers and make the sign of the cross and then think they can do as they please. When the Czar goes to church and observes all its ceremonies I wonder if he thinks of—"

A rifle shot rang out from the side of the column immediately behind them, and was followed by another and another. Men shouted and women screamed, and the order: "*Stoy* (Halt)," brought the marching line to a standstill.

CHAPTER XIV.

UNSUCCESSFUL ATTEMPT TO ESCAPE.

The cause of the firing was quickly known. Two prisoners, condemned to long terms of imprisonment with hard labor, had attempted to escape, by breaking suddenly from their guards while passing near a piece of forest. Pushkin had thought of trying the same plan, but was deterred from it by Dubayeff, to whom he proposed the attempt.

"Don't try it," said the other. "The chances are very much against success, too much for anybody who hasn't altogether abandoned hope. You are hampered by your chains, which will prevent your running fast, you know nothing of the country, the soldiers are quick with their weapons, and even if you manage to dodge the firing of the convoy guards, you will be pursued by the men on horseback. You have hundreds of miles between you and the boundary of Europe, and all that distance you will be hunted like a wild beast. Do you know what the officers sometimes say to recaptured runaways?"

"No," was the reply, "what is it?"

"They have a saying in these words: 'The Czar's cow-pasture is large, but you cannot get out of it; we find you in the end if you are alive.'"

Thus advised, Pushkin resigned himself to his fate, and gave up all thought of escape by breaking from the line of march.

The prisoners who had tried to get away were long-term politicals, and this was their first trip to Siberia. One was killed by a bullet from one of the rifles, and the other severely wounded. The wounded and dead were thrown into one of the telegas, which carried the baggage of the prisoners, and at the noon-day halt the corpse was buried a little way off from the road. The nachalnik made a formal certification of the occurrence, and obtained the signatures of several of the exiles as witnesses, in addition to the signatures of such of his men as could write their names.

"Why does he need so many witnesses?" Pushkin asked.

"Because," answered Dubayeff, "he is responsible for every man, woman and child delivered to him at starting; he must deliver them at the end of his route, at the next forwarding station, and if any are missing from the roll, he is obliged to make full explanation. If this had occurred within a day's march of the end of his route, he would have carried the corpse along as evidence that he had the complete number of the people he started with. He will keep the wounded man as long as there is any life in his body, no matter if a doctor should tell him that the prisoner's life could be saved by leaving him at the first village, but would certainly be lost by carrying him further."

"When I first went to Siberia," Dubayeff continued, "a woman fell overboard from a ferryboat while we were crossing a river. The nachalnik and his men put themselves in considerable peril to save her, not that they cared the value of a straw for her life, but because of the trouble they would be in if she were missing from the roll-call at the next station."

"Did they save her?"

"Yes, and when she was brought on board all dripping wet and hardly able to stand, the nachalnik ordered her to be bound hand and foot so that the incident might not occur again in her case. Her fall overboard was accidental, but the officer would not believe that she had not tried to commit suicide by drowning. 'She has a grudge against me,' he said, 'and wants to drown herself to have me disgraced. I know her tricks now, and will see that she doesn't play them again.'

"A good number of exiles do try to drown themselves, though," he added, "and if they were not very carefully watched, there would be many deaths in the rivers. Death is to them preferable to long exile, with all its privations and suffering, and the wonder is not that there are so many suicides, but so few. It is an even chance that the poor fellows who tried to escape to-day did so because they wanted to be shot down and make an end of their troubles. Probably the wounded man is now envying the dead one, and wishing that the rifle had made thorough work."

Inquiry among those who knew the men, confirmed Dubayeff's belief. The runways had been very despondent at the thought that they were bound for the dreaded mines beyond Lake Baikal; they realized that as they penetrated more and more into Siberia, their chances of escape were diminished, and so they determined to risk everything and make a run for liberty or death. The result of their attempt is here described.

"It is possible," said Dubayeff, before the subject of suicide was dropped, "that there are some in this very convoy who deliberately did something to cause their transfer from the dreaded prison of Petropavlovsk in St. Petersburg, to the land of exile.

"I know that suicides, or attempts at them, are quite frequent in the fortress; death is preferable to life in those gloomy bastions; and I have known several instances where prisoners tried to take their lives; after being thwarted through the vigilance of their keepers, they watched their chance to strike an officer, in order that they might be shot or sent to Siberia for life. Anything, anything, to get out of that terrestrial Hell."

Many instances of this kind are known to have occurred. As an illustration may be mentioned the case of Muishkin, a noted revolutionist. He tried to starve himself to death, and the surgeon of the fortress was sent to administer food to him by force. Muishkin deliberately struck and otherwise insulted him, and was shot accordingly. But for may months his friends knew nothing of his fate, and only learned the facts from other prisoners.

"More than once I was on the point of striking one of the officers. I made up my mind to do so, but every time I reached the determination, I had no opportunity until my anger cooled down, and I postponed the deed. But if I had been kept a week longer in the fortress than I was, I'm sure I should have been nerved to the attempt, as I was well on the road to complete despair.

"It happened that the very day I had made up my mind fully to do the worst, was the day for the departure of a convoy for Siberia. The government wanted a large number of the cells emptied to make room for persons about to be arrested, just as they sometimes dig a grave for a man before he is shot or hanged. In the middle of the night I was called by one of the guards, and ordered to follow him. He took me through a long corridor to where the blacksmith was fastening leg-fetters on another prisoner; he was an intimate friend of mine, but we did not pretend to recognize each other, lest by so doing we might betray something that the prison authorities wished to know.

"After I was fettered, I was escorted to the office of the prison, where a surgeon examined me critically, and told an officer, who proved to be the nachalnik of the convoy, that I was satisfactory. The reason of this was that the prisoners had been so badly treated in the way of food, light, air, exercise, medical attendance, and other matters which make the difference between health and disease, that not one-third of them were able to travel to Siberia, or even to the frontier. Out of thirty persons occupying one group of cells in a casemate, seven were well along in the first stages of consumption, and eleven others were not able to stand, or if they could possibly support themselves on their feet for a moment, they could not go across their cells without falling. In this state of affairs the convoy officer refused to take any who were not able to undertake the journey to Siberia, and very properly, too."

Pushkin agreed with him, and without suspecting the cause, he found the roadway through Siberia wearing a brighter aspect as he viewed it through the gloom of the fortress of Petropavlovsk that rose before his imagination.

"A convict suit was given me, and I was then taken to a waiting-room in the lower part of the prison, where

I found a dozen or more convicts, like myself, sitting around a table, on which a samovar (tea-urn) was hissing. Half of them were my acquaintances and friends, but we gave no sign of recognition for the reasons I have already told you. We had been separated for years, all the time in the walls of one and the same prison, and I found there two whom I supposed had long since been dead, and who had likewise thought me dead, too. Can you imagine anything more terrible than such a meeting? Not only were friends there, but husbands and wives, and a pair of affianced lovers, sitting almost side by side for the first time in years, and yet not daring to speak!

"But when we reached the railroad station, to which we were taken in locked vans and accompanied by guards, we were shut into the convict cars and left to ourselves. How our tongues were loosened then, and how we did talk, talk, talk, till half of the party were in hysterics. How strange and hollow was the sound of our own voices, not to speak of the strangeness of the voices which had been silent to us, and with them all other voices, for such a long, dreary time!

"Some of us were so broken down with the excitement of the change and the meeting with old friends, that when we reached Moscow we had to be lifted from the convict-cars and carried to the hospital; by the advice of the medical attendant the nachalnik of the convoy postponed the continuation of our journey for several days, to give us chance to recuperate."

Suddenly there was a cry of "*Preeval! Preeval!*" from the men at the head of the column, which was held by brodyags who had been over the road before and knew it more or less thoroughly. Dubayeff told Pushkin that some of these fellows had been there a dozen times or even more; they were in the habit of saying that they spent their time visiting their parents.

"The ostrog (prison) is my father and the taiga (forest) is my mother," says the experienced brodyag. "I honor both my parents, and when not with the one I am with the other."

The cry we have mentioned meant that the place had been reached for the noon-day halt. Pushkin looked up and saw that they were near a village; several girls and old women were waiting in the open ground close to it with provisions, which they expected to sell to the prisoners. When the column had come up to the group the order "*Stoy!*" was given, and in less than twenty seconds every man and woman of the convoy was sitting or lying on the ground, all except the soldiers, who stood ready to interfere with any attempt at escape.

The peasants had bread, milk, pirogs (pies of meat or fish), hard-boiled eggs, and other edible things for sale. Dubayeff and Pushkin had formed a "pool" with two other prisoners, and the four united their funds for the common good. They drew lots to see who should be their starosta, or purveyor for the day, and the choice fell on Dubayeff. He began bargaining for their supply of food soon after the column halted.

Pushkin was interested in observing the closeness with which his friend conducted the business, and he realized that it was necessary to make every copeck of their possessions go as far as possible. It is fair to say that it was only exceptionally the case that the peasants sought to take advantage of the necessities of the prisoners, and drive a hard bargain with hungry men.

"It's a time of plenty now," said Dubayeff, "and provisions are cheap. When I went through here before there had been a very bad season, the drought having destroyed the greater part of the crops, and everything was dear. The government allowance of five copecks a day was not enough to support a man; it would buy a two-pound loaf of rye bread and that was all. No tea, no meat or fish, nothing but bread, and not enough of that."

"How did you manage to live?" Pushkin asked.

"Live! we starved, we did not really live. Many became so weak that they fell by the wayside and were packed into the telyegas which were already filled. When we reached the forwarding stations, they were left behind in the hospitals, and not more than half of them ever recovered."

"Did the government know of the state of affairs?"

"Know of it? of course it was known. Our officers could do nothing for us, as they could not increase the allowance without orders from headquarters; the convoy officers all through the country sent letter after letter, made complaint after complaint, and recommendation after recommendation, but nothing was done. The money allowance was not increased, and so the prisoners were forced to suffer. The peasants were as kind as their means allowed them to be, but no one could expect them to sell food to us at an actual loss to themselves.

"One of the convoy officers tried in vain to have the prisoners properly fed, and when his protests went unheeded, he resigned his commission, and left the service. And he was by no means the first officer to give up his position because he could never cause the abolition of abuses which came under his personal observation.

"One naturally supposes that the government would charge itself with the feeding of the exiles on the road, but it does nothing of the kind.. It simply gives the prisoners the money allowance mentioned, and leaves them to buy of the peasants or of the soldiers as best they can. There is no particular objection to the plan, except in times of scarcity. Ordinarily, provisions are abundant and prices low enough to enable a man to live upon the allowance, but he can barely live by. careful economy. The allowance ought to be larger at all times. and especially so when there have been failures of crops, or other misfortunes that make food dear."

After a sufficient halt for rest and dinner, the march was resumed. It was unbroken by any incident of importance ; no one tried to escape during this march, and the occurrence of the forenoon had caused an appearance of gloom through the whole column, with the exception of the brodyags, whom nothing seemed to affect.

These fellows laughed and joked with each other and boasted of their exploits in eluding their officers at the mines or in making their escapes. Possibly they did not confine themselves to the lines of exact truth, but they certainly were not restrained in the least by the presence of their guards.

"You're a nice fellow," said one brodyag to another, "to run away from your good home in the Kara mines and go into the taiga (wilderness). There in the mines you had masters to look after you and see that you were sheltered at night, they gave you these decorations (leg-fetters) and a diamond-backed coat, and when you went to the taiga you lost them all."

The overcoats of hard-labor convicts are marked on the back with a double diamond, and the nature of this distinction is understood by every Siberian. Consequently, when a prisoner escapes, he must part with his overcoat, or in some way remove the mark which indicates what he is. He must also rid himself of his leg-fetters, but this is generally no great trouble to the experienced brodyag.

"I traded my overcoat for some potato-sacks," was the reply. "Potato sacks, when you know how to sew them together, make splendid coats for a tourist in the taiga."

"How did you trade?"

"I found the sacks in a stable and knew that the owner would find the coat more convenient. He didn't object to the exchange."

"Of course not, he wasn't there."

"No, he wasn't, that's a fact. But it was his stable and he might have been there if he'd wanted to be."

"I did better than that," said another brodyag. "I traded my overcoat and decorations for a whole chemidan (trunk) full of clothes."

"Cut it off the back of a tarantass, I'll warrant."

"*Nierte* (No), do you think I would do such a thing? I just climbed on the back of the tarantass when it was rolling along the road in the night, and the chemidan fell off in five minutes. I fell too and carried the chemidan off into the woods to keep it for the owner. Of course I had to examine it, to find the owner's name."

"Yes, and you can't read; what good would the name do when you found it?"

"I didn't think of that till I had all the things spread on the ground. Then it was too late, and I picked out all I could carry and left the rest."

The brodyags could have been called the life of the convoy, as they kept up a continual round of talk, of which the foregoing may be considered a sample. The politicals and those of the convicts for whom this was the first journey to the mines, were silent for the most part, and much less inclined to look upon their life from the humorous side. There is no more philosophical being in the world than the confirmed brodyag of Siberia; he goes to the mines, escapes, goes again, and again, lives and suffers in the forest, is hunted like a wild beast, but rarely profits by experience. With each arrest he takes everything as it comes and makes the best of it; his whole thoughts are devoted to how he will next escape and what he will do to make his way as smooth as possible.

The brodyag is known as "Ivan Don't-remember," for the reason that he forgets or conceals his real name in order that his identity can not be traced. When asked his name this is all he knows about it; he has no passport other than the wolf's, and if his appearance indicates that he has escaped from the mines, he is sent back there for five years. As many as two hundred Ivan Don't-remembers have been found at one time in a forwarding prison.

"A thousand or more of these vagabonds are arrested every year in Western Siberia," said Dubayeff, while talking with Pushkin on this subject. "They are sent back to the mines of Eastern Siberia, 2,000 miles towards the rising sun, and perhaps to the very mines whence they have escaped. And for every hundred thus arrested and returned to hard labor, probably thirty or more have died in the forest of cold and starvation."

"And how many get back to Europe and escape altogether out of Russia."

"Perhaps one in a hundred, not more. It is not easy to say exactly, as we never know how many have died in the forest or succeeded in getting quite away."

The weather was dry and the road was a cloud of dust. So dense was it, that often one end of the column could not be distinguished from the other, and those in the rear, whose lungs were at all weak, suffered very much from being compelled to breathe the dust-laden atmosphere in which they were constantly enveloped.

The sun was just setting when, from the head of the column, came the cry of "*Pooloo-étape!*" or Half-way station! The regular etapes or exile stations are about forty miles apart, and as this is too great a distance for a convoy to march in a single day, the government has erected the pooloo-etapes, which divide the distance into sections of twenty miles each.

Pushkin looked, and saw an inclosure of upright posts set into the ground, with the roofs of three buildings visible above the stockade. Dubayeff told him that one of these buildings was occupied by the officers of the convoy, one by the guard, and the third by the prisoners.

"Get ready for a rush after the counting is over," said he in a low voice.

"Why so," Pushkin asked.

"There will be a rush to secure sleeping-places in the kameras as soon as the gates are opened. If you don't get a place on one of the nares (sleeping-benches), you'll have to sleep on the floor, or out in the corridor, or perhaps in the yard."

CHAPTER XV.

NIGHT IN THE POOLOO-ETAPE.

In front of the pooloo-etape the party was drawn up to be counted, which was a precaution to make sure that the right number was present. It is a trick of the brodyags, when one escapes, to protect him by answering to his name at roll-call, and keeping up the deception where it is possible to do so, consequently, while the count is going, on no one is allowed to move. In this instance the counting was soon over, the number was pronounced "*horosho* (all right)," and then the gates of the yard were flung open.

There was a rush and scramble as Dubayeff had predicted and, as usually happens in such cases, the choice of sleeping-places fell to the strongest. Might makes right in Russia more than anywhere else in the world, at least such is the foundation on which nearly everything is based. The strong take from the weak, and the weak have no means of protecting themselves.

Dubayeff succeeded in obtaining a place by pre-emption, but Pushkin was less fortunate. It happened that Dubayeff found himself next to Nemo, their brodyag acquaintance, who had travelled with them from Saratov, and the latter immediately asked what had become of Pushkin.

"He didn't get a place," was the reply. "He will have to sleep in the corridor or on the floor."

"No he won't," the brodyag responded instantly; "he can afford to pay two copecks for my place, and I'll take the floor. It doesn't matter where I sleep, but I always go in for the rush so as to sell out."

The matter was soon arranged and the required price was paid. This is a frequent practice with the brodyags, and they derive a slight revenue from fastidious prisoners who are fortunate enough to have a little money.

Immediately after the sleeping-places had been secured, numerous transfers were arranged so as to bring parties of friends together, and these transactions occupied a half hour or so. Then the prisoners ate their supper, which consisted mainly of some of the food they had kept from the "preeval" or mid-day halt, or of provisions bought from peasants since the arrival at the station, or from the soldiers. The soldiers supplied hot water for making tea, charging a copeck for each kettle full, and they also drove a trade in soup from their kitchen. Many of the prisoners carried tea-kettles at their waist-belts, and some of them had metal cups, which they were careful not to allow out of their sight.

Supper was eaten on the platforms, on the floors, in the corridors, or wherever room to sit down could be found, and then the exiles, weary from their march of thirty versts, were ready for rest. The air of the kamera was foul, as there is very little ventilation and the place was crowded, but by this time Pushkin had been accustomed to the conditions of prison life and did not greatly mind his present quarters. He considered himself fortunate in having obtained a place on the platform, which, dirty as it was, was infinitely preferable to the floor or the corridor.

"It's a shame that we should be crowded into such a space as this," he remarked to Dubayeff as they were eating their supper. "Why does not the government make better provision for lodging the prisoners on their way to exile?"

"Because it is unwilling to spend the money to do so," was the reply. "The trouble is that the etapes and pooloo-etapes were built long ago, when there were fewer people going into exile than now. The accommodations were originally intended for 150 exiles, and that was the usual size of the convoys when the stations were built; now the convoys are almost never below 250, and often they are 300 or 400. The condition of the etapes has been called to the attention of the government over and over again, but nothing is done about it."

Maximof, a Russian author, who published in St. Petersburg a book upon "Siberia and Penal Servitude," which was allowed by the censor, and therefore has a semi-offical character, mentions this overcrowding of the etapes, and so does another Russian writer (Orfanof), whose book was also published in the capital of the empire. Orfanof was an officer who served for several years in Siberia, and he mentions many instances of great overcrowding that came under his own observation. In one estape, with accommodations for 140 prisoners, he found no fewer than 800! The same etape was often seen by him, and never when it contained fewer than 500 "unfortunates."

Before the prisoners were allowed to go to sleep they were summoned to the yard and the roll was called to make sure that none had escaped. Then the sentinels were placed, the exiles returned to their quarters, silence was ordered, and the doors were closed. All peasants who had been admitted to sell food were sent away before the calling of the roll, and as long as they were inside the stockade, a sharp eye was kept on them to see that they did not connive at any attempt to escape.

Sleep came to most of the prisoners through sheer weariness. A march of thirty versts (20 miles) in a day is within the powers of a robust man without excessive fatigue. But when he has been weakened by the privations of prison life, by scanty and poor food, unwholesome lodgings, and when, moreover, he is hampered by five pounds of iron chain fastening one ankle to the other, the march of thirty versts is likely to leave him utterly exhausted. This was the case with Pushkin, who fell asleep within a few seconds after stretching himself on the hard plank which formed his bed.

His sleep was troubled. He dreamed of home, and was again with his family, his wife at his side and his children seated around him. A bountiful supper lay upon the table and a steaming samovar hissed merrily as a hint that it was ready for the preparation of the fragrant tea. In the midst of their happiness, and just as they were to take their seats at the table, came a loud knocking and a summons to open the door in the name of the Czar.

With a start he waked, realized where he was, and fell back half fainting upon his bed of plank. Then, as he dozed, the incidents of his arrest, imprisonment, the midnight departure from Tambov, the convict-car of the railway, the prison at Saratov, the fastening of the leg-fetters, the "cage" on the steamboat, the railway again, the forwarding prison, and now the beginning of the dreary march of two thousand miles, all passed before him. No wonder he waked again with terror depicted on his countenance ; his chains rattled as he moved, and told him he was indeed a prisoner and that his latter dream was a horrible reality.

There was a fever in his veins when he rose in the morning and partook of the scanty breakfast which preceded the second day's march. The roll was called in the yard of the stockade ; then the gates were opened and the column filed out, as it had done on the previous day. The weather continued dry, and soon the convoy was wrapped in a cloud of dust, visible for a mile or more across the plain.

An hour or two before sunset the etape was reached ; it had been visible for some time across the plain, its dirty yellow, the prevailing color of the Siberian exile stations, and the stockade that surrounded it, rendering it impossible to be mistaken for anything else than what it was. The etape was considerably larger than the pooloo-etape already described, but the general character and arrangements were much the same. The roof was in a bad condition, the floors were rotten and broken, and the building was really unfit for human occupancy. It was very evident that in bad weather the kameras would be nearly as uncomfortable as the court-yard, so far as keeping out the rain was concerned.

"We change our escort here," said Dubayeff to Pushkin as they approached the station. "The nachalnik who has come with us from the end of the railway, goes back from here, and takes his soldiers with him ; from here to the next etape we have another nachalnik and another guard.

"This is the kind of place where you can possibly

change your name," Dubayeff whispered, with his mouth close to his friend's ear.

"Change my name! How?"

"Trade it off for another man's, some fellow who has a lighter sentence than you."

"Please explain; I don't understand."

"This is the way of it. You are sentenced to twenty years of hard labor in the mines, and are going beyond Lake Baikal. Is it not so?"

"Yes," was the reply, in a tone of sadness, as the thought of what was before him came again into Pushkin's mind.

"There are prisoners in the convoy who are sentenced for four or five years, and are going no further than Irkutsk, at least for the present. They will be distributed through the Irkutsk province, and will not be sent beyond the great lake. Some of them are gamblers and drunkards, fellows who will do anything for the sake of money; they are brodyags who have been sent to the mines before, and know the best ways of escaping.

"Now, for fi v or a hundred rubles, one of these men will change nai e, place and sentence with you; when your name is called for the next departure from the station, he will step forward, and when his name is called, you will step forward. He answers all questions as if he were you, and you follow his example. In that way, if you are not detected, he goes beyond the Baikal with your sentence, and you remain in the Irkutsk province with his."

"But is it possible to avoid detection? It seems to me that the officers would surely discover us."

"On the road with this convey it could not be done, as the officers are familiar with your personality. But when the convoy changes nachalnik and guards, it is not so difficult, provided, of course, the old escort is not standing by when the roll is called for the new one to take charge. You must get somebody that resembles you in a general way, as there is a description opposite each name, to prevent this very trick, which was formerly much more common than it is now."

"What will they do with a man when they detect him in a trade of this sort?"

"Sometimes they flog both parties to the transaction, put them on half rations, (as if the present amount of food they get were not scanty enough) and sometimes they add a year or two to the original amount of the sentence. It's a risk to run, like every other plan of escaping, but many men have taken it."

"Will you try it with me?" Pushkin asked.

"Yes, I would if I had the money to do it with. But I haven't it, unfortunately."

Pushkin thought a few moments and then said:

"If you think the risk is not too great, and are willing to share it with me, I will supply the money for the negotiation."

"No," replied Dubayeff, "it would be a loan I might never be able to repay. You have need of all the money you can carry about you, my brother, and I could not allow myself to take it from you."

"Listen," said Pushkin in reply. "Rather than go out alone, I will stay in the convoy and trust to fate. I want your companionship, your aid, your friendship, your knowledge of the country and the people. Without you, I should certainly be retaken in a few days at farthest; with you, my chances would be greatly improved and I know it. Therefore I am not only willing but desirous to furnish the money, if I have it, that will free us both. We will try the taiga together, or I will not try it at all."

Pushkin pressed the matter further, and it was at length arranged that Dubayeff would endeavor to negotiate the desired change of name and place for both.

That very evening, in the etape, the brodyag, Nemo, sidled up to Dubayeff and intimated a desire for a confidential talk. Of course he was accommodated.

"Would you and your friend like to change names with two short timers?" said Nemo.

Dubayeff thought it would be injudicious to show any eagerness to make the trade, and so he answered with an air of the greatest indifference, that he didn't believe it could be done.

"Listen," said the brodyag, "it can be done, and I know two men that will make the change with you. You are katorga (hard-labor criminals), bound for the Trans-Baikal province, and they are poselentse (penal colonists), going to Irkutsk."

"What will they change names for?"

"A hundred and fifty rubles apiece, and I want fifty rubles for my share."

Evidently Nemo had in him the material for a successful broker in the financial or other markets. He did not believe in transacting business for nothing.

"That's more money than there is in the whole world," was the reply, "or at any rate, more than in all this convoy. Say fifty rubles apiece and I'll talk with Pushkin and see if he has any money; I haven't."

"I know he has some," Nemo answered, with his finger on the side of his nose. "The money-changer is an old friend of mine, and he tipped me the wink."

But I'm keeping the secret well; nobody else knows it."

It was finally arranged that Pushkin and Dubayeff would give one hundred rubles each to the two poselentse to exchange names with them. Nemo received a ruble as a retaining fee, and retired to consult with his principals.

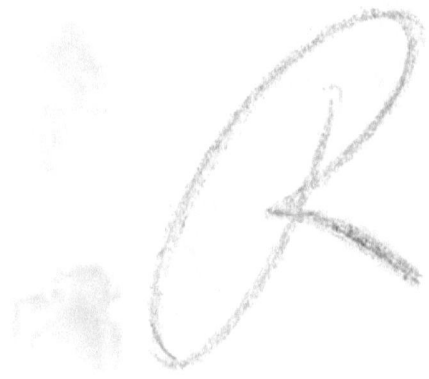

CHAPTER XVI.

HORRORS OF THE ROAD.

The bargain was closed, but not without considerable negotiation, which kept the enterprising Nemo busy. The two poselentse wanted some of the money in advance, but Dubayeff was firm in his refusal; he argued that they had the advantages of the situation, as it was in their power to fail to respond when the other names were called, and with the money in their hands, they could deny without danger to themselves that they had ever made any arrangement of the kind. Dubayeff and Pushkin would be powerless to help themselves, as they could not make complaint to the nachalnik of a circumstance that would surely bring punishment on their own heads.

"It is just possible that Nemo is trying to trick us," said Dubayeff, "he is quite capable of doing it, if he has the chance. He knows you have money in your possession, and will be on the alert all the time to get some of it. There is no danger that he will betray you to the nachalnik, as that would spoil his chance of making anything out of you, but from this time on he will be full of schemes which will cost you something. "I more than half suspect that he and his friends have formed a conspiracy in this whole business, and that if they could get the money, or any considerable part of it in their hands, difficulties would immediately arise by which the change of names would be prevented. At any rate, I'm going to see that they don't get the best of us."

As before stated, exiles, when on the road, march two days and rest one, the resting being done at the principal etapes. The convoy had been on the road two days, and therefore it did not proceed until the second morning after arriving at the station where the negotiations were made for the change of names.

During the day the prisoners lounged around the yard and in the building belonging to them, and the time of many was spent in studying the walls of the buildings, the floors, nares, and every other place where anything was cut or written.

Pushkin observed that there were messages of various kinds, nearly all of them short, and consisting principally of names and dates. Then there were curious hieroglyphics that he could not decipher, and he asked Dubay, eff what they meant.

"Nemo can probably tell you better than I," was the reply, "but I doubt if he would give you any information."

"Why so?"

"These hieroglyphics are communications that the brodyags make to one another; they have a hidden meaning, and are exactly analogous to the marks that thieves and beggars place on the door-posts of houses to inform their brethren of the character of the people living there. When one mark becomes known to the authorities another is adopted, and though the officials try to stop this mode of communication, they do not succeed for any length of time."

Nemo happened along about this time and Pushkin asked him about the signs. As Dubayeff had predicted, the fellow denied all knowledge of them, but as he did so there was a twinkle in his eye which indicated that he was lying.

"Never mind what these particular marks mean," said Pushkin. "Of course, you don't know'; but what do other travellers know about them?"

"I'll tell you a little story I've heard about them," said the brodyag, demurely.

"Well, then, what is it?"

"Ten or twelve years ago, at an etape between Krasnoyarsk and Irkutsk, one or two brodyags used to get away from nearly every convoy. They escaped in the night, and all that the officers could find out was that the number was all right when the prisoners were locked into the ostrog and all wrong when the doors were opened in the morning. The ostrog was examined everywhere, but not a hole was found where the fellows could get out; some of the superstitious soldiers thought it was the devil that did the work, and I'm not sure but a few of the brodyags thought the same thing.

"It went on for a long time, and in spite of the doubling of the guards and a patrol of Cossacks all around the outside, the escapes continued. And it wasn't until the ostrog was pulled down and rebuilt again in a different place that the thing was found out and stopped. This was the way it happened:

"The old ostrog was on some rocky ground close to a small river. At the next etape to the West there were some marks on one of the nares, which could only be found by feeling with the fingers under the end of a plank; but there were marks on the wall that directed attention to that plank. A brodyag, who was up to the tricks of the business, would find these marks, and they told him to sleep under the nares at the next station. When he got there, and looked for the place to sleep, he found some marks that told him what end of the nare to sleep under, and then other marks gave him a hint what to do. He, and perhaps a neighbor with him, managed to squeeze under a beam, and beyond this beam there was a plank that could be lifted at one end, provided you got hold of it in the right way.

"Lifting the plank made a hole in the floor, and this hole led into a sort of tunnel made by a natural crevice in the rock, where a man could creep along a hundred feet or so till he found himself stopped by a big stone. When he pushed on it the stone yielded and he found himself in the open air. He was careful to replace the stone, as the time might come when he would want to use the tunnel again. He generally got out early in the night so that he was miles away by the next morning."

"But couldn't he be tracked and run down when the snow was on the ground?" Pushkin asked.

"Certainly he could, but there was a warning mark on the plank that prevented anybody using it when snow was on the ground. A brodyag who knows these marks always respects them, and doesn't take a chance when he's told not to."

"Was it ever found out who discovered and first used the tunnel?"

"Yes, the story is that there was a sylni (person under banishment without labor) who had been sent to live three years in the neighborhood of that etape. He thought it just possible that he might be sent to Siberia again, and with a heavier sentence, and so he looked around to see if he could devise a way of getting out of that ostrog if he was ever shut up in it. He found the crevice in the rock, followed it up till it brought him under the floor of one of the kameras of the ostrog, and fixed everything all right that way. Then he managed to be engaged to repair the floor of the kamera, and he repaired it to his own satisfaction, if not to that of his employers.

"He did as he expected, and came back to Siberia sentenced to the mines. By this time he had learned all the secret marks and signs of the brodyags, and as he didn't want to keep such a good thing all to himself, he helped others in the way I've told you. He got out himself and escaped, but I don't know anything more about him."

The arrangement for exchanging names was not carried out, for the reason that the nachalnik and soldiers of the old escort were present when the convoy was called out to take the road again. Under the circumstances, any attempt at the exchange would have been detected, and the parties concerned wisely concluded that honesty was the best policy, when there was no chance of perpetrating a fraud.

It rained hard during the night and all the morning previous to the start, and the roads were converted into lanes of mud. But there was no delay on account of the rain; a Siberian exile convoy must march regardless of the weather or of the condition of the roads on which it travels. Pushkin proposed that the prisoners should address a respectful petition to the nachalnik asking that they be allowed to rest until the roads were in a fit condition, but to this suggestion Dubayeff shook his head.

"No use," said he, "not a bit of use."

"Why not?" queried his inexperienced friend. "I

know the humanity of the government towards poor unfortunates amounts to nothing, but surely the officers must be glad of an excuse to keep them from going out in such weather as this."

"If they condescend to notice your petition at all, they will tell you that to halt for such a reason would be against the regulations. They will further explain, if they are willing to take the trouble, that the movements of the convoys are arranged so that two shall never be at the same station at the same time. When we march out this morning the place will be made ready for the next convoy; if the convoys were allowed to take their own time, and travel only in fine weather, there would be great confusion and great delay in reaching our destination."

Pushkin acknowledged the force of the argument, but insisted that with the telegraph line extending from station to station, there could just as well be a little humanity in the treatment of the exiles. In which view the reader will probably agree with him.

Out into the rain and mud went the "unfortunates," their chains clanking as they dragged themselves slowly along, hurried now and then by their guards, whose temper was none of the best at being compelled to face the pitiless storm. Ankle deep was the mud, penetrating was the rain, and long before the noon halt every one of that marching party was wet to the skin. Dripping with rain, they reached the poolooetape where the night was to be passed; before their arrival Pushkin consoled himself with the reflection that his linen bag in the telyega contained a change of dry clothing, and his comrade did not undeceive him.

But when the baggage was taken from the wagons, it

was found to be no less watersoaked than the garments on the prisoners' backs.

"I might of told you so," said Dubayeff, as he saw the despairing expression of Pushkin's face, "but thought it would be cruel not to let you enjoy your delusion."

"I supposed the government would provide tarpaulins to spread over the baggage and keep it dry."

"So would any sensible man," was the reply, "but the fact is, nothing of the kind is done. It's a part of the inhumanity of our masters, and we must submit, especially as it will do no good to complain."

And so it is. The Autocrat of all the Russias sends his subjects into exile; his children have displeased him and he punishes them; but does any father with a spark of humanity in his composition deliberately resort to torture and neglect as a means of punishment? If he cared aught for the lives of his subjects he would not pursue a course that inevitably consigns many of them to premature graves. More merciful to shoot them, hang them, kill them in some way, than drive them into death by disease, as is the result of the system he follows at present.

These were thoughts that passed through Pushkin's mind as he contemplated the dripping contents of the bag in which he had expected to find dry clothing to exchange for his wet garments. All around him were prisoners in the same condition, men and women already enfeebled by scanty food and the rigors of prison life. They were cold, wet, and covered with mud from feet to knees, and their only resource was to lie down in their soaked garments and sleep as best they might.

The rain had kept the peasants from bringing a proper supply of food for sale at the noon-day halt, and it likewise kept them away from the pooloo-etape. Consequently many were unable to purchase anything and went supperless to their sleeping-places on the nares. To the cold and wet and mud was added the torture of hunger.

"I would endure it all cheerfully," said Dubayeff, "if I could have His August Majesty, the Emperor, as my companion. I could bear the hardships of the journey into exile, the rain, frost, snows, starvation, the terrible roads, the horrors of the stations, the dirt, degradation, brutality, and everything else, if he would only share them with me and I could see him as he did so. The sacred person of His Majesty would furnish a fine feeding ground for the vermin with which we are infested; how these insect pests would dance with joy when parading on and puncturing his delicate skin! And the Imperial family, the leeches that are devouring the life-blood of Russia; how they would enjoy a month or two on the road in chains and privations, and lodged in these leaky, tumble-down etapes, reeking with pestilence and permeated with the seeds of half the diseases known to civilized man!"

Pushkin was silent, but it was evident from the expression of his face that he shared the views of his companion in misfortune. How could it well be otherwise?

And day after day, with halts for the change of escort, and with halts of a few days or weeks at each of the principal cities or towns along the route, the weary column dragged along towards the dreaded mines, where the journey was to end. From the end of the railway to the mines of Kara, the destination of Pushkin and his comrade, is a distance of two thousand miles. The marching convoys average about eighty miles a week, and thus it will be seen that six months are required for the journey. The time is really more, in consequence of delays at Tomsk, Krasnoyarsk, Irkutsk, and other cities, consequent upon the making up of convoys composed of prisoners whose destination is the same.

Pushkin's march began in the summer, but long before he reached Irkutsk the autumn months had come, and with them the autumn storms and the cold winds from the north that often converted the mud of the roads into a partly or wholly frozen mass. Think of wading through half frozen mud, hour after hour, barefooted as were most of the prisoners, the miserable shoes given to them by the government having worn out in the first two or three days of their march. Over and over again have the convoy officers protested against the robbery of the prisoners by the contractors who supply shoes and clothing, but their protests are unheeded and the rascality goes on as before.

"The cost of burying those who die on the road from exposure," said Dubayeff one day, "is more than that of a tarpaulin for the baggage wagons of every convoy; and the cost of treatment and transportation of those whose feet become so sore that they cannot walk, would give every man a decent pair of shoes, instead of these miserable contrivances that do not cost a tenth part of what the contractors get for them."

An officer of high rank has made a careful calculation and sent his figures to the emperor, showing that there would be a saving to the government of fourteen rubles ($7.00) on each prisoner, if the exiles were sent in wagons or sleighs to their destinations, instead of being forced to go on foot. Formerly, all political prisoners were carried in vehicles, the criminals being the only ones required to march. But the determination of the government to subject political offenders to all possible hardship and degradation, brought about the change.

Pushkin had looked forward to some relief from fatigue and suffering during the halts at the sites named in a previous paragraph, but in this he was bitterly disappointed. If the etapes were bad, the prisons were worse, as they were crowded far beyond their capacity; each kamera contained twice as many prisoners as it was originally intended for; but even this fearful overcrowding did not suffice. There were sheds and tents in the prison-yards, and in them the prisoners, many of them ill with typhus, pneumonia, and other diseases, were packed as closely as in the kameras. There was not room in the hospitals for the sick or even for half of them; they were compelled to remain among those who, though greatly debilitated from their hardships and scanty food, were still on the list of the "able-bodied."

The tents and sheds, the latter with boarded roofs and with ends and sides of cotton cloth, were bad enough in the warm days and nights of summer, but think what they must have been as lodging-places in autumn and winter, for men and women scantily clad, wretchedly fed, and crowded together like negroes on a slave ship!

"I remember what you told me about the forwarding prison at Tomsk," said Pushkin to Dubayeff, soon after their arrival there, "but surely I had no idea of the horrors of the place."*

---

* The following statistics of the Tomsk prison, the central depot of exiles, are from an authentic source: "One prison can accommodate properly 765 men. There is space for 490 healthy persons and 275 sick ones, but the number of exiles who arrived in Tomsk in 1886 was 16,184, of whom only 14,866 were transported further. In 1887 there arrived 14,277; in 1888, 15,014;

" Have you seen the family kameras in the bologans (sheds), where the family parties of men, women and children live ?"

" No," was the reply ; "are they worse than our kazarm ?"

" Go and look for yourself, that's all," Dubayeff answered. " Get permission to see a friend there ; ask for leave to see Carl Obossoff, in the second bologan, and when you come back you will think we are in a palace."

and in 1889, up to September, over 12,000—of whom 13,522. 14,239, and 11,000 respectively, were taken to the interior. In 1886 the average daily number of prisoners was at least 1,313; in 1887, 1,120; and in 1888, 1,380. In some weeks these numbers increased in 1886 to 2,955, in 1887 to 2,755, and in 1888 even to 3,020 men. Among these the daily average on the sick list was, in 1886, 394; in 1887, 512; and in 1888, 396, the majority suffering from typhoid fever. Between 360 and 400 exiles are buried yearly."

CHAPTER XVII.

THE CHECKER-BOARD CIPHER ALPHABET.

A day or two after his interview with his sister, Ivan, in his cell at Tambov, heard a gentle tapping on the wall that separated him from the adjoining apartment.

He thought nothing of it at first, but as it was repeated over and over again, he concluded that his neighbor had something to tell him. Then he thought of the "knock alphabet" that he had heard of, and, at once he replied with a few gentle taps.

He knew nothing of the "knock alphabet," and his only idea was that the letters taken in their order should be numbered, and each letter indicated by the number of blows corresponding to its position. With this idea he counted the blows that were given on the wall, and found that his theory was correct. His unknown neighbor gave a certain number of knocks, about one second apart; then he paused four or five seconds and gave another number; then paused again and continued. By taking the number of knocks to represent a letter, Ivan was overjoyed to find that his neighbor was asking him :

" D-o-y-o-u-u-n-d-e-r-s-t-a-n-d ?"

THE "KNOCK ALPHABET."—See Page 176.

The Russian alphabet contains thirty-six letters. "D" is the fifth letter, and "a" the first, and consequently Ivan answered "*Da* (yes)" by knocking five times, then pausing and giving a single knock. But if he had been using English instead of Russian it would have required forty-nine blows on the wall to spell out the word "y-e-s"—twenty-five for "y," five for "e" and nineteen for "s."

He realized that talking in such fashion would be very slow work, and as he thought of this, his neighbor spelled out:

"Here's better way, wait."

Then he gave a hard blow at each of the four corners of the wall and followed it with the sound of scratching, as if he were drawing seven lines one after the other horizontally along the wall, so as to divide the whole space into six sections. After drawing the first line he gave one knock on the wall, two knocks after drawing the second line, three after the third, and so on. Ivan readily comprehended what was meant, viz., that the spaces were numbered from "1" to "6," beginning with the space at the top.

Then the stranger made the same number of perpendicular scratches, and thus the wall was laid off into thirty-six squares, numbers being given horizontally from left to right, from "1" to "6." Then he rapped "letters in squares," and waited for Ivan to form his diagram, which he did on a scrap of paper with the burnt ends of a match. The Russian alphabet just filled the squares—we will suppose he used the English letters—and his diagram was as follows:

	1	2	3	4	5	6
1	a	b	c	d	e	f
2	g	h	i	j	k	l
3	m	n	o	p	q	r
4	s	t	u	v	w	x
5	y	z	&			
6						

Then the unseen correspondent spelled out in the old way the syllables, "lat." and "lon.," which Ivan readily understood to mean that the letters were to be found in the intersecting squares by latitude and longitude, *i. e.*, by giving the perpendicular number and then the horizontal one. Ivan immediately replied by giving five raps and then one for "y," one rap and then five raps for "e," and finally four raps followed by one rap for "s."

Ivan had learned the knock alphabet and possessed a means of communicating with his neighbor. Even if it answered no practical purpose, it was a diversion which would enable him to drive away much of the dreariness connected with prison life.

His invisible instructor then told him to make a pause at the end of a letter twice as long as between the numbers which indicated it, and twice as long between words as between letters. When Ivan had indicated that he understood the direction, he received the follow question:

"**** ***** ** ** *** ***   * * *** ******
* *****   ***** * *** *** *** ***? (Who are you?)"

Ivan told his name, where he lived, and the circumstances that brought him to his present situation. Then he asked the name of his neighbor and what he was arrested for; the latter replied that he was Ivan Don't-remember and had been imprisoned for stealing a railway. He had secured the track all right, but was captured by the police when he went back to get the rolling-stock!

This evasive answer convinced our young friend that his neighbor was a common criminal, who did not care to reveal his identity even to a fellow prisoner. However, as the man had not said so outright, and, moreover, as they were not physically "in touch" with each other, he continued to converse with the individual who had performed what seemed a most remarkable piece of thievery. But it should be remembered that Ivan Pushkin was only twenty years of age and had never visited America. Under other circumstances, his wonder would have been not that a man had stolen a railway, rolling-stock and all, but that his crime had landed him in prison.

"Call me 'Jeleznai Doroga (Iron Road, or Railway),'" said the unknown. "It will do as well as anything else. Besides it's better than 'Ivan Don't-remember,' which is altogether too common."

The young student assented, and then his friend proposed to give him further instruction in the knock alphabet.

"You're only in your A-B-C's yet," said he; "there's a great deal to learn before you can pass as a professor."

"What's the next thing to learn?" queried Ivan.

"You must know how to change the combinations of the letters," was the reply. "We have them now in a regular form; there are thirty-six letters, and they can be placed in a great many different ways, and the lines of figures can be changed as well as the letters. That will give you numerous letter-ciphers, but they can be studied out by skillful analysis, so that they are not altogether safe."

"I see," Ivan answered. "Thank you very much."

"Wait a bit. Now I'll give you a cipher that nobody can find out, not even the man who invented this or any other alphabet, unless he has the key-word."

Ivan waited, and the system was thus explained:

"You and your friends have agreed upon the key-word 'horse.' You want to let them know that you have got out of prison and reached Warsaw—to send them the message: 'Ivan escaped; now in Warsaw.' You write the message and the key-word under it, thus:

         I v a n   e s c a p e d   n o w   i n   W a r s a w.
         h o r s   e h o r s e h   o r s   e h   o r s e h o.

"'2' and '3' are the figures for 'I.' We'll call 'I' '23,' and use the numbers for other letters in the same way. Our message, reduced to numbers and the key-word also reduced to numbers and written under it, will be like this:

23 44 11 32 15 41 13 11 34 15 14 32 33 45 23 32 45 11 36 41 11 45
22 33 36 41 15 22 33 36 41 15 22 33 36 41 15 22 33 36 41 15 22 33

"Next you add these numbers together and you get the following:

45 77 47 73 30 63 46 47 75 30 36 65 69 86 38 54 78 47 77 56 33 78

THE CHECKER-BOARD CIPHER ALPHABET. 181

"Now that's your cipher that you send to your friends. They take it and write 'horse' over it as many times as are necessary to include all the letters, and then they put the numerical equivalents of each letter of 'horse' directly under the figures of the cipher. By subtraction they get the numerical equivalents of the letters of the actual message, and the rest of the work is easy."

"I see," said Ivan. "By combining this with the changes of letters in the alphabet squares and frequently changing the key-word, it must be difficult to discover the meaning of a message sent in this way."

"Difficult!" spelled out Mr. Jeleznai Doroga, "it's absolutely impossible. The police know all about the cipher code, but they are as powerless to understand and read it as they ever were. I'll show you one of it's curious features."

"The same number may accidently stand for one letter as you see in case of ' a ' and ' e ' in ' Ivan escaped ;' in both these instances ' a ' is represented by ' 47 ' in the cipher and ' e ' by ' 30.' But ' a ' comes twice in ' Warsaw ' and it is there represented by ' 47 ' in the first instance and by ' 33 ' in the second. ' N ' in Ivan is represented by ' 41,' but in ' now ' it is ' 65.' Without a knowledge of the key-word no human being can decipher a message on this system unless he has the help of the D——l or some other supernatural power."

Ivan memorized the checker-board cipher, as the arrangement of the letters in squares is called, so that he knew on the instant the number for every letter. He was able in a few hours to repeat, instead of the ordinary A-B-C, something like the following:

"11 12 13 14 15 16 21 22 23 24 25 26," and so on to the end. When " 26 " was tapped on the wall he knew on the instant that '1' was the letter signaled; and when three blows were followed by two, he recognized 'n.'

It is not so very slow work to communicate in this way as one might at first thought imagine. An expert in cipher signaling can transmit at about one-third the speed of a good operator on the Morse telegraph.

Of course, while the prisoners were telegraphing to each other they kept careful watch to see that they were not discovered by their jailers, and several times their work came to a sudden stop owing to the presence of a warder at the "Judas" in the door. But they found a method of communicating while they were being observed; and so well did they manage it that they sometimes talked for an hour or more while the warders were regarding them through the door. This was the way they did it:

The iron beds were fastened to the walls so that they could not be moved. The rods extending into each wall, made excellent conductors of sound; lying on their beds the two men were within a foot or so of each other, separated, of course, by the stone. By tapping gently on the bed-frame close to the wall, a prisoner could make a sound audible to one who was lying on the bed in the next cell. A man might be apparently asleep for hours, lying motionless on his bed, while at the same time he was telegraphing to his neighbor, who was likewise recumbent, and receiving answers.

The checker-board cipher is often used for conversation among prisoners in the hearing of their guards, just as telegraph operators can communicate with each other in the presence of others, and keep the latter in ignorance of what they are saying. A circumstance of this kind gave Pushkin his first acquaintance with the cipher alphabet.

One evening, in one of the etapes on the road to Tomsk, a brodyag at the further end of the kamera called out to one who was lying close to Pushkin:

"Ivan Don't-remember, the scar-faced one!"

"Here I am!" was the reply. "What do you want?"

The other rattled off a string of numbers, forty or fifty of them at least, and then paused for a reply. The answer was given in the same way.

Nobody paid any attention to it, as nobody could understand it. Dubayeff was asleep at the time, and next morning Pushkin told what he had heard, and was enlightened accordingly. Dubayeff offered to teach him the system; Pushkin assented and acquired it as soon as possible.

Any one who anticipates becoming an occupant of a Russian prison is advised to make himself proficient in the use of this means of communication. It will be an important addition to his resources, and may possibly prove a means of escape. The variations of it are endless, as has been shown to the reader, and new variations will doubtless occur to every one who puts it in practice. It is known all through the prisons of the empire, from the frontiers of Germany to the shores of the Pacific Ocean, and is likely to be known as long as those prisons exist and are used as at present.

Ivan and Mr. Railway kept up frequent communication, and the former tried to talk with his neighbor on the other side of his cell. But although he rapped on the wall several times a day for some days in succession he obtained no reply, and finally concluded that the cell was empty, which was really the case.

Mr. Railway was more fortunate. On the side of his cell, opposite from Ivan's, a prisoner was lodged, who soon became proficient in the knock alphabet; he was a political, who declined to give his name when he found out Mr. Railway's character, or rather, the lack of it. He was evidently a man of influence, as he had established such relations with one of the keepers as to be intrusted with certain matters of prison news that the other could not get. Mr. Railway readily surmised that money was at the bottom of these favors, and he certainly was not far from the truth.

Whenever the political communicated anything to him, Mr. Railway promptly gave the information to Ivan, having first obtained his informant's consent to tell his neighbor on the other side. Most of the news was of no consequence to the youth, but one afternoon he learned something that caused his heart to beat violently. He realized that it might have an important bearing on his fate, and that of his mother and sister, from whom he had heard nothing since his interview with the latter.

CHAPTER XVIII.

THE PRISON OF TAMBOV AGAIN.

The information that came to Ivan from the political prisoner beyond the cell of the professor of cipher writing, was as follows :

"Woman, named Pushkin, seeing lawyer in reception-room. Spies overhearing them."

Ivan was so agitated that he could not answer promptly. When he was sufficiently calm to be able to give the signals he asked :

"Is it mother or daughter? The prisoner on the other side wants to know."

"Who is he?" was the next question.

"I'll ask if he'll let me tell you," replied the middleman. He crossed to the other side of the cell and rapped out the question.

"Certainly," was Ivan's reply. "Tell him I am Ivan Pushkin."

The middleman gave the information, and immediately the unknown political answered by means of the knock alphabet, that he was Basil Volkoff, and had know of Pushkin's arrest before he himself had been drawn into the net of the police. Later on, he admitted that this was not the first time he had been confined in prison, and under the same charge of "untrustworthiness."

Communication through the three cells was somewhat slow and kept Mr. Railway, the middleman, very busy, inasmuch, as he was obliged to cross his cell whenever he served as a repeating instrument between Pushkin and Volkoff. He was also obliged to keep an eye upon the "Judas" in the door, lest his performances should be discovered, and on several occasions he narrowly escaped detection.

Naturally, Ivan was very anxious to learn about the result of the interview between his mother and Mr. Kosavitch, the lawyer, but Volkoff was unable to tell him at that time. All he knew was that such an interview had been arranged for the afternoon, and the spies were to overhear the conversation in the corner of the reception-room.

Later in the day, Volkoff signaled that the interview lasted nearly an hour, and that the spies went away as soon as it was over, and the woman had been returned to her cell.

Ivan wished to know if his mother and sister were still together. There was some delay in ascertaining about it, but the answer finally came that they were.

But question as Ivan might, and did, it was impossible for him to ascertain the nature of the interview in the reception-room. All that he could learn on the subject, has already been stated.

As the two spies walked away from the prison after the interview was over, the expression of their faces was one of disappointment. They did not exchange a word until they were fully a block away.

We will call them Blonde and Brunette; we do not know their real names, and among those who were acquainted with them, they were often called as above, in consequence of the color of their hair and beards.

"Well," said Blonde, by way of opening the conversation; "we did not make as much out of that affair as we expected."

"That's true," said the other. "They must have suspected the trap, as there wasn't information enough in all their talk to cover a postage-stamp, or at any rate, none that we want."

"The governor will be disappointed when we tell him; perhaps he'll think we haven't attended to our duty."

"Quite likely. He's very suspicious, and he certainly wants to make out a good case against these people."

"We'll have to cook up a good story or he may send us away and put others in our places. Just now I don't want to leave Tambov."

"Nor I either. What shall we say?"

"Tell him the conversation was principally about family matters that had no bearing upon what we are trying to find out."

"Nothing could be nearer the truth than that."

"Then we will tell him that the suspicions of the untrustworthiness of the Pushkin family is confirmed, that the exile of Carl Pavloff is fully justified by the revelations which implicate his son and his neighbor, Hartmann."

"That will do very well. How about the women?"

"Oh! let them stay in prison a while longer. They will be sufficiently contrite in course of time to confess their share in the work, and give information that will lead to important arrests."

"Poor devils! it seems hard to hold them any longer. And the young one is so pretty."

"That's your weak point always—captured by a pretty face. What good can she be to you! she's engaged to Hartmann's son and wouldn't give you the fraction of a smile."

"Yes, that's so, I suppose," replied the other reflectively. "But I can't help feeling sorry to see her shut up in prison when there doesn't seem to be any reason for it."

"No reason for it! Doesn't she belong to an untrustworthy family? Besides, we must look out for ourselves, and there's no telling what mischief she might work if she could get out and be free to communicate with any one."

"I didn't think of that," was the reply. "Well, we'll let her stay."

They reported to the governor, and of course the latter followed the advice they gave, or, rather, he based his action upon the information presented by his faithful investigators. All the accused individuals remained in detention, and the governor had no pangs of conscience on the subject. On the contrary, he seemed rather to rejoice that so many untrustworthy subjects of the Czar were behind bolts and bars where they could do no harm.

In the prisons of Russia at this very day and hour, hundreds of men and women are incarcerated in order that spies and detectives may have employment. There is nothing against them but suspicion; if the real state of each case was reported to the higher officials it is quite possible the latter might realize that there was an opportunity to reduce the number of their employes. The spies are unwilling to lose the pay they are now receiving, and this circumstance is sure to influence their reports.

After his interview with Madame Pushkin, Mr. Kosavitch greatly desired to see the governor, as he thought he could induce that official to take action favorable to his clients. He had an idea that the interview would naturally lead to his being notified to come to the Chancellerie. Several days having passed without any notification reaching him, he ventured to write to the governor soliciting the honor and privilege of an audience.

Two, three. and four days passed in anxious waiting. On the morning of the fifth day he was summoned to the Chancellerie, and went at once.

The governor received him as cordially as before, and assumed the same air of ignorance as to the subject of the audience. The lawyer came at once to the point, and said he solicited official attention to the cases of his clients, and hoped the governor would cause them to be formally examined before him, either separately or together, as might seem best to His Excellency.

The governor paused, as though endeavoring to recall the case of the Pushkin family, and also that of their friend Hartmann. Ah! yes, he remembered it perfectly, but, after another pause, he said the government was not yet prepared to go on with the investigation. So many matters of importance were constantly before him for consideration that minor affairs must wait their turn.

"Pardon my presumption, Your Excellency," said Mr. Kosavitch, "but this is a matter of great importance to the persons concerned. Their liberty is in question, and their lives are imperilled by longer detention in prison."

"Their lives!" said the governor sharply; "then their

case is certainly serious, and they may have forfeited all claims to clemency by the gravity of their acts."

"Pardon me if I was not sufficiently clear," the lawyer responded. "What I meant to say was that their health is being greatly impaired by imprisonment, and danger to or loss of their health means danger to their lives."

"Yes, I see," was the reply. "You have had an interview with one of the prisoners, I believe."

"Yes, Your Excellency, and it is that interview which impels me to ask for an examination at as early a date as may be practicable. I urge it on the ground of justice and humanity."

"I will consider the matter and inform you as soon as I have reached a conclusion," was the non-committal reply of the governor. With this remark he turned to his desk, as a hint that the interview was ended. The lawyer was not slow to catch his meaning and immediately bowed himself out of the room.

Just as he opened the door he met an under-official holding a telegram in his hand. It was for the governor, and concerned the subject which had just been under discussion.

In the afternoon Mr. Kosavitch took his customary stroll along the route taken by his friend, the warder of the prison. Whenever the warder had anything to communicate he played with the buttons of his coat with the fingers of his right hand, but if he had no news to give his right arm hung by his side. Now he was making the signal agreed upon when communication was desired.

Mr. Kosavitch stopped in front of a theatrical poster that covered part of a wall, and announced that the principal theatre of Tambov was to be honored the following week by the presence of a company of players from Moscow. Griboiedoft's famous comedy, 'Gore ot Ouma,' (Grief from Wit) would be presented in a manner surpassing any previous production ever known in the city.

The warder seemed equally interested in the announcement, and ranged himself at the side of the lawyer. As he did so, he said in a low tone :

"Hartmann and young Pushkin were taken away this morning in a tarantass."

"When and where were they taken?" queried the lawyer, as soon as he could catch his breath.

"I don't know where they have gone, but they were taken before daylight, and by the same officer that escorted Carl Pushkin when he left Tambov. That is all I can tell you."

By this time he had finished his inspection of the theatrical poster and moved on. Kosavitch returned quickly to his home and sat down to think.

"Did the governor know of this when he sent for me?" was a question he asked to himself. "Of course he did, and yet he had the coolness to pretend to be as ignorant as I was. Perhaps he wanted to find out if I had any secret information from the prison, and took that plan. He knew if I had heard of their removal I would be likely to mention it, or if I did not do so, something in my manner would betray me. Well, perhaps it is quite as well that I didn't know."

"Strange I haven't heard from young Hartmann since he went to St. Petersburg. I ought to have had a letter from him before this. I will write him again and trust to my letter getting through, but must be very guarded, for the double reason of not alarming him, and also to prevent the authorities finding out that I have information from the prison. I'll say nothing about the removal, but will confine myself to the interview of the governor, with some flattery for His Excellency. Then, if the governor intercepts my letter, he will hear good of himself instead of the bad that is commonly attributed to listeners."

The Russian government exercises the paternal right of examining the correspondence of its children, and also that of foreigners who may be dwelling or visiting in Russia. Do not understand that it examines all letters, but only such as are under suspicion of containing something "prejudicial to good order," or whose writers, or the persons addressed are under police-surveillance.

An ordinary letter may be opened by holding it over a jet of steam, which softens the mucilage or gum solution, so that the flap of the envelope can be lifted without injury. If the letter is found to be entirely harmless in character, it is generally closed and sent to its destination; and the work of opening and closing is so deftly performed that only the most careful inspection will reveal that the envelope has been tampered with.

Letters to foreign newspapers are very liable to attract official attention and examination. The foreign journalists in Russia usually address their correspondence to business houses in the cities where their newspapers are situated, even when the letters contain nothing that can possibly be considered objectionable, in order that delay may be avoided. They also take the precaution to register their communications as an additional security.

Mr. Kosavitch spent the evening in writing to young Hartmann, detailing the interview with the governor and briefly mentioning his visit to the prison and his talk with Madame Pushkin. He added that Nadia was well, but suffering from her incarceration, and he hoped to interest the governor in her case so that she would not be kept in suspense any longer than was absolutely necessary. "The governor," he added, "is a man of kindly feelings, and I am sure that if he could exercise his own will, he would order her immediate release. Of course he is only doing his duty in obeying orders from St. Petersburg, and no one can blame him for that. In fact, I believe he would at once set free all those in whom you and I are interested if it were in his power to do so."

The lawyer was not exactly frank in this assertion, but we have seen that he expected the letter to go under the official eye, and therefore he desired to write something that would be agreeable reading for his Excellency.

Alexei Hartmann received the letter; whether it was tampered with and perused by the governor, we are unable to say, but it was a full day longer in making its journey to the capital than some other letters deposited at the same time.

The previous letter had suffered similar delay in its travels; in fact it had been delayed in delivery as well as in departure, and no reply had yet been sent to Mr. Kosavitch. The young man thought the lawyer would understand the silence to mean that so far he had not accomplished anything; but in this view he was not altogether correct. He discovered his error when the second

1930   The Siberian Exiles.

letter arrived, and as he had good cause to suspect that his letters had been examined, he wrote very guardedly when he sent his reply.

Chapter XIX

Ivan's Life and Experiences

Hartmann and Ivan had met the fate of Carl Pushkin; they had been sent to Siberia. But they were not in the hard-labor class of exiles as he was and therefore were not submitted to the humiliation of having their heads shaved on one side, neither were they put into leg-fetters and compelled to walk with these impediments to locomotion. They were of the class of sylni, or simple exiles, and were sent to live in Siberia for five years by order of the minister of the Interior. "Untrustworthiness" was their offence; they had associated with a man who was at that very time on his way into exile, and under a much more severe sentence than theirs, and therefore there must be something wrong about them.

It is unnecessary to recount their adventures as they travelled the road on which we have already accompanied the farther of the one, and the friend of the other. They had the solace of each other's company until they reached Tomsk, where they were retained a short time in the central depot of exiles, and then separated.

194ᵃ Ivan's Life and Experiences.

Hartmann was sent to live in a town two hundred miles to the south of Tomsk, while Ivan went about the same distance to the North. They petitioned the exile administration at Tomsk to allow them to go to the same place to live, but their petition was firmly refused.

"I suppose," said Ivan, " that the very reason why we ask to be exiled to the same place, is the reason why the authorities do not want us together. Knowing us to be friends, they think there are greater chances that we will try to escape."

"That is undoubtedly the case," Mr. Hartmann answered. After a pause, he added, that perhaps the officials were not altogether wrong in their conclusions.

When Ivan reached his destination he found that he was hedged about by a great many restrictions. He was in many ways a prisoner, although he was not confined within stone walls and behind grated windows.

Here is his account of his treatment:

"The first thing I had to do was to give up my passport and receive the 'permit to reside,' or 'wolf's passport,' as the brodyags call it. The ispravnik gave me also a copy of the regulations concerning the life I was expected to lead; these regulations are very long, and I sat down in the public square to read them.

"While I was reading the document a young man happened along; he eyed me closely and introduced himself as soon as he saw what I had in my hand. He said he was a supporter of the same Constitution, and when I looked at him as though I did not understand, he said the exiles were in the habit of calling the Code of Regulations their 'Constitution' or 'Bill of Rights.' He laughed as he said it, and I laughed too when I saw the humor of the remark.

"I found that I could not move from one house to another without notifying the police, that I could not go out of the district without police permission, and whenever I did so, I must make my journey both ways as expeditiously as possible. If I fell sick, or was otherwise detained on the road, I must send notice to the nearest police, and must also notify the police in every town or village through which I passed and show them my passport.

"I didn't care very much about this restriction at the outset, as I did not see any reason why I should want to go away from the town except to stay away forever. I had a little money left, very little, and thought I could manage to live on it until I found something to do."

Ivan then told how his heart sank when he read further and found that he was forbidden to engage in any kind of teaching, could not be employed as clerk or copyist, and could have nothing to do in any way with printing offices, libraries, or photographic establishments, and could not even keep or be employed in a grog-shop.

"What is there that one can do," he asked of the man whose acquaintance he had just made.

"You can hire out to a peasant to raise potatoes and other produce of the soil," was the reply. "I don't know of anything else."

"But, first, I must find a place to live in," said Ivan.

"You'll have hard work to do it," replied the other.

"Why so?"

"Because you are a political exile like myself. Nobody wants a lodger who is likely to be visited by the police at any day or hour, and who may be a very dangerous man to have about, apart from the trouble the police might make. When I came here, I went to nearly every house in the town before I could find a lodging, and then I only succeeded through the help of another political, who had been here a year or more. Come with me, and I'll find a place for you. I don't care who you are, but we politicals must give a helping hand to one another."

Ivan gladly accepted the invitation, and with the aid of his new friend, who introduced himself as Peter Helmanoff, he was soon at rest in a miserable room, for which he was to pay two rubles (one dollar) a month. It was in the house of a peasant who had two other lodgers of the same kind, Helmanoff being one of them. The other was a doctor, named Shulmann, who had formerly held a high position among the medical profession in a Russian city, and was exiled because his presence in European Russia was considered prejudicial to good order.

The two resident exiles did all in their power to welcome the new-comer, but there was little they could do. By way of opening the conversation, Ivan remarked to the doctor that he doubtless had something to occupy him in practicing among the people who needed the service of a medical man.

"I wish it were so," was the reply, "but I cannot practice my profession without special permission from the Minister of the Interior. I have applied for it, and my application was refused."

"Probably, because of the opposition of other doctors living here," Ivan remarked.

"Not at all. There is no doctor in the town, with the exception of a very old man who has practically given up the profession; he does not go out at night and can only leave his house in the best of weather. He prescribes for patients that go to see him, and that is all. He indorsed my application; in fact, it was at his suggestion that I asked for the permission."

Ivan bit his lip and made no reply. After a pause the doctor said :

"I practiced for a while without pay, solely in the interest of humanity, but the ispravnik forbade me to continue. I told him that when a peasant came to me with some slight ailment, or a wound to be dressed, I could see no harm in attending to his case, taking no pay for my services; but the ispravnik called my attention to the rules, and told me he would have me arrested if I did anything more of the kind.

"One day the regular doctor, the old gentleman I mentioned, sent for me to come to his house. A patient had been brought to him who needed a surgical operation which the old doctor couldn't undertake. His hands shake with palsy, his sight is feeble, and he frankly says he wants to give up practice altogether. It was quite out of the question for him to make the delicate operation required, and he sent for me to perform it."

"And did you?" queried Ivan.

"I refused at first, and told the old doctor that he must get the consent of the ispravnik before I could do anything. His son went to see that official, but he had gone to another part of the district and would be absent for several days. It was necessary to perform the operation at once to save the life of the patient, and so I performed it, while the old doctor stood over me and gave me nominal directions. His intention was to claim that I had simply acted at an assistant in the work and carried out the orders of a duly authorized surgeon."

"That ought to have satisfied the ispravnik when the case was reported to him," Ivan remarked.

"But it wasn't by any means. I spent a week in prison, and would have been there a month, or perhaps two or three months, if the old doctor hadn't laid the case before the governor of the province and secured my release. Now the ispravnik is unfriendly to us both, and is watching to catch me in another violation of the Code. I have had a chance to revenge myself on him though, this very week."

Ivan was too polite to ask in what way, but waited for the doctor to tell him or not as he chose. After a pause the latter said:

"One of his children was taken very ill in the night, and as the regular doctor couldn't go, the ispravnik sent for me. I answered that I was forbidden by the regulations to practice medicine, and much as I regretted to decline, I was obliged to do so. His messenger came again and said the ispravnik would give me leave to practice in this case. I reminded him that the authority must come from the Minister of the Interior, and continued to refuse in spite of the statement that the child was dangerously ill."

"You might have gone safely enough, could you not?" queried Ivan.

"Perhaps so," was the reply, "but I'm not entirely sure of it. The man is quite capable of calling me to attend his child and then putting me under arrest; it would have been quite in keeping with some of the methods of the police for him to do so; besides, if I had been unable to save the patient, he could accuse me of having killed it deliberately out of revenge."

"Yes, I see," said Ivan, "and he could have shown that you had good reason to harbor malice against him."

"One thing is certain," continued Dr. Shulmann, "if ever the ispravnik himself is ill, he will not think it wise to send for me to prescribe for him."

He did not say more on the subject, but quickly changed to other topics of conversation.

Ivan was unable to find any employment in which he could support himself, all practical avenues being closed by the Code. He followed the advice of his friends and applied to the government for the allowance that is doled out to administrative exiles. As this allowance is only six rubles (three dollars) a month, it required the most pinching economy to exist upon it. He and his new friends united their funds into a common purse, and in this way managed to get along without starving. Ivan was permitted to send home for a supply of clothing, which came in due time, but when delivered it was found to be ripped in nearly every seam, in the efforts of the police to make sure that it contained nothing contraband.

"All my letters," said Ivan, "those received, as well as those sent, were subject to official supervision. When I wrote a letter I was obliged to take it to the ispravnik and leave it with him. He could forward it in whole or in part as he chose, could destroy it altogether, or send it to the Minister of the Interior. When a letter came for me, and this is the case with all letters addressed to political exiles, it was handed to the ispravnik who always opened and read it. Sometimes he kept it for weeks or months, and perhaps I learned of its existence from some one who had heard it read at the club. The ispravnik has full power over all correspondence of exiles, and generally he is very quick to use it."

"I have sent to my wife asking her to write only the briefest details about family matters," said Dr. Shulmann, when speaking on this subject. "The ispravnik took some of her early letters, which were full of love and devotion, and made them the subject of jest and ribald remarks at the club, where he read them to a lot of scoundrels as depraved as himself. I determined to deprive him of this pleasure in future, and so I wrote her through the underground mail, telling what had occurred, and begging her to guard against it in future."

As he spoke, his flushed face and the tone of his voice caused Ivan to think that it would not be a good thing for the ispravnik to fall seriously ill and give Dr. Shulmann a chance to prescribe for him.

"It is to be hoped that Siberia does not contain many men of this kind," said Ivan. "This brutal ispravnik must be an exception, is he not?"

"Less an exception than you might suppose," was the reply. "Many of the ispravniks, and other small officials, are common felons, who were sent to Siberia for crime, have served out their sentences, and afterwards gone into the government service under assumed names. Most of them are coarse, ignorant fellows, and it gives them great delight to revenge upon educated men or women the ill-treatment they received when they themselves were under the ban. They have a right to come into our quarters at any hour of the day or night, look into our windows, and annoy us in other ways. It is bad enough when men are thus treated; when the victims of these insults are young women, as not infrequently happens, it is not surprising that they lead to murder or suicide. The subject is too painful to talk about; let us turn to something else."

They talked about various commonplaces, and while in the midst of their conversation were surprised by a "domiciliary visit" of the police. It did not last long, and the exiles were soon by themselves once more.

Most of the exiles have ways of communicating with their friends in the rest of the world, and with other exiles, by what is facetiously termed "the Underground Mail." In ways known only to themselves they send and receive letters, and it is safe to say that there is no event of consequence in Siberia which is not speedily known in Europe. On the other hand, news of what goes on in the outer world is conveyed to the exiles everywhere; whether they be forced colonists in the far North, simple exiles like Ivan and his friends, or hard-labor convicts like Carl Pushkin.

Ivan was not long in exile before he learned the ways of the secret mail service, and sent and received letters without official supervision. Of course he continued to conduct his correspondence, ostensibly at least, through the official channels, as any failure to do so might have aroused suspicion.

Shulmann took charge of his letters, and he was told to ask no questions. One day the doctor brought him a letter from Nadia, which told of important happenings in Tambov since his mysterious departure, an event of which she was not made aware until some time after its occurrence. The nature of those happenings we will learn in the next chapter.

CHAPTER XX.

PUSHKIN AT THE KARA MINES.

Nadia's letter to Ivan was dated "At Home," and said that her mother and herself had been set free with as little ceremony as they were arrested.

"One morning, when the warder brought us our breakfast," said she, "he said we might get ready to be tranferred from the cell in the course of an hour. He gave us the impression that we were to be moved to another cell and that was all.

"We had very little preparation, as you can believe, and were ready to make the change long before we were called for. Imagine our surprise when we were taken, not to another cell, but to the prison-yard, where a tarantass with horses attached was waiting for us. We entered the tarantass as we were told to do; then the great gate swung open and, preceded by two Cossacks on horseback, we were quickly on the road.

"On the road! and whither? How could we tell that we were not going into exile, just as Poor Father was sent? But we soon found that we were travelling towards home at a rapid pace, and in little more than two hours we were at our own door and ordered to alight.

"We stepped out of the tarantass, which was instantly

driven away, accompanied by the Cossack guard, without a word of explanation from anybody.

"Out came the servants, the governess, Francesca, Joseph, the young children, everybody in fact, and what a welcome we had! It seemed an age, yes, a whole life-time, since we went away; it seemed so to us, and from the way they greeted mother and me it was an age to them, too.

"Mother fainted when she stepped inside the doorway, and I felt my head reeling and was near fainting, as well. But the thought that she needed me buoyed me up, and I bathed her head and did everything else that was required to bring her to herself again. But when she was all right and talking clearly with the governess and the servants, I had to lie down, or I should have fallen to the floor.

"After the first excitement was over the delight of being free again was something I could never describe. I never realized such a state of happiness, and if only Dear Father and you could have been with us!—well!—the thought of what pleasure it would have been makes it difficult for me to write coherently.

"I did not know then that you and Mr. Hartmann had been sent away, nor did we know it until we heard through Mr. Kosavitch, who came to see us when he found we had been liberated. The governor did not inform him that we were out of prison, and the warder who might have told him was ill and off duty for a week when we were sent away. Oh! that awful word, 'prison!' it makes me shudder to write it.

"It seemed an age till your letter came saying that you wanted some clothing. It was brought by a gendarme, and the name of the place where you are living had been cut out; we were told that the box was to be sent to the police office in Tambov, and would be forwarded after it had been examined for prohibited articles. We were warned not to send any writing or books with it, nor anything else except the garments for personal wear that you had asked for.

"After a while your second letter came, and in that they allowed the name of your place of exile to remain. I wrote you a very formal letter in reply, as it was to undergo official inspection, but I infer from your letter, that has just come by what you call 'The Underground,' that you never received mine. I will send this one in the way you suggest, and hope it will have better fortune than the other."

Then followed a series of paragraphs which wholly concern the family of Carl Pushkin, the state of affairs at home, and other things of no special interest to strangers. The letter closed with a brief allusion to Alexei Hartmann, who was still in St. Petersburg, and had written to Nadia that the date of his return was uncertain. The sensitive girl feared that he might be in trouble, perhaps under arrest, and unwilling to distress her with bad news if he could possibly avoid doing so.

The fact was that young Hartmann was working with all his might in behalf of his father and of the Pushkin family, but with his youth and inexperience in that great beaureaucracy, he could accomplish nothing. He had few friends in the capital, and all whom he knew were without influence at court, with the single exception of the gentleman to whom Mr. Hartmann had referred in his secret communication to the lawyer at Tambov. This man's name was Lodoff; he was a wealthy contractor, who supplied the government with railway and other material, and consequently he had considerable influence in official circles, though, unfortunately, not in the direction where influence was then most required.

Had it been a matter of contract for anything Lodoff could have told at once the proper way to proceed, the officials that would need to be bribed, and the amount each would expect in return for his services. But when it came to dealing with the office of the Minister of the Interior, it was a different matter. He had given that establishment as wide a birth as possible all his life, and did not wish to have anything to do with it.

"I must be very cautious about making inquiries concerning that department," Mr. Lodoff said to Alexei, "and caution means time. We don't know whom to trust, and if we are too active we may get into trouble without accomplishing anything for those we love. Your father and I are old friends, and I'll do all in my power to help him, and also to help the family of his friend Pushkin, whose daughter is engaged to you.

"Come and take dinner with me every Wednesday," said he to Alexei, "but don't come oftener than that unless you have news to give me or questions to ask. Of course, I would like to have you here every day, but a young man coming so often to a house where there are no young women is likely to excite suspicion. When I have anything to communicate I'll send you an invitation for dinner, and you must come early so that we can have a chat before it is time to go to table. Leave my invitation on your desk, or stick it up in your mirror, so that if your rooms are examined while you are absent, the visitors will know where you are.

"Meantime," continued Mr. Lodoff, "try to get employment in the office of the Minister of the Interior. You write an excellent hand, and perhaps you could find a situation as a copyist. Never mind the rate of wages they offer, but accept anything you can get."

"But there can hardly be a chance of my finding a place there," replied the youth. "I have no friends to press me for it, and without friends an application is hopeless."

"I realize that," said the gentleman, "but you lose nothing by being refused. You certainly can get no place if you don't apply at all."

Alexei admitted the force of this suggestion and consented to make the trial. "I have a good record from the University," said he, "and believe the professors would speak well of me."

"That is in your favor," Mr. Lodoff answered, "and you may refer to me as one who knows you and your family. You may be sure I'll say everything in your behalf, if any question is asked of me."

When Alexei reached his lodgings, he found that a call had been made upon him during his absence; the visitor had not left either card or letter, and had disturbed things very little, but a sufficient number of articles had been moved from their places to indicate that whoever called there had sought to find if there was anything compromising about the room or its occupant. Alexei smiled as he thought how completely the visitor had been disappointed.

But his smile faded away as he thought that it would be a very strange proceeding for him to seek employment in the very department of the government that was keeping him under surveillance; he might be walking into danger instead of avoiding it. What should he do?

He lay awake for an hour or more meditating upon this subject. Before going to sleep, he reached the decision to give the office of the Minister of the Interior a very wide berth ; but when he woke in the morning his views had undergone a change.

"It has often happened," he said to himself, "that a man escapes a danger by boldly facing it and appearing to consider it no danger at all. Vidocq, the famous Frenchman, escaped from the galleys by walking up to the sergeant of the guard and asking for a light for his pipe, and then requesting the sergeant to send a soldier to escort him beyond a group of drunken sailors, who were quarrelling in the street.

"I will go to the bureau of the minister and seek employment, and that will be the very thing to disarm suspicion. After all, what suspicion can there be about a young fellow like me ? From the day I first set foot in the capital, I haven't exchanged a word with an 'untrustworthy' person ; at least, so far as I am aware."

After a light breakfast, he sought a young acquaintance, whom he had known at the University, to learn from him the best way of making an application for appointment. This acquaintance had occupied the position of copyist in one of the departments, and was therefore familiar with the methods of place-hunting. The position he filled was only temporary, and during the absence of an incumbent, who had been sent away for a vacation on account of his health.

While Alexei is busy in his search for employment, we will return once more to Siberia.

At last, after many hardships, perils and privations, with shattered body and drooping spirits, Carl Pushkin reached the mines, the dreaded mines of Kara (Kah-rah).

The latter part of his journey was made in winter, when the cold was intense, the thermometer often marking 35° or 40° below zero. Fortunately, the snows are not deep in the region between Lake Baikal and the Kara district, owing to the climatic peculiarities of that part of Siberia, and for the greater part of the way travelled by Pushkin, the ground was bare. But the cold winds from the north swept over the country with their pitiless breath, and the prisoners suffered terribly from their severity. Many were frost-bitten, and it became necessary to leave them in some of the larger stations where there was a permanent guard. They received scant medical attendance, and the majority of them never recovered.

For a week or more the convoy containing Pushkin and Dubayeff halted at Chita, the capital of the province of the Trans-Baikal, and about three hundred miles from the mines. It is not an unattractive place, as it is well situated on the bank of the Ingodah river, one of the head streams of the Amoor, and contains many substantial buildings.

"The history of Chita is full of horrors," said Dubayeff, "and its pretty appearance is but a mockery. It may be called the gateway of the mines of Nertchinsk, those mines which, for more than a hundred years, have been the place of banishment for so many thousands of men and women, who have displeased the autocrat of Russia, or those in power beneath him. Think of the lives that have been worn out in chains and servitude, tortured, starved, flogged, and subjected to every indignity that man can imagine!

"The prisons of Chita are the purgatory in which they prepare you for the Hades of Nertchinsk and Kara," Dubayeff continued.

"But are not the prisons of Tomsk and Irkutsk sufficient preparation for Kara?" Pushkin asked. "What worse can they do here?"

"Perhaps not so very much worse," was the reply, "but in some years the death-rate is higher than at either of the other great depots for exiles, owing to the poor food and lack of sufficient medical attendance for those who are ill. Chita is memorable for having been for several years the home of some of the Decembrists, and if we were free to walk about, we might see to-day, two of the houses they occupied about 1828. They were first sent to the mines of Nertchinsk, and after working there for two years, they were brought to Chita, and employed in a polishing mill and on the roads. The graves of those who died here may be seen in the cemetery just outside the town.

"And ever since their time Chita has been the residence of many prisoners, some of them allowed to go about under the rules that govern administrative exiles, and others held in prisons just like these at Irkutsk. Not a few have escaped from here and wandered into the wilderness, but the most of them have never gone far before they were captured and returned to the embrace of the walls that held them."

Pushkin found the condition of the prison at Chita very much like what he had experienced at Tomsk and Irkutsk. There was the same overcrowded condition, a hundred men being assigned to a kamera originally intended for forty, and sometimes the proportion was even larger than this. The air in the kameras was foul in the extreme, as the ventilation was very poor, or, rather, there was no ventilation at all. After passing a night in the kameras the prisoners were pale and apparently half-suffocated; those with weak lungs suffered terribly, far more than the stronger prisoners, and not a few were prostrated by pneumonia, typhus, and kindred ailments that sent them to the hospital and generally to the grave.

So bad was the prison, that most of the exiles in the convoy were glad to be once more on the road, although it took them to the mines where hard-labor awaited them.

For two hundred miles the road from Chita lies along the valley of the Ingodah and Shilka rivers, the former stream uniting with the latter. The Shilka and Argoon form the Amoor, the great river of Northeastern Asia, which has a volume almost as large as that of the Mississippi. It is navigable from the Pacific Ocean to Stratensk on the Shilka, a distance of 2,300 miles, and at this point the great Siberian road has its beginning. The mines of Kara are about one hundred miles from Stratensk; in summer they are reached by boats, which descend the Shilka to Ust-Kara (Mouth of the Kara) and then ascend the Kara river, while in winter the travel is upon the ice, which forms an excellent road when the rivers have become well frozen.

The winter was well advanced when Pushkin's party reached Stratensk, and therefore the rest of the journey was made on the ice of the rivers. One cold afternoon the prisoners came in sight of Ust Kara, but it was night before they entered the walls of the rough buildings, which afforded shelter from the winds, though entirely lacking in what may be called comfort, even in a prison.

"We may possibly stay here for weeks," said Dubayeff, "or we may be set at work to-morrow morning. All depends upon how much our muscle is wanted for digging or washing gold. Sometimes the placers are washed out and the colony is comparatively idle until new diggings are found. When they find them, they don't waste any time in putting us at work."

"God grant that we may not be kept here long!" exclaimed Pushkin, as he looked around him in the kamera to which they had been assigned.

"Yes, God grant it," was the reply. "Nothing could be worse than this."

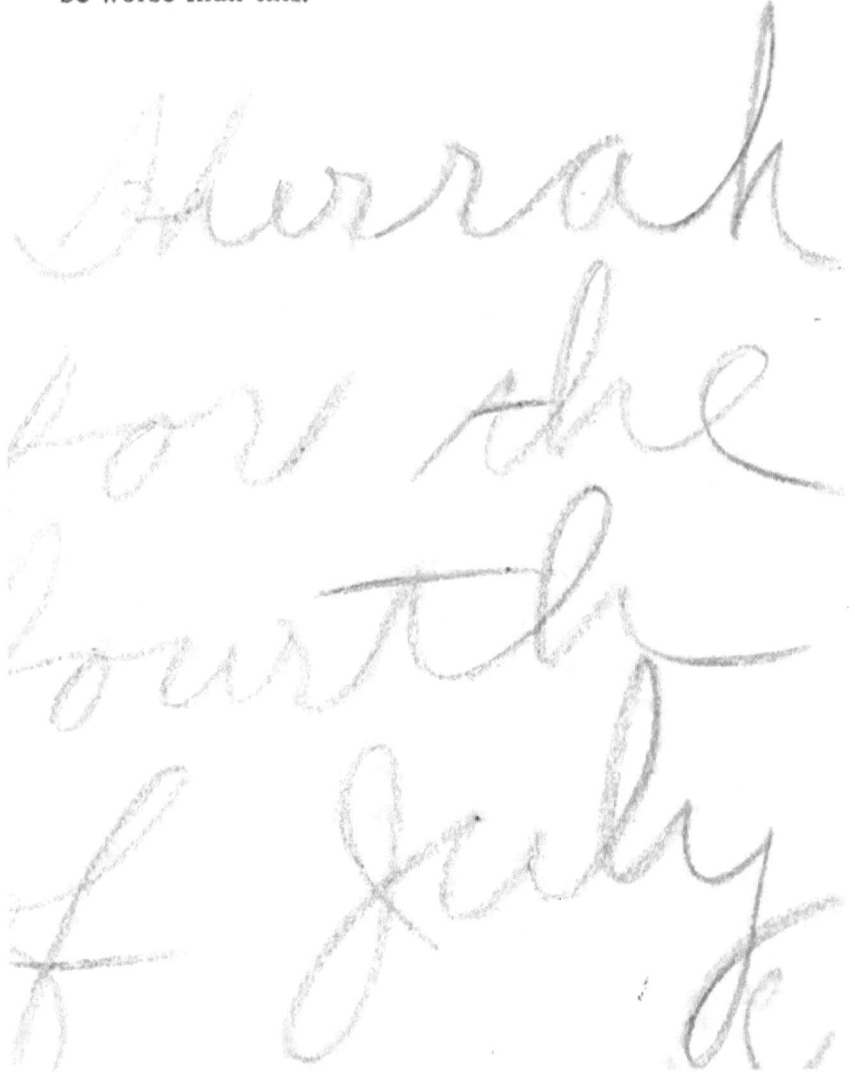

CHAPTER XXI.

PRISONERS AT WORK.

When we know what caused the exclamations of the two prisoners, given at the end of the preceding chapter, we shall have no cause for wonder.

"This is the worst we have seen yet," said Pushkin, "always excepting those family kameras at Tomsk, which I shall never try to describe to anybody, for the simple reason that all language would be inadequate."

"This prison was built a long time ago and was intended only for temporary use," Dubayeff explained. "But they have gone on using it year after year and decade after decade, and the only repairs they make are when it threatens to tumble down in the winter gales. They strengthen the outside, but leave the inside unchanged."

Imagine a low building of logs surrounded by a stockade, or, rather, having a stockade at one side of it, the building itself forming the other side. The only entrance is through a gate in the stockade; into this gateway the convicts marched, and in passing they were carefully counted by the receiving officer, who stood there note-book in hand. The heavy door closed behind the convoy, the soldiers on guard took their positions at either side of the gate, and then the prisoners were drawn up in line to be counted again.

When the count was completed, the convicts were permitted to enter the building and find their places in the kameras. There was the customary rush for precedence, and very quickly the yard was cleared of the entire party.

The prison stands on swampy ground that is moist in summer and glazed with ice in winter,—or the yard would be so glazed were it not for the unclean condition in which it is kept. In summer the exhalations from the ground are full of malaria, and a sojourn of a week or two under its influence is enough to sap a strong constitution. It is less bad in winter, but bad enough under the best circumstances.

"See here," said Pushkin, as they stepped from the yard to the corridor; "the floor is covered with filth to the depth of an inch or more. Do they ever clean this place?"

"Once a year, perhaps, not oftener."

The answer was lost, as Pushkin slipped on the floor, one of the planks having given way beneath him. The floor was dirty throughout the entire length of the corridor; dirty, broken, decaying, and giving forth smells absolutely impossible to describe so that the reader could have a fair comprehension of them. The corridor was lighted by a few small windows in one side, but very dimly lighted, so that a visitor could only grope his way. On the other side of the corridor were the heavy doors of the kameras, and it was on entering the kamera that Pushkin made the remark just quoted. Surely it was the worst they had seen, with the exception of the family kameras at Tomsk.

Filthy in every part, densely crowded, and abounding in the vilest odors, such was the kamera to which Pushkin and Dubayeff were assigned. Fifty men were crowded into a room which could decently accommodate not more than twenty, and there seemed to be very little endeavor on the part of anybody to keep the place clean. In the centre of the plank-floor there was a hole, into which garbage was swept or thrown; the hole looked and smelled like the entrance of a sewer; it was so used, but unfortunately it was simply a hole in the earth without the drainage of a sewer. And human beings were forced to live in this place! men of education and refinement, while with them were common felons who had been adjudged guilty of crimes varying from highway robbery to murder.

The prison supper was served, the roll was called, and then the prisoners were locked for the night in the kameras. Breakfast, and again the roll-call on the following morning, and then there was a day of idleness for Pushkin and his friend. They spent as much of the time as possible out of doors, in spite of the cold wind, in order to escape the foul air of the kamera.

"They used to crowd the women and men into these prisons without scruple," said Dubayeff; "but now the women are in the building on the other side of the stockade. They are not quite so badly off as we are, not that any regard is shown for their sex, but because they have more space in proportion to their numbers."

"We would be worse crowded than we are," said a prisoner who overheard their conversation, "were it not that so many have gone to the hospital and the cemetery."

"No wonder they've gone there!" exclaimed Pushkin. "The wonder is that all do not go."

"Typhus fever, pneumonia, scurvy, consumption, and other diseases of the same family, are developed here very quickly" was the reply. "When they are once started, there is little chance for one's recovery. Twenty per cent. of the prisoners at the Kara mines are now in hospital, and sometimes the proportion is much greater."

"Once there were more than a thousand deaths here in a single year," said Dubayeff, "but the great number caused the commandant to be removed, and another appointed in this place. The government thought there must be something wrong, though the officer was making an unusually large return of gold for the labor of the convicts under him."

On the third morning after their arrival the prisoners were marched out in the direction of the diggings, which are scattered along the banks of the Kara river for some twenty or thirty miles. There are also diggings on the little tributaries of the Kara, and the engineers attached to the prisons are constantly searching for new deposits. The entire region is known to be auriferous, but it is not always easy to find gold in paying quantities.

The placer diggings of Siberia are not, in a general way, unlike those of other gold-producing regions, and therefore do not merit a detailed description. The gold-bearing sand, or "pay-dirt," as the California miners call it, lies under a bed of earth and stone varying from ten to twenty feet in thickness. This bed must be removed to get at the "pay-dirt;" it consists of gravel, clay and stones, and often the stones are of considerable size, so that the labor of removal is very severe. Some of the Siberian gold mines are underground, and are worked by tunneling, as in American

THE SZA IS a DEVI

By E.

CHAINED TO A WHEELBARROW.—*See Page* 217.

mining regions. Work in the underground mines is worse than in the open cuttings, for the reason that the air is almost always bad and the mines are very imperfectly drained. The prisoners often work in mud that is nearly if not quite knee deep, their clothes become wet through and through and in this condition they come out of the mines into the piercing air when the day is ended and march to their prisons. No wonder their health breaks down under such conditions, to which must be added the scanty and unwholesome food and the terribly vitiated air they must breathe at night in the overcrowded kameras.

Pushkin and Dubayeff were placed in a gang at an open cutting and supplied with the tools of their occupation. Their work was to break up the hard gravel and clay above the auriferous sands and wheel it away. Their chains were not removed, guards with loaded rifles stood constantly over them, and the overseer ordered them in exactly the tone of a driver of slaves. And to all intents and purposes they were slaves, as much so as any negro who ever wore out his existence in Cuba or Brazil.

"Let us be thankful that we are not chained to our wheelbarrows," said Dubayeff, when they reached the mine and stood waiting to begin their work. "Look at that poor fellow at the other end of the cutting."

Pushkin looked in the direction indicated and saw a man who was fastened to a wheelbarrow; a chain extended from it to the middle link of his leg-fetters, and no matter at what work he was employed, or where he went, he was obliged to take his barrow with him.

"It is taken off at night when the day's work is over, I suppose," Pushkin remarked, as he ceased looking at the "unfortunate."

"No," replied Dubayeff ; "he must have it with him day and night, month in and month out, in prison or at work in the mine. He cannot take more than a single step without it, cannot even cross from one side to the other of a prison cell, and if he is ordered from this place to one a hundred or a thousand miles away, he must trundle the barrow before him."

Pushkin stood speechless as Dubayeff continued :

"One prisoner, named Shedrin, who had been a schoolteacher in Russia, and was sent to Siberia as a dangerous revolutionist, was chained to a wheelbarrow here in the mines. Orders came one day that he and some other politicals should be sent to St. Petersburg to be shut up for life in one of the fortresses. He was thrown into a wagon, with the wheelbarrow still chained to him, and was compelled to carry it all the way to the Imperial capital."

"Is such a thing possible ?" said Pushkin, in astonishment.

"Not only possible, but actual," was the reply. "When the roads were rough and the prisoners were riding instead of marching, the officers found that the wheelbarrow caused great inconvenience to the occupants of the vehicle. It was consequently removed and fastened behind the telyega, but it was chained again to Shedrin at every halt at the etapes and in the trains and steamboats that completed the long journey."

"What had the man done that caused such brutality?"

"He struck an officer," was the reply, "and the way he came to do so was this :

"Two women, political prisoners, on their way to the mines, managed to escape from the prison at Irkutsk, where their convoy was halted. They were captured a few hours later and brought back to prison, and an officer of the governor-general's staff, a colonel, happened to be in the office of the prison when they were brought in. He ordered them to be searched, and he stood by and looked on while they were stripped naked by the rough soldiers who obeyed his orders. Not only did he stand there, but he insulted them outrageously by his remarks, and he afterwards went to one of the kameras and boasted to the prisoners there about what he had done. Shedrin was so angry when he listened to this, that he called the colonel a coward and scoundrel and struck him in the face. This was the offence for which he was chained to a wheelbarrow."

"And men like that colonel are our masters!" said Pushkin with indignation.

"Unhappily, yes," was the response. "Occasionally there are humane officers in charge of these prisons, and the men and women are treated as well as the severe rules of the discipline will allow. But for one who is humane there are five or more even who are brutes; some are cruel but honest; some are cruel and at the same time are thieves, and still others are cruel, dishonest and confirmed drunkards or libertines. When all the bad qualities are combined, what can we expect?"

"Yes, you may well say that," Pushkin remarked as his friend paused. "What *can* we expect?"

"There was one commandant of Kara who destroyed the letters sent to the prisoners, and stole all the money that was intended for them. It was not being sent surreptitiously, but in the manner provided by the government, to be retained by the commandant and expended for the benefit of the prisoners in any lawful manner they may designate. He destroyed the letters which notified them of remittances, and then gambled away the money as soon as it reached his hands."

"But was he allowed to remain here after his conduct became known?"

"It took some time to remove him, longer than it did to cause one of the most humane officers ever known here to resign, for the reason that his conscience would not allow him to carry out some of the orders that he received from St. Petersburg or from the governor-general of Eastern Siberia. He considered these orders brutal and wholly unnecessary, and endeavored to have them recalled. When he found it impossible to do so, he tendered his resignation, and subsequently left the service altogether. He tried to have some of the conspirators who were robbing the government brought to justice; in revenge, his house was burned and he escaped in his night clothes, and with difficulty saved his life. Some of the guilty officers made false charges against him, and came very near having him sent into the mines as a hard-labor convict. And all this because he was honest and humane!"

This conversation occurred while the prisoners were waiting directions to begin work; it was brought to an end by an order from the overseer, and thus began Pushkin's first day at the mines.

The days followed one after another, there being no respite except on the first and fifteenth day of each month, and also on the principal saints' days of the Russian calendar. Every morning, at seven, the prisoners were marched out to their toil, and at five in the afternoon the work was stopped and they returned to the prison. This was the winter schedule; in summer the time of work was much longer, beginning at five in the morning and ending at seven in the evening. When the deep snows fell, mining operations were altogether suspended, and then the prisoners had nothing to do but sit in the pestilential kameras or walk in the prison-yard.

Spring approached, and some of the prisoners laid plans for escaping as soon as the weather was mild enough for them to live in the open air. Dubayeff and Pushkin eagerly considered the various schemes that were proposed, and through the advice of the latter, the one that had the greatest promise of success was adopted. Its result was certainly highly creditable to our friend's sagacity.

CHAPTER XXII.

STORY OF AN ESCAPED CONVICT.

The prisoners expected to be set at work again in the mines, but before the snows had melted, an order came from St. Petersburg that they were to be kept in close confinement, their chains were to be removed, and all work in the mines was to be performed by the criminal convicts. This facilitated the carrying out of the plot to escape, which was already well under way.

The change from winter to spring, in many parts of Siberia, is like a transformation scene in a theatre. On a certain Sunday, Puskkin relates that the ground was covered with snow, and the rivers were frozen as they had been for months. Suddenly, on Monday, a strong and warm 'wind from the south set in, and by nightfall the snow and ice were melting rapidly. By Thursday the snow was gone from the hills and valleys, and the rivers were filled with floating ice, which was making its way with the swift current towards the sea. The melting snows turned the river into a flood, and by the following Sunday the stream was clear of ice. In a few days the trees were budding, and the ground was green with the up-springing grass, and in less than a fortnight it was thickly carpeted with flowers. Birds were singing among the trees, and the cuckoo sounded his familiar call in every direction. It was the call for the prisoner to escape; at least, such is the Siberian interpretation.

The cuckoo is known among the convicts as "General Kukushka," and when they hear his call, they say that the General is summoning them to assemble under his banners, and it is their duty to obey. At such times, if there is any chance of escape, they eagerly embrace it, though well knowing they are very likely to be re-captured and returned to prison with severe punishment for what they have done.

"Why did you run away?" said a prison official to an old convict, who had won the friendship of everybody by his good conduct, and received many favors in consequence. He had been relieved of all supervision, and was employed about the stable of one of the officers; he was well fed, and had very light work, and was so old that it was supposed he would be entirely contented to remain where he was.

"General Kukushka called me, and I was obliged to go," was his reply. "I hear him calling again, and if you want to keep me you must lock me up, so that I can't get away."

Instances have been known where exiles in what is known as "the Free Command," have gone to the officers in the early spring-time and asked to be sent to prison "until General Kukushka has stopped calling." They did not want to run away, but felt that they could ⁺ resist the summons of their sylvan commander.

The Free Command consists of those who are allowed to live outside of prison, in houses designated for them to occupy. They must report daily to the police, and be subject to domiciliary visits at any time. They are practically in the condition described in the settlement where Ivan and his friends were living when we last saw them. Those who have been followed to Siberia by their families may live with them, all the members of the families being under the same regulations as the exiles themselves.

Escape from the Free Command is not at all difficult, as no guards are kept about the houses, and if an exile departs immediately after reporting at the police office, or being visited in his house, he can get several hours start before his absence is discovered. But if he is brought back he is punished, perhaps with a flogging, and certainly he will be sent again to the prison of whose horrors he knows by practical experience.

Among the prisoners in the kamera occupied by Pushkin and Dubayeff, there were several who had heeded the summons of the cuckoo, and "taken to the woods" in the hope of getting away from Siberia. As the plan for escaping was discussed, each of these men told his story in the fullest confidence that it would not be repeated to official ears.

"I was in the Free Command," said one, whom we will call Onossoff, though that was not his real name, "and did a little gold-washing on my own account. You know it is against the rule for any convict to have golden wheat in his possession, and the same rule applies to all the traders who deal with us. But they and we are willing to run the risk, the trader gets a large profit, as we are obliged to take what he will give us, and neither party to the transaction is likely to make any complaint about the other. Well, I had a good run of luck, as I found a little placer only a short distance from the village, where

I could work three or four hours a day without being discovered.

"With the gold, I bought a passport; it was a forged one, but as it was on paper bearing the government stamp, it answered my purpose.

"Then I bought some clothes that suited the person described in the document. I became for the time a low-bred peasant, a regular mujik, unable to read or write, and in order to represent him fully it was necessary for me to have a wig, which I made myself. My hair would have enabled any one to detect me, even if there had been nothing else in my appearance to arouse suspicion."

"How did you manage to make it?" one of his auditors asked.

Onossoff paused a moment, as though it was a secret he did not care to reveal. His questioner apologized for the interrogatory, and promised to ask no more questions.

"I may as well tell you," said Onossoff, "as the hint may be useful, though I don't care to try the ruse again, and certainly nobody can undertake it often.

"A mujik with just the head of hair that I wanted was killed in a drunken row. He had no friends, and was hastily buried, and I volunteered to dig his grave, on the pretense that he had been kind to me on several occasions. I dug the grave, and didn't dig it deep, and the night after he was buried I went out, re-opened the grave, and took off his entire scalp. You see he had no further need for his hair, while I could make it very useful; besides, I wanted to make good my words that the man had been kind to me."

The listeners shook their heads as if intimating that a wig obtained in that way would hardly be an agreeable article of wear. Onossoff divined their thoughts and continued:

"That wig certainly helped me very much, but I had constantly before me the thought of how I got it. Whenever I wore it my head used to ache, and you may be sure I threw it away as soon as I could. No, I didn't throw it away, but gave it decent burial, though its grave was a long distance from where I obtained it.

"After I got the wig, a difficulty that I had not thought of confronted me. You see, my beard is black, while that mujik's hair was red. He had a red beard, too, but I left that alone in the grave, as I didn't believe I could attach it to my face so as to defy detection. A false beard will answer on the stage of a theatre, but not in actual every-day life.

"I hunted around for red hair-dye, but my search was a failure. That kind doesn't seem to be made, and so I was forced to fall back on a decoction of laurel bark and lime water, in addition to allowing my beard to be constantly dirty. In this way I got along very well.

"It was from the Nertchinsk mines that I escaped, and not from Kara, and it was two or three weeks from the time I was all ready that I ventured to start. I had managed to get a fair map of the country between the mines and the town of Nertchinsk, and after selling all my gold dust I had nearly a hundred rubles left, with everything paid for.

"One night I started out with a large loaf of bread, a few pieces of meat, and a little salt in a packet. I determined to avoid the road, though I would keep near it, and the most of my travelling was done at night. I lived on my bread and meat and such edible roots as I could find in the forest or along the stretches of open country that I was often obliged to cross. The stars at night were my guides, and the sun by day, whenever I ventured out in the daytime. But even without them, I could have found my way, as the road follows the valley of the Nertcha to where it joins the Shilka at Nertchinsk.

"Not once did I go near a house until I had passed beyond Nertchinsk and was on the road to Chita. I saw two or three groups of mounted soldiers passing along the road, and knew that they were scouring the country in hope of finding me. By the time I had passed Nertchinsk, to which I gave a wide berth, not going near enough to see more than the dome of the church, I was out of food, and could find nothing in the ground to sustain life. The case was desperate, and I found I must risk my freedom or starve.

"I was on the top of a hill whence, looking down the valley in the direction of Nertchinsk, I saw a common telyega, which was evidently the property of a peasant. It was going the way I wanted to go, and before it got to the top of the hill I was waiting for it at the roadside. My guess was correct, as it contained nobody except the driver, who proved to be its owner.

"'Where are you going, brother?' I asked.

"'To Chita.'

"'So am I. My brother lives there. I started to walk all the way from Stratensk to Chita, but have got tired of walking and want to ride.'

"'I'll take you there for a ruble.'

"'Too much,' I said. 'Will give you fifty copecks and help drive when you want to sleep.'

"'All right, jump in.'

"In I jumped, and the telyega rattled down the hill. I asked my new friend for some bread and offered to replace it at the next village. Fortunately he had a loaf and my hunger was soon satisfied.

"At the top of the next hill," continued Onossoff, "my friend got down to fix the harness and I looked from the rear of the telyega. On the top of the hill over which we had just come I saw a squad of mounted soldiers that were evidently following us. My friend did not see them, and after he had adjusted the harness, I asked if he did not wish to have me drive awhile.

"He was only too glad to have me do so, but just as he was getting inside the telyega he looked around and discovered the soldiers descending the last hill. He seemed somewhat alarmed, and I immediately concluded that he had done something that was not in conformity with the law. Here was my opportunity.

"'Before I go further with you,' said I, 'I must know who you are, and you want to know who I am. Here is my passport; let me see yours.'

"He drew his passport from the breast of his coat, where it was wrapped in a dirty rag, very much like the one in which my passport was inclosed. I saw that his paper was genuine, and as he could not read, I managed to change the documents while they were in my hands. He received my forged paper, rolled it carefully in his rag, and returned the package to his coat.

"Then he suggested that he didn't want the soldiers to see him, and if I had no objections he would hide in a clump of bushes until they had passed. I readily consented, and he jumped out and disappeared while the soldiers were concealed from view by the top of the hill which was between us and the slope they were ascending.

"I was busy with a piece of broken harness as they came up, and the sergeant in command demanded my passport. I handed out the paper, which he examined carefully, while two of his men overhauled the vehicle to make sure that no one was concealed in it. The sergeant asked if I had seen anybody on foot; I answered in the negative, and he then gave the order to move on.

" Lucky for me he didn't ask me my name, as I hadn't yet had time to memorize the contents of my new passport, and in the excitement of the moment, I had not learned from my new acquaintance what it was. Soon as the soldiers were out of sight I called him, and he came out of his place of concealment.

" Exactly why he was so fearful of being seen by the soldiers he would not tell, and it was no business of mine to know. In fact, I didn't consider it wise to appear inquisitive on the subject, and I merely remarked that probably he was afraid of the conscription, to which he joyfully assented. What I suspected was, that he had been dealing in the products of an illicit distillery, and was afraid of arrest on that account, or possibly he might have been buying gold from the convicts at the mines and had some of it in his possession.

"We got to Chita without further trouble. I was worried about the passports, as the police might have orders to arrest the holder of the one I carried, and also of the forged one I had given to my friend. On the whole, I concluded that the forged paper would be the safer document to have, and under pretense of looking at them to see how much they looked alike (neither of us being supposed to know how to read), I managed to trade back again.

" At Chita I dropped the fellow after paying him the fifty copecks agreed upon, and from that time on saw nothing more of him. Then I looked around for some kind of employment that would help me in getting away. The police were very vigilant and might fall upon me at any moment, but anyhow they didn't, and in a few days I succeeded in hiring out to a man who had a contract to deliver some goods to a merchant at Verkne Udinsk. The goods consisted of German wines and spirits and American canned provisions, that had been brought up the Amoor and Shilka by steamboat, and from Stratensk to Chita in wagons. My employer took my passport to have it properly indorsed, along with the papers of his other drivers, and I had the satisfaction of having it pass through the ordeal without suspicion. I was greatly relieved, as the indorsement by the Police Master at Chita would make the paper go readily in the other offices where I was required to present it.

"In this way I went from place to place, and was never once under suspicion as far as I know. I constantly had a perfectly plausible story at the end of my tongue, but it always gave me a cold shiver when the gendarmes suddenly came around to examine our passports lest there might be something to indicate that my papers were forgeries.

"On and on I went, sometimes hiring out as a driver of horses to the contractors, who do such a large business in Siberia; I always accepted every offer of wages, no matter how low, and generally for the sake of throwing any possible inquisitor off the track, I stipulated for employment for the return trip, offering to engage for lower pay per month than for the single journey. Of course a return was the farthest thing possible from my wishes, and my apparent anxiety to get back was a complete foil if one were needed.

"Eventually, I got to Moscow; but two or three times,

between Tomsk and Kazan, I thought my fate was sealed.

"At the first large town west of Tomsk our train, or caravan, was detained, to enable the police to search every man in the party. They made a thorough search, too, and evidently suspected that a runaway convict was among us. They took all the drivers into a room in the police station, and there we were stripped to the skin one after the other. My wig fairly rose on my head when the operation began, and I already saw myself in chains and on my way back to the mines."

"How did you escape the discovery of your false hair?" queried one of the listeners.

"Luckily the marks they sought for were on the body of the runaway and not on his head," replied Onossoff, "and they had no occasion to look above our shoulders. I had bound a rag close around my skull, a very common device of the Russian peasants in cold weather, and so it attracted no attention."

CHAPTER XXIII.

PERILS AND PRIVATIONS.

At another time Onossoff was roused in the middle of the night to show his papers and answer some very searching questions that were put to him. He accounted satisfactorily for his presence in every place, and was able to describe the towns and cities with such accuracy, that the police were convinced of his honesty. The men they sought for were exiles who had escaped from Tobolsk in Western Siberia; they had never been at Irkutsk or Chita, and consequently Onossoff's ability to describe those places was greatly to his advantage.

When he had completed his narrative, another of the prisoners told how he and companion had escaped from penal servitude in Yeneseisk, in the province of the same name. They had been unable to procure passports, and therefore were afraid to venture near any of the towns or villages, or even show themselves by day for days and weeks at a time. "We should have died in the wilderness," said he, "if we had not fallen in with two brodyags; in point of fact, we came near losing our lives at the time they fell in with us, as they thought we were spies sent out to catch them. We were able to undeceive them very quickly, or they might have killed us to ensure their own safety.

"We were obliged to conceal our real characters and pretend that we were brodyags and criminals instead of politicals. I claimed to have been a counterfeiter, while my companion was a thief whose special line was to rob houses and apartments while the owners were away. I explained the secrets of my profession as well as I could, and promised to take them into partnership in case we got safely to St. Petersburg. I told them they were just the kind of men I needed for partners, as they could pass the false coin at the lafkas (drinking shops), and other places, where they could tender the spurious money and obtain good in change.

"We had four months of hardship before we reached the banks of the Dwina, which we wished to descend in order to reach Archangel. A good many people were waiting there for the opening of navigation, and we pretended that we were pilgrims on our way to the monastery of Solovetsk. We were very careful about saying our prayers in the regular orthodox fashion, lest we might be discovered; our money was very scant, and we were forced to beg, but this enabled us to carry out the idea of our being pilgrims, and therefore was quite in the line of our deception.

"The commerce on the Dwina is mainly in corn and other products, that are rafted down the stream to the market of Archangel. We hired out on one of the rafts, where we were to assist at rowing in return for a free passage and two rubles in money, in addition to our food. The voyage occupied two weeks. When we came in sight of Archangel, every one of us broke his oar against the side of the raft, in accordance with the custom that has prevailed among the boatmen of the Dwina from time immemorial.

"The police don't give much attention to the pilgrims, but we dared not show ourselves interested in anything but the monastery of Solovetsk, lest we might be discovered. We decided that it was best to separate into couples, and so my friend and myself said good-by to our brodyag comrades, and set about finding a passage out of the country.

"An English steamer was taking in a cargo of tallow, bristles, and other exports of Archangel; in fact, there were several English steamers doing exactly the same thing. We got on board of one of them, by helping the crew to handle the bags of tallow, and managed to get below without being discovered. She was just completing her load, and it wasn't more than two or three hours after we got stowed away, that the hold was closed. She was a freight steamer and had no passengers to wait for, and therefore it wasn't long after her cargo was complete that she got under way.

"It was dark and hot below deck, and we were almost suffocated. Each of us had taken the precaution to conceal a large bottle of water under his coat, and it is well we did so, or we might have perished of thirst. We had bread enough for several days, and we dug into one of the bags of tallow and ate of that. Tallow, and bread and water furnished our only subsistence for four days, in a hole where we could not turn around without pressing hard against each other.

"By this time we felt sure that we were quite out of reach of Russia, as the steamer ought to have rounded the North Cape and entered the Atlantic. We rapped on the deck to attract attention, but it was two or three hours before the sound we made was heard. Then the hatch was taken off, and we crawled out into the light of day. Never did the light seem so blessed as at that moment.

"'Who are you?' said the gruff voice of the captain of the steamer, as he surveyed us from head to foot.

"'Water! water!' we cried, as we fell to the deck, unable to speak more.

"Water was brought, and after we had satisfied our thirst the question was repeated.

"'May we talk to you aside?' I asked.

"The captain took us to his cabin, and then I told him frankly who we were and why we had stolen a passage on his vessel. I offered to give him our little store of money, and if that was not enough, we would work our passage to England.

"'You may work your passage and keep your money,' said he, as he took us by the hand, ' and I won't turn you over to any policeman for having stolen your way on board. We happen to be short-handed, as we lost two men overboard on the way out, and you can take their places. I'll pay you when we get to London, but you must get ashore when I don't see you, just as you got on board.'

"At London he gave each of us a sovereign, and we sneaked ashore after thanking him for his kindness to a pair of escaping exiles. After awhile we went to Paris, and you can't guess whom we encountered there one day, six or eight months after we left Archangel."

"Your brodyag acquaintances, probably," said one of the listeners.

"Yes, and they turned out to be politicals like ourselves. You can see how well the four of us had to play our parts in order to keep up the deception that we did. Each pair supposed the others to be ordinary convicts, criminals, without education or refinement, and full of criminal intent for the future."

Other stories of escape were told, but we have no place for them at present. Let us turn to the plan which had been made to get away from the Kara prison.

As the prisoners were not allowed outside the enclosure, work having been wholly suspended at the mines so far as the politicals were concerned, the guards had become somewhat careless in roll-calls, and in counting the prisoners before the kameras were closed for the night. From requiring all to be ranged in line while the count was made, they fell into the plan of standing in the doorway of the kamera and enumerating the prisoners as one might count pigs in a pen or sheep in a fold. If any prisoner was lying down, and appeared to be asleep, he was not disturbed, but counted where he lay.

We are well aware that the air in the kameras was foul, and it is no wonder that the officers who counted the prisoners were quite willing to avoid the necessity of breathing it. Hence their readiness to drop into the practice described.

Pushkin suggested that a pile of rubbish should be allowed to accumulate in the prison-yard, in a corner made by the junction of one of the buildings with the stockade. They readily obtained permission to clear up the yard, and threw the rubbish in the place selected for it. It was arranged in such a way that two men could be concealed beneath it without attracting attention.

This was done two or three weeks before putting the

plan of escape into execution. Then lots were drawn to determine who should be the first to get out.

The choice fell upon two young men from St. Petersburgh. One had been for a short time in the naval service, and the other was a graduate of the Imperial University and had taken his degree only a few months before the trouble which led to his arrest and exile to Siberia.

It was arranged with friends in the Free Command outside the prison to place two suits of ordinary clothing, such as the peasants wear, in a spot agreed upon. This would enable the runaways to exchange their prison garb for something that would not reveal their character, and the friends would secure the prison suits as soon as possible, and destroy them. They were also to leave a supply of food, so that the escaping prisoners might have a supply for several days, and thus facilitate their flight.

On the night fixed for the escape everything was ready both in and outside of the prison. The young men took an affectionate leave of their companions, as it was more than probable they might never meet again. "We certainly hope we are not destined to meet for many months at least," said Pushkin, as he took them by the hand, "since an early meeting means that you will not succeed."

Just before the hour of going into the kameras for the night, the men concealed themselves beneath the pile of rubbish. Their places on the sleeping-bench were occupied by two dummy figures, carefully made up to resemble sleeping men.

The officer came and made the verification by counting. Then the kamera was closed, the night-guard was set and the place was quiet.

The men outside crept cautiously from beneath the rubbish, scaled the stockade, slipped quietly down the outside and got away without making the least noise. They found the clothing and food as agreed upon, left their prison garb in the same place of concealment, and before the next morning dawned they were far away on their route to freedom.

Carrying out Pushkin's plan they travelled eastward, following as near as they dared the bank of the Shilka to its junction with the Argoon to form the Amoor. From this point to its junction with the Usuree river, the country on the south bank of the Amoor belongs to China, while that on the North side is Russian territory. Along the Russian bank there are settlements at various distances from each other ; they were established there for the purpose of developing the country and supplying the steamers navigating the river with fuel, and some of them have grown to considerable importance.

The southern bank is occupied here and there by villages of aboriginals of Mongolian origin, and there is one Chinese city, Igoon, with about twenty thousand inhabitants. The Chinese and the original natives are not particularly friendly to the Russians, though there is no actual hostility between them.

The scheme was to steal a boat in the night time at one of the Russian villages on the north bank, and then float down the river with the current until an hour or so before daylight, when a refuge would be sought on the southern shore until darkness came again. At the first opportunity the boat would be exchanged for a native canoe, and then, the runaways, by disguising themselves so as to resemble natives, might proceed in the daytime, being careful always not to approach the

Garden near
the bridge
n we will be
up, the Library
Signed
Black Hawk

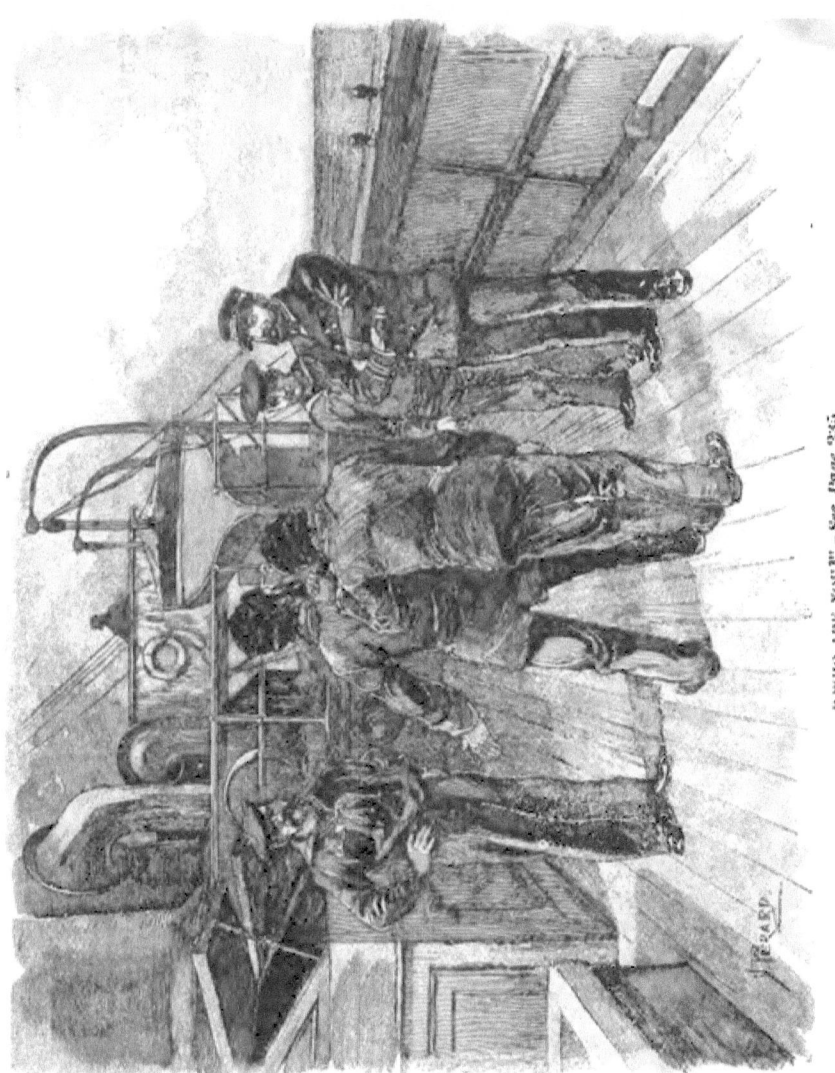

"WHO ARE YOU?"—See Page 235.

northern shore and to keep as far as possible from any steamboats they might see. All the larger towns of the Russians were to be passed in the night, as the officers of the garrisons might examine them with telescopes and detect their disguises.

They had many narrow escapes from detection and arrest, but succeeded in reaching the coast at De Castries Bay, below the mouth of the Amoor. A Japanese steamer happened to be there when they arrived, and through the connivance of some of her crew, they were smuggled on board and hidden in her hold until the vessel was well down the Gulf of Tartary, on her way to Hakodadi. Japan had no reason to feel very amiable towards the Russian bear, and when the captain found who his unauthorized passengers were, he simply told them he should put them ashore at the first port he reached. As this port was a Japanese one, they had no reason to object to this way of ridding himself of their presence.

We have seen these unfortunates in a land of safety and will now return to the prison at Kara.

A few nights after the first escape, two other prisoners got away and afterwards two more. Those who remained were careful to place the required number of dummies on the sleeping-benches every night, so that the verification before the shutting up of the kameras did not reveal what had happened.

Now came the turn of Pushkin and Dubayeff to avail themselves of the road to liberty.

The preparations for departure were made, and there was an affecting scene in the kamera an hour or two before nightfall, when our friends said farewell to those who had so long been their companions in misfortune. All day Pushkin had seemed greatly depressed, and more than once he was half determined to abandon the enterprise and remain in prison. He was cheered by Dubayeff, but all that the latter was able to say could not wholly restore his spirits, which, down to that day, had been buoyant.

The leave-taking was suddenly interrupted by the entrance of the commandant of the prison, accompanied by a strong guard. It was customary for one of the warders to notify the prisoners a few moments before the coming of an officer, but in this case no warning was given.

CHAPTER XXIV.

FLOGGING WITH THE "PLET."

The prisoners were ordered into the yard, and their movements were hastened by the soldiers, who had orders to drive them out of the kameras at the point of the bayonet in case of resistance. Then the kameras were searched and the dummy figures were found under the sleeping-benches. This was the first information that the officers had that any one had escaped.

An immediate enumeration was ordered, and it was found that six prisoners were missing; the presence of the eight dummies showed that two more were on the point of flight, and the commandant immediately set about ascertaining their names.

All were questioned one by one. Each man declined to give any information other than that the choice to go out had been decided by lot, so that all were equally guilty. This had been agreed to at the inception of the plot, and was so stated by every prisoner when his turn came to pass under the inquisition.

Finding he could learn nothing in this way, the commandant offered exemption from all punishment to the man who would reveal the names of the two prisoners whose turn it was to escape.

There was silence along the whole line. Not a man moved or indicated his willingness to accept the proffered bribe.

"Once more!" said the commandant. "Unless I know those names within ten minutes, every man will go into leg-fetters and handcuffs."

Then he walked away, leaving the prisoners to consult among themselves. They broke the rank and gathered in a group out of earshot of the soldiers.

"I will acknowledge that I was to leave this evening and would go out alone," said Pushkin. "That will save the rest from punishment."

"No! no! you shall not," came in a suppressed but fierce whisper from the lips of all his companions. "It will not save us, and would make you suffer more than the rest."

"Perhaps it would be better," said Pushkin.

The others declared that he should not. He persisted, and then Dubayeff added that he, too, would confess that he was to accompany Pushkin.

Another man spoke and said he would announce to the commandant that the lot had not yet been drawn for the escape of that night. But the others said they would not be believed, and they might as well remain faithful to the promise which had been sworn to at the start.

Convinced that they could do no real good by acknowledging their part in the matter, Pushkin and Dubayeff yielded to the importunity of their comrades and consented to stand by the original agreement.

"Time is up," said the commandant. "*Stroisa!*"

The rank was formed again and the commandant addressed the first man in the line:

"Have you decided?"

"Yes, we have."

"Well, who are the men?"

"We answer as before, that everything is decided by lot and all are equally guilty."

Then they were ordered to their kameras, which had been stripped in the meantime of everything belonging to the prisoners. They had only the clothing they wore, all their extra garments and everything they had been allowed to buy with their own money, or had received from their friends or from benevolent people outside, was gone. Nothing was left save the vermin that infested the place, as it infests every prison in Siberia, often to the extent of driving prisoners to despair and suicide.

As a preliminary, the prisoners were deprived of supper, not a particle of food being given them before the kamera was closed. The commandant had a purpose in thus depriving them of nourishment, beyond the mere idea of punishing them for wrongdoing. He hoped that hunger would drive them to desperate acts, and thus he would have a reason for shooting down all who showed themselves insubordinate. Then he would report that there had been a serious "*boont* (insurrection)," which he had been compelled to suppress by severe measures.

As soon as the prisoners were ordered to their kameras, the news of the escape was flashed by the telegraph in every direction where the wire extended. Descriptions of the missing men accompanied the news of their flight, and by the mail that left the next day their photographs were forwarded to the principal centres of police activity.

The second couple was not recaptured, but the third and last that left was overtaken and brought back.

They had succeeded in crossing the Shilka, and had almost reached the frontier of Mongolia before they were apprehended. Word was sent throughout the country that they had been retaken, and naming the place of their capture, and the officers naturally supposed that the others had taken the same course. Consequently, the search was redoubled in that quarter and slackened elsewhere, and this enabled the others to avoid recapture. This was a part of Pushkin's scheme; the first couple was to descend the Amoor, the second go westward towards Lake Baikal, and the third seek to reach safety on the soil of China. If he and Dubayeff had succeeded in getting away, they would have tried to reach the Okhotsk sea by travelling to the north and east of the Yablonnoi mountains. Once on the shores of that sea, they hoped to be picked up by an American or English whaling vessel, and carried to the Sandwich Islands or other friendly land.

On the morning after the scene in the prison-yard, which has just been described, all the prisoners were put in leg-fetters. There was the clanking of chains everywhere, and as the blacksmith's hammer closed the rivets one after another, the hearts of the victims sank within them. Their heads were half-shaved as when they were first condemned, and they were ordered to remain in close confinement, except for a limited time during the day. When they were taken into the prison-yard they were handcuffed, and if they lagged at all in their steps, the soldiers had orders to prod them with their bayonets.

Five or six days passed, and then the two escaped prisoners were brought to the prison, ironed hand and foot. From the place where they were retaken they were compelled to make a forced march back to the banks of the Shilka; they had been scantily fed and rudely treated, and their physical condition was so low that the medical attendant at the prison said they must be allowed a period of rest before receiving any physical punishment.

They were sent to the hospital, where they were fed and treated fairly well, not on account of any feeling of pity on the part of those who had them in charge, but in order to bring them up to the necessary condition to be flogged.

Down to quite recent years it has not been the custom in Siberian prisons to flog the political convicts. They were punished for infractions of duty in a variety of ways, such as shutting them up in secret cells, reducing their allowance of food, confining them hand and foot with heavy irons, depriving them of all privileges of books, writing materials or communication with friends, but never by flogging. This punishment was reserved for the criminal classes only. Whenever a political prisoner had done anything that, were he a criminal, would have rendered him liable to a flogging, it was the custom for the prison surgeon to certify that the physical condition of the accused was such that flogging would be dangerous to his life. In this way he escaped the degradation.

But in recent times, the government determined to put the political convicts on the same footing as the criminal ones; including flogging and all other degradations. When the orders to that effect were received, some of the officers connected with the management of the prisons resigned their positions, and sought transfers to other departments, rather than act as they had been directed. But it was not difficult to fill their places, and the regulations were carried out with the utmost rigor.

Down to about the middle of this century flogging in Russia was performed with the knout (noot). This weapon of cruelty is a thong of thick leather, twelve or fifteen feet long, cut in a triangular shape, and hammered until it is very nearly as hard as a piece of wood; sometimes iron filings or bits of wire are hammered into it to give it additional hardness and to tear the flesh of the victim. By law, the number of blows was limited to one hundred and one, but when these were given with the full strength of the executioner, very few persons ever survived them. If the victim died during the administration of the punishment, the flogging continued until the full number of blows ordered had been given.

. Though the use of the knout was abolished by imperial order, it continued " in exceptional cases ;" Russians generally deny that it is used at all, and certainly the cases are rare during the past twenty years.

It was rumored among the prisoners at the Kara mines, that the captured runaways were to be flogged, and naturally the report caused much discussion.

"It is possible that they may use the knout, as in olden times," said Dubayeff, "but more likely they will employ what they consider its humane substitute, the plet."

"I would rather be knouted at once, if I cannot be shot," said one of the prisoners. "The knout is more merciful than the plet, though apparently more cruel. Better die under a hundred blows than under a thousand."

"A thousand!" exclaimed Dubayeff. "They can give you six thousand blows, or even more."

"Yes, but it generally takes about a thousand blows

to cause death," was the reply, " and the remainder are applied to the corpse."

When the medical attendant at the prison certified that the men were sufficiently strong to undergo the punishment of the plet, the execution of the sentence was ordered by the commandant. Five hundred blows were to be given to each prisoner; the original order was for double that number, but the commandant was warned that they would be likely to cause death, and this was not what he desired. He preferred that his victims should live and suffer.

The flogging was performed just outside the prison-yard; the prisoners were not required to be present, as the commandant feared that their indignation might lead them to revolt then and there, regardless of the consequences.

One hundred soldiers were drawn up in double lines facing each other, and about six feet apart. Each soldier had laid aside his rifle and was armed with a plet or birch rod, four feet in length, and about the size of a man's little finger.

The first of the victims was named Rodanoff, a native of Kiev, and the son of a prominent citizen of that place. He was brought from the hospital in a cart, and wore his leg-fetters, which rattled as he stepped to the ground. His lower limbs were covered with trowsers, held in place by a cord at his hips; the rest of his body was naked, though it was covered on the way from the hospital by his coat, which lay loosely upon his shoulders. His hands were securely tied in front of him, and as he descended from the cart, they were fastened in the angle of a pair of crossed muskets (with fixed bayonets), that were held by two non-commissioned officers. The commissioned officers and all others, excepting those who held the muskets, were distributed along the line to see that every soldier gave the heaviest blow with the plet that it was in his power to give.

When all was ready, the sentence was read to Rodanoff, and he was informed that by the clemency of the commandant the number of blows had been reduced one-half. Instead of a thousand he would only receive five hundred.

He said nothing, but stood with his teeth firmly clenched, and was evidently determined to bear as bravely as possible the punishment that had been decreed. Then the order to proceed was given, and the two sergeants walked slowly backwards between the files of men, and as they passed along each soldier administered a vigorous blow with the stick upon the naked back of the prisoner.

The reader will observe that the sergeants walked slowly. There would be mercy in allowing them to move rapidly, and thus get through the ordeal as quickly as possible; but such is not the intention of the inventor of punishment with the plet. There is the prisoner, bound between the crossed muskets; he must walk as those who hold the muskets walk, and they move at a slow pace in order that the punishment may be prolonged, and every soldier can do his work thoroughly.

The supple birches cut deep into the flesh, drawing the blood at every stroke, and before the end of the line was reached, the prisoner's back was a mass of gore. His face was crimson, his eyes seemed starting from their sockets, many of the blows were received with a convulsive shudder, but he did not utter a sound. Not a cry escaped his lips, which were red to bursting, but soon assumed a tinge of purple.

At the end of the lines the sergeants turned and

retraced their steps; as one hundred soldiers were in line and each man was to administer but a single blow when the prisoner passed him, it was necessary to go five times along the line to carry out the sentence.

Blood poured down his limbs as he walked, and the blows were applied to raw and quivering flesh, but the punishment continued. Near the three-hundredth blow the color left the prisoner's face and blood spurted from his nostrils; he fainted and fell forward, so that the two sergeants were unable to hold him upright.

Then the cart was brought forward and Rodanoff, quite insensible, was placed within it, and laid flat on his face upon a truss of straw. The cart was led slowly along the lines till the remaining blows had been given, and then the poor wretch was carried away to the hospital to be restored and healed, provided he lived. Sometimes, in such cases, when a victim faints, he is carried to the hospital at once, the punishment being suspended. A careful record is kept of the number of blows he has received, and when, weeks or months later, the surgeon certifies that he is sufficiently restored, he is brought out and receives the remainder.

Enough of this horrible scene, which the Russians appear to consider a humane substitute for the application of the knout. The punishment of the plet is sometimes called "running the gauntlet;" this would imply that the victim is allowed to *run* between the files of men and avoid the blows if possible, which is very far from being the case. Special care is taken that he shall not run, nor can he even proceed at an ordinary walking pace. And if any soldier should, out of compassion, deliver aught but a vigorous blow, he is liable to receive a dozen strokes of the plet on his own back in order to teach him his duty.

After Rodanoff was carried to the hospital, his comrade was tied to the crossed muskets and received his punishment. The scene was exactly like that which preceded it, save that the victim endured the infliction without fainting, although his back was not less lacerated than was that of his friend. Both men were in hospital for nearly five months before the surgeon certified that they were sufficiently restored to be returned to prison.

CHAPTER XXV.

THE HUNGER STRIKE.

Until the hour when the flogging was performed the prisoners expected to be compelled to witness it. They had agreed that if they were ordered out they would go, but each man was to stand with his eyes shut, and his fingers in his ears, provided he were not handcuffed, while the flogging took place. No plan was formed for offering resistance, as it was plain that they would be shot down in case of failure to do as they were ordered.

"There's an old adage," said Pushkin, "that one man may take a horse to water, but ten can't make him drink."

"Yes," replied one, who was standing near him, "they may compel us to go out, but we will not see or hear what takes place."

"If they handcuff us we will have to hear the sound of the plet as it falls," said Dubayeff.

"We will stuff our ears with pellets of dough from our bread," said one of the party, "and can do it when we are ordered into the yard where the handcuffing will take place."

Rye bread, commonly called black bread (chorney

kleb) in Russia, is a very plastic material, and the listeners readily saw that its use in the manner suggested was feasible. Happily there was no occasion to try it.

Many of the prisoners whose tastes are artistic devote their time to fashioning little statuettes and other figures out of the black bread, which forms an important part of their rations. The writer has seen many of these works of exile hands; one of the best he remembers was shown to him at Chita, and consisted of a set of chessmen, wholly made of the material described. It was the work of a Polish exile, and had been purchased by one of the officers of the garrison.

One of the ways of adding to the unhappiness of prisoners is an order occasionally issued in Russian prisons, forbidding the inmates to indulge in any artistic work of this sort. The object of the order has no other purpose than to enforce absolute idleness regardless of the result.

But if the prisoners at Kara were not compelled to witness the punishment of their recent companions, they were treated with the greatest rigor. On the day following the incident just described, they were ordered into the yard early in the morning, and carpenters were set at work erecting partitions in the kameras, so as to convert each of them into three or four cells. The prisoners were then divided into squads of six or eight, and a cell was assigned to each squad. There was no chance to walk about, as the sleeping-benches occupied the greater part of the space; not more than three steps could be taken in any one direction, and the prisoners had their choice to lie or sit on the benches, or stand in the narrow space left between the foot of a bench and the wall.

They were allowed no bedding of any kind; they had their prison clothing and nothing more. Their food, which had been scanty enough, and wretched in quality, was reduced; they were not allowed to exercise in the yard, in fact, they were not allowed to go outside their narrow cells on any account whatever. Life, under such conditions, was unbearable, and the men set about planning a revolt.

"It is better to be shot down at once and make an end of things, than endure this treatment," said one of them.

"Yes," said another; "I'm ready for anything, no matter how desperate."

Various plans were proposed. One suggested that each should watch his opportunity to strike an officer, and be shot or hanged for his offense; but it was decided that this was impracticable, for the reason that opportunities for doing so would be rare, and it would take a long time for the scheme to be carried out. Another proposed that they should tear up the benches, and use the planks as weapons with which to attack the soldiers, the attack to be made simultaneously in all parts of the prison, just as the doors were locked for the night. But the same objections were raised to this as to the previous plan.

"I have it!" exclaimed another.

"Yes! what?"

"Set fire to the prison and burn ourselves and our guards together. The building is so watersoaked by the rains and by the ooze from the marshy grounds it stands on, that if it burns at all it will burn very slowly. The guards can easily put out the fire, or, if they do not, they can stand by and see us roasted, while they stand ready to capture us in case we escape from the flames."

The proposition did not meet with favor, partly on account of its impracticability and partly because of the horror possessed by the whole human race at such a form of death. Of all the savage methods of taking life that by burning at the stake is regarded as the most fiendish.

There was a pause, and at length Dubayeff spoke. His face was pale, and it was easy to see that his words were momentous.

"Brothers," said he, "we are at our last extremity. There is only one mode of remonstrance left."

He paused again. No one spoke. It was two or three minutes before he continued.

"We have nothing left but the hunger strike."

The rest assented, and the word was passed through the other cells, partly by means of their voices and partly through the aid of the knock alphabet. The proposal was agreed to, and the hunger strike was to begin on the following morning.

Pushkin suggested that a last opportunity should be given to the commandant to cease his barbarity, and he volunteered to be the spokesman for the despairing men. So, when the guard came on its next round of inspection, he told the officer in command that he had a petition to make on behalf of all the prisoners, and not on his own account.

In a little while the officer returned, accompanied by two soldiers, and Pushkin was escorted to the commandant's room. The commandant looked up from some papers he was examining and gruffly said:

"Well, what do you want?"

"We ask that your Excellency will remove the partitions that were recently put up in the kameras, and restore us to the conditions under which we lived before the attempt to escape was made. We feel that we have been sufficiently punished for violating the rules of the prison, and will give our word of honor that no further attempt to escape will be made while we are here."

"That's what you want, is it?" said the commandant with a sneer. "Go back, and say that the prison conditions will not be changed, and every man will be flogged if another petition is sent here. The one who brings it will be the first for the flogging, and get a thousand blows of the plet."

Pushkin was taken back to the cell, where he repeated the words of the commandant. Then the word passed about, and it was agreed that the hunger strike should begin on the following morning.

The golodofka, or "hunger strike," is an attempt of prisoners to bring their authorities to terms by refusing food and dying of hunger unless their demands are met. It is the last resort in Russian prisons; when everything else has failed, the golodofka succeeds.

"Our masters are a strange race of men," said Dubayeff to Pushkin, as they were discussing the subject one day. Though they have abandoned the death penalty in the Civil Code, and are constantly boasting of their humanity in this regard, they permit men and women to be hanged or shot by order of courts-martial. They boast of having abolished the knout, but they flog and kill with the plet; they put men in solitary confinement, and let them die a lingering death in the fortresses of St. Petersburg, and in other prisons; they kill us with scanty food and wretched lodgings that they would consider unfit for a dog or pig; they see us perish of consumption, fever and other diseases, which any man knows are caused by the conditions into which we are forced ; they drive us into the winter's cold with insufficient clothing ; see us devoured by vermin ; deprive us of employment ; will not allow us to read, write or study, and so force us into insanity ; and torture us in other ways that shorten our lives. But when prisoners have to starve themselves as a protest against extreme cruelty, they have invariably carried their point."

On the morning following the making of the agreement the food that was brought to the prisoners in the cells, or kameras, was handed back untouched to the warders. The men sat, or lay, on the sleeping-benches, and talked with one another in low tones. Some had already shown signs of insanity, and as hunger made itself manifest, the signs increased. Their language was incoherent ; some babbled incessantly, while others became moody and spoke but rarely.

The warders reported to the commandant that the prisoners refused their food.

"They'll be tired of that soon enough," was his comment. "Take it to them regularly, at the exact time they've been accustomed to get it."

His orders were obeyed, but the men remained firm. All that day, and the next, and the next, and still they refused.

Then the commandant became alarmed. He sent an officer to say to the prisoners that if they would end the hunger strike at once, he would see what could be done towards meeting their demands.

This was a vague promise, to which the men listened in silence. The officer did as he was ordered and retired to make his report. At the next service of food the prisoners saw that the articles were of better quality than usual, and more liberal in quantity, but they refused as before.

On the fifth day the commandant came in person and offered to telegraph to the Minister of the Interior in their behalf, provided they would declare the strike at an end, and receive the food which was waiting for them in the prison kitchen. He addressed himself directly to Pushkin, evidently recognizing him as the leader, and assured him that there had never been any intention of flogging the entire party, or himself, the threat having been made merely for the purpose of frightening them into obedience to orders.

"I have no authority to act for my comrades in this matter," Pushkin replied. "I did not suggest the hunger strike, and therefore cannot advise that it be stopped."

"Who did suggest it?" asked the commandant, in a tone of anger.

"I must decline to answer Your Excellency's question," replied the prisoner. Then the commandant turned on his heel and left the kamera.

He immediately telegraphed to the minister that the political prisoners had made a hunger strike. He asked for instructions, and stated in the customary brevity of the telegraph, the demands that had been made. He waited anxiously for the minister's response, which did not come until just as the sun was setting behind the hills that enclosed the valley of the Kara river.

CHAPTER XXVI.

PROGRESS OF THE HUNGER STRIKE.

"I very much doubt if there will be a favorable response from the Minister of the Interior," said Dubayeff to Pushkin, when it became known that the commandant had telegraphed to the capital for instructions.

"Why so?" the latter asked.

"Because the party of action has been creating considerable trouble of late, and the ministry is very much irritated. At any rate, this is the time when active measures were to be undertaken, and we may hear of them any day."

"What were they intending to do?"

To this interrogation Dubayeff did not give a direct answer. Pushkin changed his question to an inquiry as to what the party of action expected to accomplish in the work in which it was engaged.

"We are divided in our opinions," was the reply, "and probably no ten men could be brought together who would agree exactly as to the objects we wish to attain. In a general way, we want the government to be based on representation, rather than upon tyranny; the people must have a voice in the plan of government, and to this end they ask that the provinces, through the existing zemtsvos, or provincial assemblies, should be allowed to send representatives to a national assembly, in which the public welfare may be discussed, and suggestions made for the improvement of the condition of the hundred millions of inhabitants of which Russia can boast.

"For a long time," continued Dubayeff, "we acted without hostility to the government, and sought to bring about reforms without violence of any kind. Our young men and women 'went to the people;' they sought to educate the peasants, and for this purpose they went among them in their villages and workshops, instructed them in the schools, established 'circles,' or debating societies, and acted in the most open manner in doing what they did not think would meet with any objection. They were patriotic in the fullest sense of the word; they wanted to see Russia take a place among the civilized nations, with an intelligent population, ruled by men who could be respected throughout the empire, and have the confidence and friendship of all their subjects."

"And how were these efforts met?"

"If an official in the service of the government ventured to suggest the formation of an assembly, in which its affairs could be discussed, he was removed from office and sent to a distant part of the empire, there to be watched by the police who had him under strict surveillance. The young men and women who had gone among the people were required to give up their work of teaching ignorant peasants how to read and write; some were allowed to return to their homes or leave the country, but the majority of them were arrested and sent into exile. Arrests were without open charges; exile was without trial, but by the far more expeditious 'administrative process,' the same which brought you to Siberia."

"Was this before the party had shown any violence toward the Czar and his officials?" Pushkin asked.

"Yes, not a hand had been lifted against anybody, nor was there any intention of violence. There is a mistaken impression, which the government has taken pains to spread as widely as possible, that all Liberals are terrorists. The majority of the Liberals are opposed to violence altogether; a small minority adopted the policy of violence, but they only did so after it had been clearly shown that the government would not grant reforms through peaceful means. There was no violence until after hundreds of liberals had been sent to Siberia, for no other reason than that they wished well for their country, and hoped to see the ignorant mass of the population educated up to the ability of helping to govern themselves. Some of those who were not arrested and banished became angry at the treatment of their friends and determined upon revenge."

The reader who is familiar with the history of the troubles in Russia during the last twenty years, will remember that the work of violence began with the assassination of General Mezzentseff, Chief of Gendarmes, in St. Petersburg, in 1878, and was followed by several other assassinations or attempts at murder in the next two or three years, culminating in the death of the emperor Alexander II., in March, 1881. Before the first of the assassinations, the prisons of Russia were crowded with the victims of arrest, and hundreds had been sent to Siberia without trial.

"These people were Nihilists," is a natural comment upon the foregoing paragraph.

The term " Nihilist " is one that is not acknowledged by any of the Russian liberals. It was invented by the novelist Turgenef to describe a character in one of his stories; it was caught up by the government and the anti-liberals and applied indiscriminately. According to them it includes all classes of liberals; it may apply to some of them, such as the murderers of the emperor and their special sympathizers, but is an undeserved stigma upon all those who have opposed violence from the beginning and still oppose it as vigorously as ever.

"I was never a terrorist," continued Dubayeff, "and deprecated every kind of violence. But you see that made no difference in my case; this is my second visit to Siberia, and there are many others in this very prison who believe with me, and their actions have always been consistent with their beliefs.

" The death of the emperor Alexander II. was decreed by the terrorists, because they believed that a notable example should be given that all the world would talk about. They had no special hatred for *him;* it was the imperial system that they attacked, and as he was its representative, it was his fate to be killed. And in killing him they set back the cause of reform, instead of advancing it. He was the friend of reform; he liberated the serfs, established trial by jury, and did other things for the good of the country. He received a petition asking for freedom of the press, and other liberties, such as are found in most other countries, and not only received it, but took it under consideration."

" That was just before his death, was it not ?"

"Yes, he drew up and signed a proclamation to the people, telling them he intended to summon a national assembly to take steps for forming a constitutional government. He signed it on the 12th of March, 1881."

"That was the day before his death."

"Just one day before his death," said Dubayeff, in a tone of sadness. "The proclamation would have been issued on the 14th of March if Alexander had lived. But he was assassinated by the terrorists, and thus the hopes of the liberals were doomed to disappointment.

"If any men should be termed Nihilists," he continued, "they are those who have held back the cause of reform by the murder of Alexander Nicolaievitch, and by other murders that have disgraced the cause. And the worst of the business is, that the regicides really acted from honorable motives, and thought they were doing good work for their country. They were carried away with the idea that a notable example must be made to call the attention of the whole world, out of Russia as well as in it, to the abuses of despotism and the sufferings of the people. They argued that nothing short of this would answer; it was impossible to control them, and you know the result."

"Wasn't it possible for the moderate liberals to persuade them to hope for reform through peaceable means?" Pushkin asked.

"That was tried in several instances, but it failed every time. And the men who undertook to convince the terrorists that reform was possible without violence, and who tried to get them to abandon that policy, were sent to Siberia in consequence. The mayor of Kharkoff, and other prominent men, were among the victims of the government, who punished them because they tried to induce the terrorists to desist from carrying out their project. They caused the Zemtsvo of Kharkoff to send a petition to the Crown, in which were stated the grievances of the people, and respectfully asking that they be investigated. That was their offense, and for it they were exiled to Siberia, and so were prominent men in other provinces who did the same thing."

The conversation was interrupted by a rumor through the prison that the commandant had received orders from St. Petersburg relative to the treatment of the prisoners who had made the hunger strike. Exactly how it came no one could or would say, but it came as do many other rumors from the outside world, through the medium of the guards.

The conduct of the party of action, to which Dubayeff referred at the time the hunger strike was inaugurated, was as follows:

A paper called *The Will of the People* was extensively circulated. It was in every sense a revolutionary sheet, as it breathed hostility to the government in every line, and discussed the reforms which were demanded in no mistaken tone. The paper was printed abroad, sometimes in London and sometimes in Switzerland, and was smuggled into the country, packed in merchandise, wrapped around parcels, and in a hundred other ways. Now and then a printing-office was established in a cellar in St. Petersburg or Moscow, and the printing was done there; but sooner or later the police made a descent and arrested all persons connected with the establishment. The arrest was speedily followed by exile, and almost always without a trial; to be found in the office of a clandestine press was sufficent evidence of guilt to render a trial quite unnecessary.

Attempts had been made on the life of the Czar, and also on the lives of several men high in authority. The Czar was virtually a close prisoner in his palace; he could not venture out of doors without a powerful guard, and whenever he did go out, the streets in every direction were virtually closed to the public. Assemblages on the corners were forbidden; there was a hedge of troops lining both sides of every street through which the emperor passed, and his safety was further secured by his carriage often taking a different route from the one that had been made public.

All his personal attendants were more or less under suspicion, and the autocrat of all the Russias did not know whom to trust. So great was the dread that he would be poisoned, that all his food was prepared under the eye of a high official, who literally stood over the cook and watched his every movement. When a meal was brought to table it was necessary for this same high official to come forward and partake of each dish before it was served to the Czar. Only in this way could safety from arsenic, strychnine, or other deadly ingredient be assured.

While stepping from his carriage one day, the Minister of the Interior was greeted by the explosion of a hand-grenade which fell at his feet. Happily for his safety none of the fragments touched him, though they buried themselves in the side of the carriage and wounded two attendants who were at his side. And this was the day on which the Minister received the information that the prisoners at the Kara settlement had started a hunger strike.

More pressing matters demanded his attention, and the telegram was placed on the table to wait its turn for consideration. When he reached it, the Minister thought a few moments on the subject, and then answered:

"Let the strike continue, but use your discretion."

This virtually placed the power in the hands of the

commandant, though he read between the lines that the Minister was not relenting in any of the harsh orders previously given relative to the Kara prison. That the prisoners should suffer was a foregone conclusion; the commandant was to see that they did not carry matters too far.

He waited until the next day and then went in person to make another appeal to the prisoners.

"If you will bring the strike to an end this moment," said he, "I will do all in my power to mitigate your restrictions, and make the rules as favorable as possible. No man shall be punished for what has occurred in the past, and the efforts to escape shall be wholly forgotten."

It was evident to the prisoners that the ministry had not relented, as the offer of the commandant was not at all definite. He proposed to do "all in his power," which might be much, little, or nothing at all. Their answer was ready, without any consultation on their part, and was in the negative.

It would have been almost an impossibility for them to get together to consult upon any subject, as all were greatly weakened by their self-starvation. More than half their number were unable to stand, some could not speak, some were delirious and raved incessantly, but their ravings were scarcely audible beyond their narrow kameras in consequence of their lack of strength. One man, whose insanity at first took a violent turn, was now unable to articulate above a whisper, and the whisper was so weak that more than half his words would have been indistinct to a listener close by his side.

Every day the surgeon passed through the kameras and made a careful inspection of every "case." On the ninth day he reported to the commandant that several of the prisoners were so low that they might die at any time; on the tenth day two were reduced to a condition of insensibility, and others were falling into a comatose state from which they could be roused only by hypodermic application of stimulants, and by giving them food by force.

Not wishing to take the responsibility of ending the strike, although it was in his power to do so, the commandant telegraphed to the Minister of the Interior as follows:

"Golodofka continues, several deaths imminent."

He waited anxiously for the reply, which came, as did its predecessor, near the close of the day. It was in these words:

"Concede demands. Prevent news of strike becoming known."

Immediately, the commandant went to the prison and told the sufferers that he had received orders from St. Petersburg that gave him full power to act. He promised that the request made through Pushkin before the inauguration of the hunger strike should be granted; the partitions in the kameras would be taken down on the following morning, the prisoners might exercise in the yard during the day and would only be locked up at night, their books would be restored to them, they could communicate with their friends as before, there should be no further punishment on account of the escapes, and in every way they were to be under the same conditions of existence as before the escapes were discovered. He would make two conditions only: the first was the one they had themselves offered, that they would pledge their word of honor not to make any new attempts to run away, and the second was that they should not inform any one outside the prison as to what had occurred. In other words, they were not to tell of the golodofka and its results.

This last condition was rejected, and for a while it seemed as though the hunger strike would continue. Finding the prisoners determined in their resistance, the commandant yielded the point, and the protest by self-starvation was declared at an end.

All night the surgeon and his assistants were busy in endeavoring to save the sufferers from further torture through hunger. Stimulants were applied, food was given sparingly, the worst cases were removed to the hospital, the kameras were ventilated as much as it was possible to ventilate them, and on the following morning the obnoxious partitions were removed.

CHAPTER XXVII.

THE FREE COMMAND.

The skill and care of the surgeon was rewarded by the recovery of all the prisoners, though several had very narrow escapes from death. Among these was Pushkin; he had held up until the end, retaining his faculties throughout; at the final visit of the commandant he was able to talk coherently, though scarcely above a whisper, but when the decision was announced that the request of the prisoners was granted and they would take food, he fell off into a complete faint and the hospital attendant who had him in charge thought he had expired.

Hypodermic injections of brandy gave strength to his almost imperceptible pulse, and the food which was judiciously given under medical supervision had the desired effect. He was carried to the hospital and placed in a bed, and there he remained for several days, scarcely able to move. By degrees he regained his strength; in due time the surgeon certified that he was sufficiently restored to be sent from the hospital, and he was accordingly returned to the prison.

For some time after this occurred, the prisoners had no just cause to complain of their treatment. Their food was better and more abundant than before the escapes were made, and the commandant was faithful to his promise that the former conditions should be restored. They were allowed to communicate with their friends as before, all their letters passing under the eye of the commandant or one of his subordinates to make sure that they contained no allusion to the golodofka.

"We may gain a point," said Dubayeff to Pushkin one day, "by notifying the commandant that we will not refer to the hunger strike. We may gain a point with him and shall not lose anything by it."

"How do you make that out?" queried the latter.

"This is the way of it," Dubayeff replied. "The hunger strike is already known to our friends in Kara outside the prison, and you may be sure they have sent news of it to Moscow and St. Petersburg. By this time every revolutionist in Russia has heard of it, if I am not greatly mistaken. The strike and its results are known by telegraph, you may be sure, and the details of the whole matter will reach our friends by mail."

"In that case," said Pushkin, "we have no real occasion to allude to it. I agree with you that a point can be made with the commandant by voluntarily acceding to his request."

There was a general consultation among the prisoners, and it was agreed that Pushkin should again act as their spokesman. Since he was the bearer of an offer, instead of a demand, it was likely that he would be more civilly treated than on his previous visit.

At the next change of guard, Pushkin said to the officer:

"Please say to His Excellency, that the prisoners have asked me to present a proposition to him on their behalf."

Exactly what passed in the mind of His Excellency, when he heard the request, it is impossible to say, but he did not hesitate at receiving the embassador of those in his charge. Pushkin was escorted to the office of the commandant, and that official was noticeably less gruff in manner than at the previous visit.

Instead of demanding, "What do you want?" he put his question in the words, "What do you wish to say?"

"Your Excellency demanded that we should not inform our friends of the golodofka," said Pushkin. "We refused at the time, and Your Excellency did not press the condition."

"Yes," said the commandant, in a tone of inquiry, as though he would say, "What has that to do with your mission?"

"My comrades have sent me to say that they respect Your Excellency's demand," Pushkin answered. "They have not informed their friends of the golodofka, and they will not do so. They give the same honorable promise that they did about attempting to escape."

Doubtless the commandant was fully capable of seeing the stroke of policy that his prisoners were endeavoring to make. He knew that the story of the hunger strike was already known outside the prison, as it was sure to have leaked out through the soldiers of the guard and the attendants at the hospital. But he was too good a diplomat to let Pushkin know his thoughts on the subject; he believed, with Talleyrand, that language was given to man for the concealment of thought.

"Very well," he answered, with a slight nod. "Is there anything that the prisoners desire?"

"Nothing, Your Excellency. I came as the bearer of this offer and not to bring a petition."

"Is there anything you wish to suggest?"

"Nothing, Your Excellency. But if I might be allowed a suggestion, it would be that we may have some employment. If we could build a shed in the prison-yard, and have a carpenter's bench with a few tools, and perhaps a few tools for blacksmithing, we should find it a great relief from idleness."

"I will see what can be done," was the reply, and this non-committal answer terminated the interview.

Two or three days later some lumber was brought into the yard and the prisoners set about the construction of a shed. The principal tool of a Russian carpenter is a small axe, and with it he often accomplishes wonders. The axe serves often as plane, saw and chisel, in addition to performing the usual work of the axe in other lands. Houses may be wholly constructed with this tool; very comfortable houses they often are, and a defiance to the rigors of winter.

A certain number of axes was distributed to the prisoners, but they were carefully counted two or three times every day and at night were handed over to the guard. It was against the rules for a prisoner to be intrusted with a weapon, and certainly this innocent tool of industry would make a formidable article of offense in the hands of a determined man. The prisoners were under promise not to attempt to escape and it was not feared they would undertake it, but the commandant rightly judged that they must not be placed under temptation.

The shed was soon in place, and then the prisoners were supplied with materials, which they fashioned into chairs, tables, bureaus and other things that might be sold in the neighboring town. Unfortunately the town was small and the market was restricted, but it was made to yield something. The same was the case with the blacksmith's shop which they were allowed to establish, but in this case, as in that of the other, all the tools were carefully enumerated daily and handed over to the guard at nightfall. Every ounce of iron was accounted for ; the iron given out was carefully weighed, and so were the articles into which it was fashioned. Had there been a disposition to secrete it for future violations of the prison rules, there would have been little chance to do so.

All through Russia the same care is taken to prevent the possession by a prisoner of anything that may be used as a weapon. When a female prisoner obtains permission to sew, she must account for every needle intrusted to her, and she is not allowed to have scissors in her possession. The scissors are kept by her guard, and when she has occasion to cut the material on which she is working, she must call the guard and indicate where the cutting is to be made. He is supposed to cut the material himself, but if kindly disposed he allows her to handle the scissors, though he stands ready to snatch them from her at any instant. Scissors in the hands of a woman are regarded as dangerous in two ways ; she may use them as a weapon against her jailors, or for stabbing herself to death if she has resolved upon ending her troubles by suicide.

Life in the Kara prison as it was after the hunger strike is not absolutely unendurable, and the prisoners did not give their keepers any cause to complain of their conduct. They were permitted to improve the condition of their kameras ; they bought various articles of bedding and clothing, and if the place could have been freed of the vermin that infested it, much of its horror would have disappeared. Hot water and lime were occasionally applied to the walls, floors and sleeping-benches, and the evil was somewhat mitigated, but vermin increase and multiply like other living things and only a short time was required to restore their numbers.

"It is not imprisonment under proper sanitary conditions that we complain of," said Dubayeff, "but the deliberate torture to which we are subjected. Men who conspire against the government take Chance in their hands, and they expect to be punished if they are caught and convicted of their offenses. Justice may be hard; it may sentence us to death or to exile for life, but as long as it is justice we have no right to murmur. If we are convicted after a fair trial, which follows speedily upon our arrest, we must take our fate as we find it, and he would be a coward who complains, even though his sentence may be death on the scaffold.

"Though we may be the worst offenders, we are entitled to humane treatment. We do not expect choice food, but we have a right to receive what will support life, and to have that food clean and properly prepared. We ask and expect to be treated as well as a farmer treats his cattle and pigs, but you know for yourself that we are not."

"True," answered Pushkin, "but the consciousness of having deserved his punishment does not lessen a prisoner's desire to escape and be free again."

"Not by any means," was the reply. "Every man under restraint, no matter how just it may be, longs to escape, and the subject is rarely out of his thoughts. How much more is it present with him when he is innocent of any crime, has been kept for years, maybe, in prison without being allowed to know the charge against him, and is finally sent into exile without trial, solely upon the order of the Minister of the Interior, who cannot possibly have any knowledge of a twentieth of the cases upon which he acts so summarily."

The reader may accept the foregoing as the grievance of many thousands of Russian subjects at this very day. Arrest upon suspicion only, and often without tangible foundation for suspicion, imprisonment without charges being made known to the accused, trials where no defense is allowed, or more frequently no trials whatever, but sentences under arbitrary order, long detentions, solitary confinement under conditions that often cause insanity or bodily ailments, exile accompanied by great physical suffering, intentional exposure to inclemencies of weather, confinement in prisons reeking with seeds of disease and swarming with vermin, improper and insufficient food, scanty clothing, heavy chains, flogging and other cruelties, these are the things of which complaint is made. No one has a right to expect that a prison will resemble a palace and abound in luxuries, but he certainly has a right to expect that he will not be treated worse than the brutes, no matter what may have been his offense.

The wives and children of some of the prisoners were living in Kara, and formed a part of the Free Command which has been mentioned in a previous chapter. These men were specially exemplary in their conduct, as this was one of the conditions on which they were released from prison conditions, and allowed to live with their families in the Free Command.

Anxiously they counted the days when their prison term would be ended and permission granted for them to live outside. According to the regulations, they were to be under strict surveillance; they would be obliged to report daily to the police, perhaps several times a day, and at any moment the police might visit their houses and take note of anything they observed there. Any infraction of the rules rendered them liable to be returned to prison. Disagreeable as were the restrictions under which they lived, they were far more acceptable than life within prison walls, and the police rarely had occasion to complain of violations.

Life in the Free Command is a sort of probation for the convict who is to be sent, after the probationary term is ended, to become a colonist in some inhospitable part of Siberia. To a man who has been followed or accompanied by his family, it is a boon of the highest value; it is welcome, of course, to the man without family, as a relief from chains and prison conditions, but in many cases it leads to demoralization. The criminal part of the Free Command is much given to drunkenness and social disorder; the political prisoners refuse to associate with the criminals and hold themselves strickly aloof; but not infrequently despair makes one of them desperate and he falls into evil ways.

One day it became known that in the beginning of the following week a selection was to be made of prisoners assigned to the Free Command. It was rumored that the selection would be a large one, not on account of any special feeling of kindness on the part of the officers, but because the prison was needed for a convoy of hard-labor convicts that was expected very shortly.

But the next day come rumors of an occurrence which filled every heart with indignation and fear. Event followed event in rapid succession; the last in the list was a terrible tragedy, terrible even for the wilds of Siberia, with all the horrors contained in the history of that dreaded land.

CHAPTER XXVIII.

IVAN BANISHED TO THE ARCTIC CIRCLE.

Dr. Shulmann and Ivan Pushkin formed a close friendship in the little town where they were domiciled together. As the ispravnik was on unpleasant terms with the doctor, the former very soon formed a dislike for the latter's young friend, and kept a careful watch in the hope of catching him in a violation of the rules, so that due punishment could be inflicted. Ivan was equally watchful to avoid giving an opportunity for complaint, and, therefore, carried out every regulation to the letter.

At noon every day, he was required to report in person to the police. He was careful to time his movements, so that he should be at the official bureau a few minutes before the designated hour, regardless of the weather or of any occupation in which he was engaged.

One day, while on his way to make his report, he was startled by an outcry of the people on the street, combined with feminine screams. A horse attached to a telyega, containing two women, had become frightened,

IVAN STOPPING THE FRIGHTENED HORSE.—See page 277.

bermen convict

and was running away, dragging the vehicle after him at a terrific pace. One of the women fainted and fell to the bottom of the telyega, and the other was screaming with all the power of her lungs.

As Ivan saw the horse approaching, he made ready to spring forward and seize the runaway by the bridle. He succeeded in catching the bridle and stopping the frightened animal, but he was severely bruised in accomplishing what he did, and his clothes were badly torn, as he was dragged for quite a distance, and almost thrown under the wheels of the telyega. He assisted in lifting out the fainting woman and helping the other to the ground, and then he resumed his journey to the police station.

He arrived several minutes past the hour when he should have reported. The ispravnik was in the police office when Ivan arrived, and as the young man made his appearance the official glanced at the clock, and then at the clothing of the exile.

"You have violated the regulations," said the ispravnik, severely, "and it will be necessary to punish you."

"I have been delayed by a work of humanity," Ivan responded. "I was stopping a runaway horse, and saving two women from possible death."

"A very plausible story!" said the ispravnik, in a sneering tone.

"It can be proved by several witnesses," the young man answered, "and I can also prove by them that my clothes were torn while I was clinging to the horse."

"Is there anything in the regulations that says an exile may stop runaway horses?" the ispravnik asked.

"There is nothing I am aware of that forbids it," Ivan replied.

"We will see about that," said the official. Then he

turned to the regulations, and pointed out a clause in section 24, in which administrative exiles are forbidden to exercise any public activity.

Stopping a runaway horse in the principal street of a town in mid-day, certainly requires an exercise of public activity, but it is doubtful if the framers of the Code ever intended this particular clause to be interpreted as the ispravnik chose to construe it. Ivan suggested as much to the official, but was brought up sharply with an order to hold his tongue or it might be worse for him.

Silent, but indignant, he stood in front of the ispravnik, and was glad when he was told to go. He went straight home and told Dr. Shulmann what had occurred.

"The scoundrel means mischief," said the doctor, "and you can now understand why I thought him capable of calling me to attend his sick child and then punishing me for violating the regulations. You will hear from him before many hours, or at all events, as soon as he can communicate with the governor of the province."

Dr. Shulmann's prediction was verified. The ispravnik informed the governor that the exile, Ivan Pushkin, son of a political convict, who had been sent to the Kara mines, was guilty of "pernicious public activity," and had sought to obtain undue influence over certain loyal subjects of the Czar, then residing in that town. His acts were "a menace to public peace and order," (Section 28 of the regulations) and the ispravnik recommended that he be sent to reside in a Yakut village in the northern part of the province, beyond the Arctic circle.

The governor acted upon the suggestion of the ispravnik, and in due time, Ivan was exiled to the place which the ispravnik designated. Exile in a village of Siberian peasants is bad enough, but it is a hundred times worse among the Yakuts or Tungusians.

These are the aboriginal inhabitants of Siberia. They are mostly nomads or wanderers, moving from place to place to catch fish and fur-bearing animals, and to find food for their reindeer, which constitute their only wealth. They live in yourts or tents; the summer yourt is made of the skins of animals, stretched upon poles, like the tents of the American Indians, while their winter yourts are built of logs, poles and earth, so that they bear a strong resemblance to tents. The summer yourt is entered at the side like an ordinary tent, but the winter yourt is entered through a hole in the roof, which serves alike for doorway and chimney.

Imagine a man of refinement sent to live among the lowest tribes of Indians on the Western plains of the United States, and the reader can have a fair idea of what exile must be among the Yakuts and Tunguse. And it was exile of this sort that had been decreed to an educated and refined young Russian for "exercising public activity."

"Existence did not seem worth having," said Ivan, "and many times I seriously contemplated putting an end to it; only the thought of my parents, and my brother and sister, caused me to stay my hand. The Yakuts had orders to keep me constantly in sight, lest I might escape. Whenever I stepped out of doors I was followed, and not a moment was I allowed to be alone. In the yourts I was obliged to mingle with the whole family, men, women, children and dogs; the air was stifling and foul, what with the lack of ventilation, and the fires that were constantly burning in the middle of the circular space which formed the interior.

"Nothing but extreme hunger could induce me to eat of the native food, which was more repulsive than what was served to us at the etapes along the great road when we came to Siberia. When I could get raw fish I ate it in preference to anything else, as it certainly had the merit of cleanliness, but when fish were not to be had, we lived upon the flesh of the reindeer. And it was the way of cooking this flesh that disgusted me, and made me loathe my food.

"No part of the deer is wasted. They cook the flesh, entrails and feet, in the same pot, and with them the half-digested moss that they find in the stomach of the deer. This moss they consider a special delicacy, while I always regarded it with horror; it reminded me of the old adage, 'There's no accounting for tastes.'

"At first I was regarded with suspicion, but after a while established friendly relations with my custodians as I learned something of their language. The head man of the little village was a decent sort of fellow, and wanted me to instruct him so that he could read Russian; I would have done so gladly for the sake of occupation, had it not been for the requirement in the 24th article of the Code, that administrative exiles must not engage in any kind of pedagogic work. To instruct a Yakut in the Russian alphabet, would be a violation of the law, and I might be sent further north, perhaps into the Arctic Ocean, or to the Pole. Who knows?

"I used to accompany the natives when they went to trap fur-bearing animals. Of course there was nothing that I could teach them in the way of wood-craft, in which they are adepts, but there were some points in mechanics of which they were ignorant, and I was able to show them. Then I built a regular ladder for them to use in descending through the roof into the yourt in place of the notched stick, to which they were accustomed. I planned a winter yourt which was something like a regular house, as it had a door for entering it, and there was a chimney opposite the door, so that the place was not filled with smoke. I wanted to put the door on the level of the ground, but to this they would not listen. I put it about half way up one side of the yourt, and made an entry or vestibule out of some reindeer skins, and then I made a sloping walk from the entry to the floor of the yourt, so that the ladder in either its old or new form was not required. In this way I secured the friendship of all of them, and especially of the old and infirm ones, for whom climbing was a matter of difficulty.

"They rewarded my efforts by giving me clothing like what they wore themselves. It was made of reindeer skin, and consisted of a shirt or frock of thin skin from which the hair had been scraped, trowsers with the hair still on and worn outside, and akukhlankah, or frock, which was put on over the head just like a civilized shirt, and tied tight around the neck. The trowsers were kept in place by a wide thong around the waist, and I had boots made of deerskin, the thickest part being used for the soles. When dressed in these garments I looked very much like a native, and the people seemed pleased when I adopted their costume. I laid my old clothing away very carefully to keep it safe against the time when I should be allowed to go back to live among the Russians again. I vowed that I would never show any more public activity by stopping a runaway horse, even if the ispravnik himself was in the telyega and in danger of having his neck broken.

"There was no mail communication with the place where I lived, and so there was no way in which I could send or receive letters. I had been consigned to the care of these natives 'until called for,' as a parcel may be left in a store-house, and nobody could tell when I might be wanted by my masters, the police. All they knew was that I might be sent for at any time, and they were bound to deliver me alive or give conclusive proof that I was dead. I formed a hundred different plans of escape, but never one that was practicable. In spite of the friendly terms that had been established between us I was watched just as closely as ever, and never was I permitted to go out of sight."

While Ivan was thus leading a life of deprivation his friend Hartmann was passing a varied existence in the town to which he had been sent when they separated at Tomsk. He was under the same restrictions as those which controlled the movements and occupations of the administrative exiles whose condition we have studied, with the difference that his ispravnik was an intelligent and humane man, and not a brute and scoundrel like the one who sent Dr. Shulmann to prison for an act of humanity, and secured Ivan's banishment to a sub-Arctic village of aboriginals in the manner described.

There were about twenty-five political exiles residing in the town, all of whom had been sent to Siberia without trial for terms varying from three to six years. They had not been charged with anything more serious than "untrustworthiness;" one was a friend of a man who had been found to have a copy of a contraband book in his possession; another had asked at a booksellers for a volume that had recently been placed under the ban of the censor, though it had formerly been allowed; a third was the younger brother of a man who had given a copy of *The Will of the People* to a police spy; a fourth was acquainted with somebody who was under surveillance, and a fifth was the owner of a house which he rented to a provision-dealer, who was afterwards said to be intimate with members of the revolutionary party. Several were in total ignorance of the causes which brought them to Siberia; they had repeatedly asked what were the charges against them, but had been unable to find out.

Some of the exiles received money from their friends, others were able to earn something through the kindness of the ispravnik, who permitted them to engage in occupations which were really prohibited by the Code. They were allowed to teach music, drawing, arithmetic, grammar and other matters that would not trench upon politics, provided there was always some one present to bear witness that there was nothing seditious in the instruction they gave. History and geography they were forbidden to teach, and the same rule applied to political economy and certain branches of natural and other philosophy.

Several exiles supported themselves by manual labor, in addition to receiving the monthly allowance of six rubles from the government, a sum that was totally inadequate to their wants. There were two young married women who accompanied their husbands into exile, two others were married women who had themselves been exiled, and in the same category were two girls, each under eighteen years of age, who had been sent to Siberia from the boarding-schools where they were being educated. What a frail structure must be the empire of the Czar, when it is imperilled by two school-girls yet in their teens!

At the suggestion of Hartmann, the exiles asked and obtained permission to cultivate a piece of government land just outside the town, and as he knew more about the practical work of the farmer than did any one else of the party, he was made the chief. The farm more than realized their expectations; they produced considerable quantities of garden vegetables, which they sold in the market-place or utilized for their own tables, and they had a goodly sized field of grain. Altogether, their lot was an easy one compared with that of many other exile communities; they were on the best of terms with their ispravnik, gave him no trouble whatever, and did not need to be watched. They gave him their word of honor that they would not take advantage of his leniency to run away; he accepted their promise, and only required that they should report in person twice each week at the bureau of the police. Even this regulation was not really enforced, as he occasionally dropped in upon them when they were assembled in the evening, and allowed them to consider this call as the equivalent of a personal report at the bureau.

They were allowed to receive books from their friends in European Russia, provided, of course, they were such as had been approved by the censor; they clubbed their books together, and with the addition of some that had belonged to former exiles, and some that were presented by the officials or residents of the town, the Exiles Library numbered nearly three hundred volumes. Among the works in the library were Darwin's Descent of Man, Shakespeare's plays, novels by various American, English, French and German authors, Macauley's History of England, Grote's History of Greece, and several histories of Russia by native authors. More than half the number of books were in Russian, but all the principal languages of Europe were represented.

The exiles had little use for the Underground Mail, as their letters were not under rigid surveillance either going or coming, but occasionally they wished to write about matters that they were not willing to pass under an official eye, no matter how friendly it might be. At such times they had recourse to the 'Underground,' and their communications came and went safely. They had not been required to make any promise concerning their correspondence, and therefore were violating no stipulation.

But this comparatively Arcadian form of banishment could not last. In some way news was conveyed to the authorities at St. Petersburg that the kind-hearted ispravnik was robbing exile of its terrors, and turning it into something actually enviable. This was contrary to the will of the Czar and his ministry, and forthwith an order was issued for the removal of the ispravnik to a place where there were no exiles, and the appointment of one who would take care that the law was properly enforced.

CHAPTER XXIX.

A CHANGE OF RULERS.

The blow fell without a moment's warning. One day a new ispravnik arrived and exhibited his commission to him of the tender heart, together with an order for the latter to leave as soon as he could close his affairs, and proceed to take possession of his new post.

The new arrival was to assume command immediately, and he did so within twenty hours of his arrival. The rumor quickly spread among the exiles, and they were greatly alarmed on hearing it. That evening they met at the house where four of them lived, and it will readily be understood that the change which was likely to affect them very deeply, was the only subject of conversation.

Their forebodings were gloomy, as they knew that their ispravnik was of a type not often found in Siberia. They surmised that the removal had been made on account of his kindness to them, and this thought touched them to the heart.

While they were discussing his merits, and hoping, though against hope, that his successor might resemble him, there was a knock at the door. It announced the coming of their friend, whose sorrow was as great as theirs at being obliged to go away. But military orders, the world over, leave no discretion to him who is ordered, and it was idle to think of securing a modification of the action of the government.

"I come to say farewell," said he, " and before leaving, I want to express my appreciation of your uniformly good conduct. I believed that you were honorable men and women; the extent of your complicity in political troubles was no affair of mine; but, whatever views you may entertain on the subject of the government of Russia, does not debar you from being honest and upright. I have sought to treat you kindly, trust to your honor, and do everything in my power to enable you to support yourselves. I shall give you a thoroughly good character to my successor, and hope he will continue the policy which I have found so satisfactory."

Then one of his auditors spake a few words of farewell, which drew tears from nearly all eyes in the room. Everyone realized that he was saying good-bye to one who had shown himself their friend, although he had not the slightest trace of sympathy with revolutionary ideas, and his loyalty to the imperial crown could not be questioned.

With a warm clasp of the hand for each one of that sorrowing party, the ispravnik left the house and returned to his own residence. The next morning he was the ispravnik of —— no longer.

He kept his promise to the exiles by giving them a thoroughly good character to his successor. He told how he had treated them, how they had acted with most scrupulous honor in all their relations with him, how they were liked by the citizens, and the enterprise they had shown in various ways.

"Should you carry out the same policy," said he, in

closing, "I am entirely sure that you will never regret it. It will save you a great deal of trouble in governing them, to have them do the most of the governing, so far as they are concerned, without requiring any help from you."

The other made a non-committal reply, and said he could not settle upon any policy until he thoroughly understood the situation. But, for the present, he would leave matters unchanged, or, at any rate, as far as he could do so consistent with the orders he had received.

He did leave them unchanged—for a whole week. The exiles began to believe that they would really be allowed to live as before, and that their forebodings were idle. They were congratulating themselves to this effect, when one day they received notice that the regulations concerning persons living in administrative exile would be rigidly enforced. No exile would be allowed to give instruction of any kind, and therefore they must abandon the lessons which were bringing them remuneration. Those that were cultivating government land must abandon that employment, and if they wished to labor as agriculturists, they must hire themselves to peasants who might need their services. The cultivation of land as a speculative enterprise, such as they had undertaken, was nowhere sanctioned by the Code, and must be given up at once.

Sad was the meeting of the exiles on the evening after the promulgation of this order, and it was rendered doubly sad by reason of the buoyant hopes they had entertained, when an entire week elasped without any intimation of a change in their situation.

It was evident that the new ispravnik intended to construe the Code against the exiles, rather than in their favor, when there was any opportunity for doubt.

Their former ruler had said, "You can do anything that you are not forbidden to do, and you may do some forbidden things, provided you do them in such a way as to leave no possibility for harm." The new ruler said substantially, "You can do nothing that is not specially sanctioned by the Code; wherever it is silent upon any point, you are prohibited."

They addressed a respectful letter to the ispravnik, in which they referred to his predecessor regarding their conduct; they called attention to the manner in which they had given instruction so that, supposing them to have been disposed to evil, they were powerless to commit any wrong. They referred to the cultivation of the land and said they had carefully read the regulations and could not find that it was forbidden. They prayed to be allowed to continue in the same occupations as before, and promised that they would guarantee, each for all and all for each, that the most perfect order and obedience would prevail among them.

The letter was returned to them with the word "Impertinent" written in large letters across its face.

From this time on their existence was one of misery. The ispravnik exercised his ingenuity to devise means to make their life wretched by humiliating them as much as possible. They were ordered to report to the police twice every day; they were visited at all hours of the night; were forbidden to have curtains upon their windows, so that the officers or soldiers might be able to look in at any time they chose; and they were obliged to account for every hour of their time whenever the ispravnik chose to ask them what they were doing. The sleeping-rooms of the women were not exempt from intrusion on the part of the officers; several times, when the young girls that have been referred to came home from calling on other exiles, they found some of the ispravnik's officers asleep on their beds, and similar insults were offered to the two married women, whose husbands were not with them.

"They required our neighbors to keep an eye upon us," said Hartmann, "and to report all our movements. Not content with this, the officers and soldiers listened at our doors, looked in at our windows, both day and night, and occasionally they posted sentinels with orders to allow no one to enter or leave the house until morning. When several of us met together to spend the evening we would find ourselves compelled to stay all night, and during our absence from our quarters they were carefully searched.

"If the searches had been decently conducted, they would have not been of serious consequence, setting aside the humiliation of our being thus under surveillance. But it seemed as though the police were instructed to make the searches as troublesome as they could, for they overturned everything, scattered our books and other belongings on the floor, tore open every parcel, upset our beds, and left the place in as much confusion as though it had been visited by burglars with plenty of time at their disposal. At nearly every visit we missed some trifling things, trifling in themselves, but very dear to us, who had so little that we could call our own."

Under these circumstances, the exiles determined to send a petition to the governor of the province, setting forth the conditions under which they were living, and asking that they should be relieved from the petty annoyances that have been mentioned. They repeated the guarantees they had already offered to the ispravnik, and referred to the fact that his predecessor had never found occasion to complain of them or place them under punishment.

While they are waiting his response to their appeal, we will return to the mines at Kara. We will remark that the governor's reply gave them no opportunity to hope for an improvement in their condition.

Soon after the hunger strike among the men came to an end, the women convicts (all politicals) were transferred to a prison several miles away. They were marched out early one morning, after a notice of only a few minutes, barely sufficient to enable them to pack up the few trifles and comforts in their possession. The wind from the North was bitterly cold, and when they reached their destination, some of them were more dead than alive.

They had hoped that the prison to which they were sent would be more comfortable than the one they left behind, but great was their disappointment when they found it worse. The floors were rotten and broken, the walls were dripping wet and covered here and there with thick mildew, the place swarmed with vermin, and the space allotted to the prisoners was smaller than in the other prison. Some of the women sat down and cried in true feminine fashion, or threw themselves on the dirty platforms, and vented their grief in loud lamentations. But others set their teeth firmly in their despair, and gave an example for the others, by enduring, without a murmur, what was forced upon them.

The food supplied to the prisoners was in keeping with their surroundings; it was scanty in quantity, wretched in quality, and very badly prepared. The service of the prison was performed by soldiers, who could enter the kameras at any time without warning. To the credit of the soldiers be it said, they were less rude than the officers who commanded them, and very often showed that their lack of education and their rough exterior, had not deprived them of sympathy for the unfortunates under their charge.

A few days after their arrival at the prison, the women were notified that they must lay aside their own garments, which they had been permitted to wear, and return to the costume of convicts.

Some of the women were so ill that they were unable to stand, others did not believe the order would be enforced, and therefore did not make the change when the convict clothing was brought to them. Their conduct was considered rebellious, and the commandant proceeded to measures that would reduce them to submission.

CHAPTER XXX.

A WOMAN FLOGGED TO DEATH.

About nine o'clock one evening the kameras of the women were entered by several soldiers, under the command of a lieutenant. Several of the women were asleep, and nearly all were lying on the sleeping-platforms; some in their night clothing, others in their own day garments, and two or three in the prison garb, which they had donned in obedience to orders.

Those who had put on the convict dress were told to remain where they were; the others were ordered to rise and deliver up their own clothing at once.

Several obeyed, as they saw that resistance would be useless; some cried and became hysterical, and others did not move, either on account of their inability to stand or out of a determination not to submit to the humiliation.

"Come!" said the officer; "there must be no further nonsense. Unless you get up at once, you'll be helped."

"Leave us for ten minutes," said one of the women, "and give us the chance to make the change."

"Not a minute or a second," was the gruff reply. "Get up at once!"

[293]

No one moved. Then the lieutenant took a list from his pocket and read four names of prisoners who were under the surgeon's care and against whom the order would not be immediately enforced. There remained three who refused to don the prison-dress in the presence of the officer and soldiers, though they all said they would do so if left alone until morning.

Refusal to obey a specific order of this kind was "mutinous conduct" and could not be permitted with safety to the imperial dynasty. Then the officer proceeded to do as he had been instructed.

At his command two of the soldiers seized one of the women by the arms, dragged her to her feet and into the passage-way outside of the kamera. She was clad only in her night-dress; her own clothing had been spread above her, and it dropped to the floor as she was lifted up.

"Take her to the commandant's room," the officer ordered.

The woman screamed, but no heed was paid to her screaming. She was dragged, wearing only her night-gown, along the corridor and into the commandant's office. The lieutenant followed with the rest of the soldiers, and as he entered the presence of his superior, he made a military salute and signified that he had followed his instructions.

The woman's only garment was then stripped from her by the soldiers and a convict's dress was thrown over her shoulders. She struggled and resisted, but her strength was nothing compared to that of the Cossacks who were doing the bidding of the brute wearing epaulettes, the commandant or director of the prison.

"How many more have you who refuse?" queried the commandant.

"Two," answered his subordinate, again making the military salute.

"Take this one back and bring them along," was the order which followed. "We'll have no more sentimental nonsense about this business."

The lieutenant departed to carry out his instructions. By the time he reached the kamera the other women had donned the prison costume, knowing that unless they did so, they would be submitted to the same outrage as the one they had just witnessed.

Bear in mind that these prisoners were not untutored savages, accustomed to scanty apparel and having very crude notions in regard to modesty. All were refined women of good families, well educated, accustomed to good society in European Russia, gentle in birth and breeding, and with sensibilities of the highest type. Two were the wives of officers in the army, two were the wives of lawyers, one was the daughter of a prominent physician in Moscow, and another the daughter of a wealthy merchant of Odessa. One had trod the boards of the imperial opera-house as a prima donna of song, another bore a high reputation as a soubrette, and others were school-teachers, thoroughly educated for the duties of their profession. These were the women who were treated by brutal soldiers in the manner described!

Madame Soluzeff, the victim of this official outrage, was dragged back to her kamera and flung senseless on the sleeping-bench whence she had been taken. All night she lay in a swoon, out of which she was occasionally roused only to scream hysterically and swoon again. Her grief-stricken companions endeavored to soothe her, but without avail. In the morning she recovered and began to talk incoherently, and it was soon apparent to her friends that her mind had given way under the terrible strain.

The doctor was called, and after hearing the account of how she had passed the night, he administered an opiate. Under its influence she fell off into a heavy sleep; he came again at noon, administered another dose of the same drug, and said he thought that when she recovered from its effect her mind would be in its proper state.

His prognostication was incorrect. She did not recover; her intellect was blotted out forever, and her physical system had undergone such a shock that she was unable to rise to her feet. She was carried to the hospital, and four days later was a corpse. Doubtless the protectors of the imperial throne breathed more freely when they learned that Madame Soluzeff, exiled for life because she was a member of a " Circle for Self-Instruction," where liberal views were occasionally discussed, was no more.

In the kamera with Madame Soluzeff at the time the order to don the apparel of the convict was issued, there was a married woman named Shihida. She was twenty-seven years of age, a vivacious, excitable and withal a brilliant personage, the daughter of a merchant of Taganrog. Her education took place at the gymnasium in that city, and after passing the examinations with high honors she became a school-teacher in Taganrog. One who knew her describes her as a brunette of medium size, with a thoroughly Russian physiognomy, and a pair of large black eyes that fascinated every one with their powers of penetration and the look of intelligence which lay within them. The same friend says she was so excitable in her character that she was often called a bundle of nerves; she was an idealist who demanded the most unswerving adherence to principle, and would allow no excuse for a deviation from it. And this adhesion to principle she demanded in the most trivial matters as well as in affairs of the greatest importance; whenever a promise of any kind was broken, she accepted no explanation and never granted forgiveness.

Such a woman is certain to have possessed liberal ideas, and it is no surprise that she fell under suspicion and was sent to Siberia, because of her frankly avowed belief that the affairs of the empire required improvement. She was transported to the Kara gold mines, whence she would be sent to the North as a forced colonist at the expiration of her term of penal servitude.

When the order to don the prison clothing was issued, she was one of the first to refuse, and she persisted in her refusal up to the time when Madame Soluzeff was dragged out in the manner we have described. She was one of the two who was left behind by the lieutenant, and it was only by the earnest entreaties of her companions that she was induced to put on the hated garments. She did so under protest, and declared that she would not wear them many days. What her plan was she refused to say, but bided her time for action.

A few days later she violated one of the minor rules of the prison, and was taken to the office of the commandant for reprimand and punishment. While the commandant was reprimanding her, and using most abusive language, she stepped suddenly in front of him and slapped him in the face.

She expected to be hanged for this infraction of discipline, and had evidently planned her action with deliberation, though some of her friends think she struck the officer under an impulse of indignation at his insults. The commandant was determined not to let her off by the usual method of execution, but ordered that she should be flogged. He sentenced her to receive one hundred blows of the plet, "humane" substitute of the Russians for the knout.

She was sent to a solitary cell and not allowed to communicate with her companions. The next day the flogging took place in the prison-yard. A woman was flogged with the plet by command of an officer of the imperial forces of Russia, in his presence and in that of the other officers of the garrison.

No, all the other officers were not present. The prison surgeon would not certify that Madame Shihida was in proper physical condition to enable her to be flogged without danger to life, and when told that the flogging would take place without his professional certificate, he refused to be present. The commandant threatened to place him under arrest, but he persisted and said he would prefer to be court-martialed for disobedience of orders, rather than appear to sanction the affair by witnessing it.

Madame Shihida was brought to the commandant's office from the cell where she had passed the night alone. She was weak from the poor food and the wretched conditions under which she had been living, but her step was firm and she offered no resistance until the soldiers began stripping the clothing from her back; then she struggled and resisted, she fought with all the strength of desperation, but was soon overpowered and her body was bared to the waist.

Her long black hair streamed loosely down her

shoulders as she was half led and half carried by two Cossacks from the office of the commandant to the prison-yard, where the soldiers and officers were drawn up in line to witness one of the most revolting spectacles known to this last half of the nineteenth century.

In the centre of the square of soldiers a blanket had been spread on the ground. On this blanket the woman was thrown, face downward; four soldiers held her limbs to prevent her struggling, a fifth held her head, and then the commandant gave the order for the executioner to begin.

The supple birch cut a deep furrow into the tender flesh at the first blow, and as each stroke fell, other furrows were made, until the woman's back was a mass of gore. The flesh quivered, the body shuddered convulsively, and the first half-dozen blows were followed by screams from the victim, who could not unflinchingly endure the horrible pain. But after a short time she was silent, and with good reason, for she had fainted, and was no longer aware of the punishment she was receiving.

The hundred blows were given, and then the executioner stayed his hand. The insensible body was lifted to a stretcher, a cloak was thrown over it, and the men carried the burden to the hospital. The surgeon did all in his power to restore Madame Shihida to consciousness, but his efforts were of no avail.

The flogging took place on Wednesday morning. She never recovered from the shock, though she continued to live until Friday morning, when her last breath was drawn. She found the death that she deliberately sought, though not in the form in which she sought it.

When her fate became known among her late companions in misery, four of them committed suicide by poison. Two others took poison with the same intent, but were saved through the efforts of the surgeons.

Then the women organized a hunger strike which lasted seventeen days. During the last days of the strike they were saved from death by the forcible administration of food by the surgeons, but they persistently refused to take food voluntarily, until the odious edict forbidding them to wear their own clothing was recalled.

Of course the report of the occurrences in the women's prison was carried to the male prisoners very speedily. It caused great excitement and indignation, and the anger of the men ran to such a height that some lost control over themselves and attacked their guards. An attack upon the guards could hardly terminate other than in defeat, as it was without any preparation or previous plan, and was made under excitement. Some were shot down, and the rest were pounded with the butt ends of rifles, stabbed with bayonets, or otherwise subdued. The "boont," or insurrection, was soon over, and the commandant telegraphed an exaggerated account of it to his superiors, in which he represented it to be an affair that was long contemplated, and prepared for.

In consequence of the "insurrection" the draft for the Free Command was stopped, and orders came to the commandant to distribute the political prisoners in small parties among the gangs of criminal convicts in the various mines of the Kara district.

The command was carried out, and brutally, too. The next morning the prisoners were ordered out before breakfast and immediately marched away in leg-fetters to their destination. They protested against the cruelty of compelling them to go on the road without food, and asked the commander of their escort to allow them to rest on the way long enough to obtain and eat something. This request was refused, and the men were prodded with the bayonets of their guards. This angered them so, that they picked up stones and attacked the soldiers. As might be expected, the latter made quick use of their weapons, shooting two or three of the prisoners and knocking down others who resisted. Further resistance was rendered impossible by tying every prisoner's hands behind his back, and in this plight they finished their journey. Starving, bruised, bleeding, and weary, they reached their destinations among the criminal convicts.

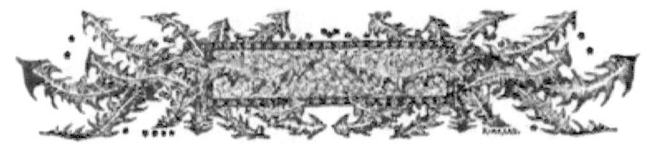

CHAPTER XXXI.

ASSASSINATION OF THE GOVERNOR.

Pushkin and Dubayeff were among the cooler-headed prisoners who saw the futility of resistance, and they took no part in the demonstrations at the prison or on the road. But they did not escape without injury, as Dubayeff was one of those knocked down with the butt of a rifle, while Pushkin received a bullet that was intended for another prisoner. Fortunately for him, his wound was slight and confined to the flesh, so that it healed in a few days. Dubayeff's injury was more severe, but he, too, recovered, and was able to take his place among his companions.

For some eight or ten weeks the prisoners were held under "dungeon conditions," as a punishment for their resistance to the cruelty of their guards, and no distinction was made among them. Those who had taken no part in the affair were treated in the same way as the others, but they were too honorable to make any complaint, lest it might cause greater inhumanity to be shown towards the active participants in the "boont."

When a prisoner is under dungeon conditions he is placed in solitary confinement, and allowed no luxuries or privileges whatever. We have seen what dungeon conditions are in the prisons of European Russia;

they are very much the same in Siberia, but if there is any difference, it is against the Siberian prisons, which are not as well built as those of the older part of the empire.

It happened that Pushkin and Dubayeff occupied contiguous cells in the prison to which they were assigned, and as both know the knock alphabet, they were able to communicate with each other. This was their only resource for beguiling the long days, as they were not permitted to have books or writing materials, could not walk in the yard, and were rarely allowed to pass beyond the boundaries of their cells. Whenever they were taken out, it was for the purpose of examining the cells to make sure that no preparations had been made for escape. They were obliged to exercise great caution in communicating by means of the knock alphabet, as their discovery in using it would have led to a change of their cells.

Scurvy broke out among the prisoners, whose food consisted only of rye bread and water, with an occasional allowance of thin soup with boiled barley. The disease was so prevalent among them, that the commandant of the prison became alarmed, and ordered the men to be collected in one of the prisons, where they were placed in kameras and supplied with more nourishing food. Several of the worst cases were sent to the hospital, and two men never recovered. The prisoners asked that their money, which was in the hands of the authorities, should be expended in buying things that were greatly needed by the sick; but the request went unheeded. While living in dungeon conditions, they had no beds or bedding, but when scurvy became so prevalent, they were allowed thin mattresses of straw, which they spread upon the sleeping-benches.

In spite of the vigilance with which they were watched the unfortunates managed to keep up communication with the outside world, through the aid of such of their guards as were corruptible. Any intelligence obtained by one was shared with all, and thus the knock alphabet performed an important service while they were under dungeon conditions. After the return to the kameras the necessity of communication by sound was removed.

In corresponding with their friends in the Free Command the prisoners used the checker-board cipher, which has been elsewhere described. Nothing was ever written in plain language, lest it might fall into the hands of the authorities, and as the key to the code was frequently changed, the possession of a message in cipher would do the authorities very little good.

The guards had various ways of concealing the missives intrusted to them. The letters were nearly always enclosed in bread pills; the guards concealed these pills in their hair, in their garments or boots, or wherever else they could find a secure place. There was one soldier who had a very capacious mouth, garnished with teeth proportioned to the size of the buccal orifice, and he was one of the most successful mail carriers of which the place could boast. One of his teeth was hollow, and the cavity was of a size sufficient to take in a bread pill of liberal dimensions. He utilized this hollow to advantage, and though he suffered occasionally from toothache, he never went to the surgeon or dentist for relief, lest the pulling or filling of the tooth would deprive him of an important vehicle of transport.

He would come into the kamera with one or more of his fellows, and drop the pill at the feet of a prisoner without being observed by his comrades, although they might have their eyes on him all the time.

One evening, when he came with others to shut up the prisoners for the night, he signified that he had a letter for them. While the verification was going on he dropped the pill on the floor, and as soon as the men were left to themselves they picked it up and proceeded to decipher the communication it contained.

The message was brief but of great importance. It consisted of the following words:

"Governor killed yesterday by Vera Paskovitch."

The governor of the province was a brute, and all rejoiced to hear of his death. But what of Vera Paskovitch, and how did she accomplish it?

"They will be more strict with us than ever," said Dubayeff, "and it may be some time before we can get the particulars."

"Yes," replied Pushkin, "but they must rack their ingenuity to invent a new torture."

"Vera is a saint," remarked another. "She has done a noble work, and will probably be hanged or flogged to death for it."

"Let us hope she escaped," said Pushkin. "We will offer thanks to God, and pray for the poor girl's escape."

All assented to the proposal, though a considerable number of the prisoners were quite indifferent on the subject of religion, or anything relating to it. Some were skeptical to the last degree, and said they saw no use in a deity who would allow them to endure everything they were undergoing, solely because of their difference of opinion with the authorities at St. Petersburg. But in this instance, they set aside their unbelief, and joined as fervently as the rest in a prayer for the deliverance from peril, of the girl who had rid them of one of their persecutors.

As Dubayeff predicted, it was several days before they learned the full story of the death of the governor of the province in which the Kara mines are situated.

Vera Paskovitch had been sent to Siberia for fifteen years as a punishment for being a member of a secret society which had for its object the establishment of a parliament, or National assembly, in Russia. She had served her probationary term in prison, then lived in the Free Command for a time, and on the expiration of her term there, she was sent to a small town in the Trans-Baikal province, to live as a colonist.

Miss Paskovitch had suffered much during her imprisonment, and passed through two hunger strikes in as many penal establishments ; her guards had robbed her of what money she possessed at different times, and her treatment on several occasions was similar to that of the women in the political prison at Kara.

In the village to which she was assigned, she heard about the flogging and death of Madame Shihida, and of the sufferings of the other women in the same prison. Brooding on these horrible occurrences she determined to assassinate the governor, whom she regarded as the cause of the greater part of this brutality. She reasoned that his death at her hands would call attention to the condition of the Siberian prisons, and though she expected to be hanged for her crime, she did not hesitate a moment in carrying it out.

She confided her purpose to no one. Her first step was to buy a pistol, and this was by no means easy. It is necessary for any one who wishes to carry fire-arms in Siberia to have a permit from the police to do so, and such a permit could never be obtained by a young woman living under exile conditions. She went to a criminal colonist in the town, and asked if he could buy a pistol for her.

"Perhaps I can," was his guarded reply, "but what do you want it for?"

"I want it to scare away thieves from the house where I live," she answered.

"Have you been troubled by them?" he asked, in a tone of surprise.

"Yes," she answered, "twice within the month they have tried to get into the house, but have been scared away by the big dog at our neighbor's. I'm afraid they'll come again and so I want a pistol. What they could find to steal I cannot imagine, as there's nothing in the house worth taking away."

"That's what I was thinking, myself," said the ex-criminal, who had doubtless done some stealing on his own account before coming to Siberia. Like most men in his profession he always took good care to know that there was something worth having before he entered a house or assaulted a traveller.

"I'll get you a pistol," he said, after a pause, " but it will cost ten rubles."

She agreed to the price and soon had the pistol in her possession. It was a very common affair, worth not more than two or three rubles, but forbidden goods cost dear in any part of the world.

Vera obtained permission of the police to visit a friend in a village some twenty versts away and spend a fortnight with her. But instead of going to the village, she made the best of her way to Nertchinsk, intending to proceed thence to Chita, the provincial capital, where the governor lived. She learned on reaching Nertchinsk that the governor was then on a visit to Kara, and would remain two or three days at the town on his return.

The girl concluded to wait for his arrival, but had considerable difficulty in evading the police. She found some administrative exiles living in the town, and through their aid she was concealed. She did not reveal to these people the object of her visit, lest they might try to dissuade her.

The governor came at the time designated and was the object of much attention on the part of the citizens. She sought an audience with him in order to present a petition of some peasant women who had been evicted from their houses by a wealthy landowner, and felt that the case should be laid before the governor by one of their number. She enacted her *rôle* to perfection ; her dress was of the coarsest description and her manner was that of a peasant girl who had never yet looked upon a governor except at a distance. The governor's adjutant had no suspicions of her object or he would have caused her to be searched ; moreover, he knew that the governor had a favorable eye for pretty girls, and Vera Paskovitch possessed a very attractive face.

Several citizens were in the audience-room when she entered, timid and shrinking, and hesitated near the door. After disposing of the cases to which he was listening, His Excellency turned to the new visitor, and said :

" Well, my pretty girl, what do you want ?"

The girl was standing with the pistol concealed in her handkerchief and ready cocked. As she stood full in front of him, she raised the weapon and discharged it at his breast, saying, as she did so :

" Remember Kara !"

"НЕМЕМНЕН КАRА!"—*See Page* 308

Died in 1792

The bystanders rushed forward to seize and disarm her, but it was too late. The bullet had done its work and the governor was fatally wounded. He died the next day, and but for the opiates administered by the surgeon he would have suffered great pain previous to his death.

Miss Paskovitch was taken immediately to the prison and thrown into a solitary cell. A few days later she was carried under a strong guard to Chita, where her trial was ordered to take place before a military court some three or four months later.

While awaiting her trial she was kept in a " secret " cell, which the other occupants of the prison said was a cruel place to shut a dog in. It was not more than six feet square and as many in height; it had no windows, and the only place where light and air could enter, was through a hole about ten inches square in the door. The room had not been swept or cleaned for years, and contained not a single article of furniture; there was no bedding, and when she asked for a truss of straw to lie upon, she was told that there was no straw for murderers.

How she lived during these three months under such conditions one can hardly comprehend; she must have possessed great vitality to endure so long. But endure she did, and in due time she was brought before the military court, which quickly condemned her to be hanged.

An effort was made to show that her act was part of a plot, and it was quite natural that the government officials should suspect the existence of a widespread scheme.

She was promised leniency if she would reveal the extent of the plot and name the conspirators in it, and especially the one who suggested the murder of the governor.

"There is no plot," she replied, "and there are no conspirators. I alone planned what I have done, and no one knew anything about it but myself."

"What was your motive?" the presiding officer asked. "Had the governor wronged you?"

"I never saw the governor before," she replied, "and have no knowledge that he ever knew my name. He may have seen it in a list of prisoners, but that is all."

"Then why did you select him as the mark of your pistol?"

"In order that the attention of Russia, and the whole world, might be drawn to the sufferings of the men and women now imprisoned in this province, to whom death would be a blessing, far better than life as they find it. I believe that when the rest of the empire knows of the wrongs that are perpetrated in Siberia there will be a change for the better. I gladly give my life for the good of those whom I leave behind me."

The decree was entered that see be hanged a month after the trial. She was sent back to her miserable cell, and at the end of the month was told that in view of her youth and sex, the sentence had been commuted to imprisonment for life. She refused to take food from the time this announcement was made, and died not long afterwards.

How widely the knowledge of her act, and the causes that led to it, became known in the empire, is difficult to say. These matters are not published in the newspapers, as they do not meet the approval of the censor, and the only way they can reach the public is through repetition from one person to another, or through manuscript accounts which circulate surreptitiously. It is fair to say that the readers of the *London Times*, and of daily newspapers generally throughout the world, have a better knowledge of the political and social troubles of Russia than the majority of the people whose whole lives have been spent there. It is emphatically the case with Russians, that they must go from home to hear the news.

In the prisons at Kara it was an anxious time as from day to day, or at irregular intervals, they learned the details of the dramatic act of Vera Paskovitch, her imprisonment, trial and sentence, and the commutation that was given by the government in its great clemency. Then a little later they learned that she was dead and the circumstances under which she died.

The reader will ask if the death of the governor resulted in any amelioration of the condition of the prisoners.

Yes, that was the result, though not directly due to intent on the part of any one in particular. The removal, by death or otherwise, of a high official the world over, generally causes many changes in the list of his subordinates. It was so in the present instance, and the commandant at the prison where Pushkin and Dubayeff were confined, was relieved of his duties and sent elsewhere. His successor was a more humane man, perhaps we should say he was less a brute, and consequently the prisoners were gainers by the change.

Most of their old privileges were restored, one by one, and they were looking forward to the time when they would be allowed to live in the Free Command preparatory to being sent to settle as colonists. The new commandant acquainted himself with the history of the so-called insurrection; though he expressed no opinion, it was evident that he did not hold his predecessor altogether blameless for its occurrence.

There was little difficulty in holding communication with their friends outside, as the guards were not closely watched and the hollow tooth was no longer needed. Short letters, and sometimes long ones, were sent or received, and the prisoners were fairly well informed concerning the world from which they were so completely secluded.

One day there came a letter which told of occurrences in other parts of Siberia. It was in cipher, like all the contraband letters, and as it was slowly reduced, sentence by sentence, to intelligible language, those who heard it realized that after all theirs was not the only place where brutes rule over men and the feelings of humanity are known only to those who suffer.

Dubayeff and Pushkin stood with their hands linked together as the translators spelled out the words and composed the sentences that made up the communication. Dubayeff whispered to his friend that the letter deserved to be written in blood, to which Pushkin made no response other than a feeble nod.

When the end was reached, the man who translated it said that the original, from which this account had been abridged, was written in the blood of one of the victims of the tragedy which was described. Dubayeff shuddered and turned pale when he heard this, and thought of the words he had spoken a few minutes before.

CHAPTER XXXII.

THE MASSACRE AT YAKUTSK.

The tragedy referred to in the preceding chapter occurred in Yakutsk, the chief town of the province of the same name. It is a place of about five thousand inhabitants, in latitude 62° 1′ North, and has the reputation of being the coldest town of its size on the face of the globe. Its mean annual temperature is a trifle above thirteen degrees; in winter the thermometer has remained sixty degrees below zero for weeks together, while in summer the earth thaws only a few inches below the surface. At the beginning of winter, those of the inhabitants who cannot afford glass windows make use of thin sheets of ice as a substitute, and the cold is so intense and sustained, that there is not often any occasion for renewing the frozen panes during the entire season.

The inhospitable climate of Yakutsk, and the hardships of existence there, make the place attractive in the eyes of the Exile Administration of Russia. The province annually receives many exiles, some of whom are sent to reside in the town just mentioned, while the rest are scattered over the vast province, which extends to the shores of the Arctic Ocean. Yakutsk is one of the oldest towns in Siberia; it existed before Irkutsk was founded, and its ruined fort can boast an age of two centuries. The town is a conglomeration of native yourts and Russian houses, and its largest building is a stone cathedral, which reflects great credit upon its builders, when its locality is considered. About one-half the inhabitants are Russians and the rest aboriginal Yakuts. Throughout the province the aboriginals are far more numerous than their conquerors, with whom they have long lived on terms of perfect friendship.

At the time of which we write, the prison of Yakutsk, an edifice scarcely less noticeable than the cathedral, was crowded with exiles sentenced to perpetual banishment in that rigorous region. The greater number of them were politicals, of the same class as those we have seen at the Kara mines, and they had been waiting for the order for their distribution among the villages where they were to reside. The general conditions of the prison of Yakutsk were so much like those we have alrerdy seen, that they do not merit a special description. Suffice it is to say that all the exiies were quite ready to be sent to their destinations, as they realized they could hardly be worse off in their new homes, and would certainly have the advantages of pure air and exercise.

In one part of the prison were thirty politicals, who had been there for several months. Ordinarily, they had the privilege of being together in one of the kameras, but for the slightest infraction of the rules, and not infrequently upon the mere caprice of their custodians, they were separated and shut up in the "secret" cells for days or weeks at a time. An order came for the transportation of the thirty to a point further up the Lena, the river on whose banks Yakutsk is built. They were notified that they could be allowed no more than five pounds of baggage to each person, and no one would be permitted to have any money, either in his possession or in the hands of the officers of the convoy.

"When we received this notice," said the writer of the letter giving an account of the tragedy, "we drew up a petition to the governor, asking him to rescind the order, as it was simply impossible for us to exist on the government allowance. We explained that if the command should be enforced, not one of us would be able to live; it meant starvation for us all, though we said in our petition we did not suppose the government so intended it.

"Every prisoner in our company signed the petition, which we handed to the chief of police to give to the governor. The chief looked at the paper and handed it back to us; then he called his deputy, who ordered us into the yard and then took the petition to the governor.

"He came back in a little while and told us that our conduct was rebellious, and the governor had ordered us to be put in leg-fetters. The prison blacksmith came and ironed us, and then we were sent again into the prison. In about four hours we were ordered into the yard once more, where we found a strong force of police soldiers, commanded by a lieutenant.

"The police building is close to the general prison, and we were told that we were to go there, and then set out on our journey. Some of us protested, and said we wanted to wait in the yard until we had a final answer from the governor.

"The police lieutenant frowned and shouted:

"'What! you refuse to obey orders?'

"Then he said to his soldiers, 'Give it to them, boys!' and immediately the soldiers fired upon us, and followed up their volley with the use of the bayonet. We tried to break through the ranks, but could not, as we were impeded by our irons and hemmed in by the bayonets.

"In a few minutes the ground in the prison-yard was covered with dead and wounded prisoners. The noise of the firing brought the governor to the spot. Zotoff, one of our brave fellows, snatched a revolver from a soldier and tried to shoot the governor. Then the soldiers fired another volley at the prisoners, and Zotoff fell severely wounded among those already on the ground.

"Those whom the bullets and bayonets had spared were beaten with the butts of the rifles, so that not one of the thirty escaped injury. Bruised and bleeding all who could walk were driven into the prison building, the wounded who could not stand were carried to the hospital, and the dead were taken away for burial, or, at all events, they disappeared.

"One of our party, Bernstein, had been followed to Siberia by his wife, who lived outside in a house near the prison. Bernstein was wounded in the *melee*, and when his wife came into the yard and tried to reach him, to bind up his wounds, she was beaten by the soldiers, and next day she was flogged by the governor's order.

"Of our whole number of thirty, six were killed by bullets, bayonets, or beating, and nine are so badly wounded that they are in the hospital. Sophie Gurewitz is among the dead, killed by the thrust of a bayonet while she was on her knees begging for life; Anna Zoroastrova is one of the wounded, and she is not likely to recover.

"Next day we were brought up for trial in the prison-yard. You might suppose our trial would take considerable time, but it didn't. We were not allowed any defense, and the witnesses against us were the soldiers who had attacked us by order of the lieutenant of police. Here is the formality that each went through :

"'What is your name ?'

"'Nicolai Zotoff.'

"'What is your age ?'

"'Thirty-two.'

"'What is your religion ?'

"'The Greek Church.'

"'What defense have you to make ?'

"'What is the charge against me ?'

"'Armed rebellion against authority.'

"'What are the proofs against me ?'

"'You have already heard the proofs given by the witnesses who were present at the time.'

"'I deny that I made any rebellion, I had no arms and was assaulted by the soldiers.'

"'That is all you have to say. Stand aside. The next.'

"This was all the trial they gave us, and a week later they called us into the yard again to hear our sentences. Zotoff and Bernstein were sentenced to be hanged; Zotoff because he had fired a pistol at the governor, and the other because his name was first on the petition, and also because he resisted the attack of the soldiers. When the time came for the execution Zotoff was still in bed with his wounds, and we thought a respite would be given him until he could stand. But he had no respite; he was brought out on a stretcher and the noose was placed around his neck while he was held above the heads of four tall soldiers. When all was ready they dropped the stretcher, and the body of our poor friend hung in the air.

"The others were sentenced to hard labor in the mines for terms of ten, fifteen, or twenty years; four of them were women who had not lifted a hand in the fight, except to beg the soldiers to stop the shooting and stabbing. We are to be taken to the mines very soon, so they tell us, though some of the soldiers say the women and two or three of the men will be distributed as colonists among the Yakut villages to the north. It matters little what they do with us, as none are likely to live much longer.

"Just before Bernstein was taken to execution he was allowed to see the others, and give us his last message. As we shook hands and embraced, he said, 'May this last parting be lightened by hopes for a better future for our unhappy country. Never an atom of Nature's matter can be lost, and thus a human life sacrificed to-day will benefit those who yet live. Never grieve about the dead; you have a great, a living issue before you. Our sufferings will benefit humanity; we are suffering in behalf of a down-trodden people, and we die a sacrifice upon the altar of Liberty.'"

Bernstein and Zotoff were personally known to some of the prisoners at Kara. As the letter was read there was deep and audible sorrow on the part of the listeners, and especially of those to whom the victims of the massacre were more than mere names. It would have required little to raise a revolt then and there; so frenzied were the prisoners with what they had heard, that they were ready for anything, no matter how desperate or hopeless. Happily, no one suggested an insurrection, or volunteered to lead an assault upon the guards.

"After this," said Pushkin to Dubayeff, "I shall bear with less repining my imprisonment here. Bad as Kara has proved itself, it is not such a hell as Yakutsk."

"Yes," was the reply, "and the mystery I have mentioned heretofore rises again before me. If our masters seek our deaths, why do they not kill us at once instead of dragging us to Siberia and wearing out our lives in the way they do."

Similar comments were made among the other prisoners, and in the midst of their conversation on the subject the attendants came bringing the suppers for the occupants of the kamera. While they remained within hearing there was no allusion to the tragic news that had touched all hearts.

The reader doubtless wonders how such a letter as the foregoing was brought from Yakutsk. As before stated, the original communication was written in blood with a splinter of wood instead of a pen. The paper on which it appeared was smuggled into the prison by one of the soldiers, who subsequently carried the letter to an administrative exile living in the town of Yakutsk. The latter made several copies, and these he transmitted to exile friends in Irkutsk and Chita; their transit took a long time, as opportunities for sending by safe hand were rare and Yakutsk is more than two thousand miles from Irkutsk. The route follows the Lena; in summer navigation is by boats along the river, and in winter a road is kept open along the icy surface. There is little travel other than that of exiles and their convoys, and of the exiles who go there only a small proportion ever return to European Russia.

When these letters reached Irkutsk and Chita fresh copies were multiplied and sent wherever they could be conveyed. Some of them fell into official hands and were destroyed, but others reached their destinations. Considerable time was consumed, but in less than a year the details of the outrage were in every prison of

Siberia, and also of European Russia, and had been printed in the newspapers of the outside world. Try as best he may, the autocrat of all the Russias cannot suppress the spread of intelligence; if the spirit of the martyred Bernstein can visit this world, it will know that the story of that terrible tragedy has been spread far and wide.

The Russian censorship, with all its activity, is not able to suppress the circulation of forbidden literature. Manuscript stories are passed from hand to hand in the same way as printed books, and some manuscripts have had thousands of readers before they fell into official hands and were destroyed. In the meantime other copies were made, so that the destruction of one did not avail towards suppression of the works.

"At one time," said Dubayeff to Pushkin, when they were discussing the censorship, "I was employed in the office of a newspaper, and in this way I happened to know how the censor does his work. Everything has to pass under his eye, and his will is as autocratic as that of the Czar in regard to what shall not be published.

"The censor used to come to the office about eleven o'clock at night to look over the proof-slips of what had been written and put in type. He examined everything—editorials, news matters in and out of Russia, local happenings, advertisements, and even the notices of marriages and deaths. If anything seemed objectionable, he drew a line through it with red ink, and wrote the word "Forbidden" on the margin. Sometimes he blotted out entire articles, sometimes he destroyed a part of an article and allowed the rest to stand, and occasionally his objections related to only a few lines or words."

"What did you do when he destroyed only a part of an article?" Pushkin asked.

"If the article would be readable after the forbidden matter was left out," Dubayeff answered, "we patched it up and used it; but it very often happened that the matter was of no further use. In that case it was destroyed at once. Where changes were suggested, or a few lines taken out here and there, the article was returned to the man who wrote it, so that he could throw it into shape."

"It must have happened sometimes," Pushkin remarked, "that a great part of the work you had prepared was rejected. How did the paper fill its columns in that case?"

"That didn't give much trouble," was the reply. "We always had a large amount of what the printers call 'standing matter,' which had been approved by the censor, and when much of our work in a day was marked out, we fell back upon the reserved stock already in type. This consisted of stories, descriptive articles, editorials about feeding cattle, making roads, killing fleas on dogs, or other subjects that could not be regarded as breeders of discontent among the subjects of the Czar or 'prejudical to social order.'"

"Did the censor stay at the office till the paper went to press?"

"No, he went home after returning the proof-slips. After he had gone we couldn't insert a single item of news or an advertisement of a horse for sale or a cook wanting a situation. Nothing could go in the paper without the censor's approval, no matter what might be its importance.

"Treatment of this sort is very apt to give an editor a feeling of contempt for the government, and more.

than one who has started out on his career with the most unbounded loyalty has ended by becoming an advanced liberal and having his paper suppressed for 'untrustworthiness.' I've known several cases of exactly that sort.

"Sometimes they stop the circulation of a paper when everything in it has been approved by the censor. An official higher in authority discovers something wrong, and we get orders to stop the sale of copies and burn all we have on hand at the time. All copies that can be found are seized and destroyed, and the government rests in peace. The same thing happens with books, and whole editions have been officially burned after the censor had consented to their publication. But the books circulate in manuscript, and the ideas, aspirations, thoughts and hopes of the writers live and grow and have their effect."

The government endeavored by every means in its power to prevent the news of the massacre at Yakutsk, and the floggings at Kara, from reaching the outer world, as well as from their being known outside of the localities where they occurred. We have seen how its efforts were unsuccessful. Truth is mighty and will prevail.

One day a soldier, who came to aid in the "verification" of the number of prisoners, managed to intimate to Pushkin that he had a communication for him. He was unable to deliver it at the time, but during the course of the day the precious missive was placed in the prisoner's hands. It was in cipher, and he did not know the key-word. As he looked at the paper on which it was written, his heart sank within him, as he did not see how he would be able to ascertain its purport.

Dubayeff came to his aid with a practical suggestion.

"Can you tell by the shape of the letters, or any other indication, from whom this note has come?"

"I think it is from my son, but I don't know positively."

"Very well," Dubayeff responded. "Let us start with the supposition that he wrote it. What's his name?"

"Ivan. Ivan Carlovitch."

"All right. Let us try 'Ivan' and see how we come out. It's a custom we have where no key-word is understood between us, that we will use the first name of the writer.";

They made the trial and sure enough the guess was correct. "Ivan" was the key-word.

CHAPTER XXXIII.

AFFAIRS AT HOME.

Necessarily the letter was brief, as it was on a small scrap of paper and closely written on both sides. It gave Pushkin the first information that his son and his neighbor Hartmann had been exiled to Siberia, and it also contained news from home to the effect that his wife and children were deeply mourning his absence and lamenting the cruelties they knew he must be undergoing. There was also a hint that Alexei Hartmann was in St. Petersburg, endeavoring in some way to unravel the mystery which surrounded his family and that of the girl to whom he was betrothed.

Pushkin's joy at receiving news from his family was saddened by the knowledge that his son was, like himself, a forced inhabitant of Siberia, and, that his friend and neighbor, Hartmann, had suffered a similar misfortune. But he took consolation from the fact that they were not degraded and tortured by chains and the insults and cruelties of Kara, and, in comparing their condition with his, he felt that it would be the height of happiness if he could share his son's exile, and be relieved from the horrors of the Trans-Baikal province and its mines and prisons.

Happily for his peace of mind, he did know of Ivan's banishment to the Yakut village in the far north; the letter was written in the town where Ivan was living with Dr. Shulmann and other administrative exiles, before the exercise of " pernicious public activity " that led to his transfer to a far more inhospitable place.

All the night after receiving the letter Pushkin lay awake, pondering upon the varied misfortunes that had fallen upon himself and his family and friends. His conscience was deeply troubled to think that his neighbor, Hartmann, had suffered as we have seen, solely because he endeavored to aid one who was in trouble. Repeatedly he wept as he thought of this, and in the morning Dubayeff asked why his eyes were so red and what had caused his tears to flow.

Pushkin told him, whereupon Dubayeff said:

"Friendship in Russia is more dangerous than anywhere else in the world. Elsewhere it may possibly result in loss of social position, or of money, but this is about the worst that can befall us. Here, in Russia, it often means imprisonment, separation from family, home, and everything else that we prize, together with financial ruin, exile, years of suffering, and death at last. When we reflect upon what friendship may bring, we may well wonder why anybody ever allows himself to form an attachment for any one else, or to perform a single kindly act."

"Yes, you are right," replied Pushkin, "but on the other hand, should not our friendships be stronger than anywhere else in the world, for the reason that they are so much more precious? There is an old adage to the effect that 'What costs nothing is worth nothing;' surely that cannot be said of our friendships, when they cost us all so dearly as they do."

Dubayeff admitted the force of the argument. The entrance of their keepers at this point put an end to the dialogue.

There was nothing in the letter from Ivan to indicate that Pushkin's whereabouts was known to his wife and daughter, and he was left in doubt as to whether they had received the two or three letters he had sent to them by the "Underground Mail." In these missives, which were very brief, he had purposely avoided giving any account of his sufferings, as he did not wish to cause them more mental pain than was absolutely necessary; he simply said that he was at the Kara prison, and had a warm friend in Dubayeff. In fact, he said more about his companions in misery, than of himself and what he was obliged to undergo.

But this forbearance on his part, though it may have served to deceive Nadia, was no deception to Madame Pushkin. She knew from its general repute what the Kara prison was; never did she hear it mentioned without a shudder, and day after day, and night after night, she thought of what her husband was suffering and enduring in that far away region beyond Lake Baikal. She knew that he had gone to Siberia in chains, knew that he had dragged his weary limbs for thousands of versts over dreary wastes, through mud and frost and snow, and knew also that he was an inmate of the prison whose name has been for more than a century a terror throughout the length and breadth of Russia.

She had thought and wept and prayed and lamented through all that weary time. Well was it that she was a woman of great strength of character, and had the consolation and support of her daughter's presence, or she might have yielded to despair and welcomed death as a relief from her sorrow. Hope and faith were hers, and in her darkest hours she was sustained by the belief that all would yet be well. Every cloud, despite its blackness, had a silver lining; every night, however gloomy, was followed by the sunrise and the glorious light of day.

From time to time she instructed Mr. Kosavitch, the lawyer at Tambov, to send money through the hands of the officials to the mines of Kara, where it was to be expended in the purchase of such comforts for Pushkin as the rules of the prison would permit him to have. Of these remittances not one in five was ever heard of afterwards; we have elsewhere seen how the prison officials and attendants rob the unfortunates under their care, and their conduct towards Pushkin was no exception to the rule. She devoted much of her time to the care of the estate, and in the hope of keeping it in good condition against the time of her husband's return, she found a partial solace of her grief.

Nadia's affection was most tender and devoted; the love that she bore for father, mother and brother, seemed to be concentrated on the only one of the three that remained at home. But this must not be understood as saying that the others were forgotten, or were less in her thoughts than ever before. Morning and night her prayers rose for them both and she shared her mother's hope that they would some day be again under the roof where they had passed so many happy hours. Night and day her thoughts were concentrated upon measures for their release and return, and it is needless to say they always included the father of the young man to whom her hand and heart were pledged.

She was in frequent correspondence with Alexei Hartmann, but owing to the possibility of their letters being examined, the missives of both were of a more formal character than is usually the case with notes that pass between young lovers. There were vows of eternal fidelity, and many tender words ; now and then there were allusions to the unfortunates beyond the Ural Mountains, and ardent hopes in their behalf, but never was there any reference to the real object of Alexei's mission to the capital of the empire, and the progress, or the lack of it, that he was making towards the desired end.

Whatever information she received on this subject was obtained from Mr. Kosavitch, who occasionally visited them to consult Madame Pushkin concerning business matters connected with the estate, and to consider any possible means of benefitting the exiled father and son. Nadia repeatedly sought an interview with him apart from her mother, but it was a long time before a favorable opportunity occurred.

One day, when the lawyer came, Madame Pushkin was away at the house of a neighbor. Nadia received him with her accustomed grace of manner, and after a few polite preliminaries she came at once to the subject that was nearest her heart.

"Do you think, Mr. Kosavitch, that I could go to Siberia?" she suddenly asked.

"What!" he exclaimed. "You go to Siberia? Impossible, unless the government sends you there. Absolutely impossible."

"But couldn't I go and comfort dear father. He needs some one to comfort him, I'm sure he does."

"Yes, my dear child, that is quite true; but your mother needs your comfort and care. You do not know how dear you are to her, and how lonely she would be without you."

"Wouldn't the knowledge that I had gone to be at father's side console her for my absence?"

"Perhaps it might, but it could not fill your place. And think of what a terrible journey it would be for a young girl to go to the mines of Kara, alone and unprotected."

"I have thought of that," Nadia answered, "and know it would be a great hardship. But I feel that I could accomplish it, and perhaps I could find some one who was going there on just such a mission as mine. That's one thing I wanted to ask you about; do you know of any woman who is going to Kara to join her husband, son or daughter, there?"

"No, I do not," replied the lawyer. "Let me urge you to drop all idea of going to Siberia, not only for the reasons I have given you, but because you can be of more real service to your father by remaining at home."

"How can that be?" she asked.

"In the first place, you will be a comfort to your mother, and what comforts her will be a service to him. I feel confident that in some way you will have an opportunity to unravel the mystery that surrounds your father, and bring him back to you once again; his return will bring Ivan and Mr. Hartmann home, too, as they were sent into exile for no faults of their own, but on your father's account. I have been working in every way I could to bring light out of darkness; thus far I have not made much progress, but I shall leave no opportunity unimproved, and hope steadily that I shall be able to bring you good news."

Then he told the girl that he was on better terms with the governor of Tambov than formerly, and expected through him to ascertain the charges against Carl Pushkin, which up to that time had been steadily refused. The governor had promised to ask that they be sent from St. Petersburg, as they had not been supplied to him; he had only acted upon orders, at least, so he said, and did not know upon what the orders were based.

While he was talking on this subject, Madame Pushkin returned from her neighborly visit, and the business for which the lawyer had come was speedily concluded. It related entirely to affairs of the estate, and when it was concluded, the conversation naturally turned upon the subject in which all were so much interested—that of the exile of Carl Pushkin and his son.

Nadia rose to leave, but her mother told the girl to remain. The latter resumed her seat, and then, with some hesitation, related what she had been saying to Mr. Kosavitch.

"I didn't intend to deceive you in any way, dearest mother," she said, "but I have been thinking of this for some time, and wished to have the views of our good friend, Mr. Kosavitch, on the subject, before I mentioned it to you. Now I have talked with him, and am keeping my little secret no longer."

She turned to the lawyer, who repeated what he had said when Nadia mentioned her plan of going to Siberia. The mother listened in a sort of dazed way, as if she could hardly believe what she was hearing, and while she listened, Nadia moved to her side, and threw her arm lovingly around her neck.

"You are a good, noble, dutiful girl," said the mother, kissing her child as she clasped her to her heart. "You were ready to brave everything for love of your father, and in the hope of bringing him back to us. But Mr. Kosavitch is right; you had best remain here at home, to comfort and help me, and take whatever opportunity offers of restoring your father to his home. I could not bear to have you go ; I should be lonely. Oh ! so lonely, and the thought that you were in peril, through all that long journey, would drive me wild. I have need of all my strength, and of all that you can give, to help me bear up to the end. Do not think of going away from me ; drop all thought of it, and I'm sure that when your father hears of it, he will approve most heartily the advice of our good friend."

"I shall do as you say, dear mother, and I should have done nothing without your approval."

"I understand, my child. I have known that something was in your thoughts, and felt sure you had an idea of a noble and heroic action in your father's behalf. I did not imagine that you contemplated going to Siberia, but thought you would some day propose to go to St. Petersburg and intercede with the emperor or the empress for your father's pardon. I have seen you reading the story of ' Elisabeth,' and supposed you contemplated following her example."

Madame Cottin's charming romance, which has been translated into many languages, is well known in Russia, as it is one of the books permitted by the censorship. Many editions have been published in Russian, some of them liberally illustrated by the best artists of the country. It is no wonder that Nadia turned to the book in order to learn something of the life of exiles in Siberia, and it was but natural that the mother should suspect her daughter of a desire to act like the heroine of the story, and seek an opportunity to plead her father's cause before the emperor in person.

Mr. Kosavitch soon took his leave. His words made a deep impression upon Nadia, and especially the suggestion that she might find the occasion to unravel the mystery that surrounded her father and ensure his return to his home.

That night she lay awake for a long time, thinking of a thousand ways in which she might act. Every plan that she thought of was found impracticable when she carefully considered it, but she determined to present to her mother those schemes that were the least unfavorable and submit them to her mature judgment.

The mother listened eagerly to the plans which Nadia had formed, but one after another she showed the impossibility of their success. The girl was somewhat disappointed, but she concealed her feelings, and set about her daily duties as usual. Before the day was over she received a letter from Alexei, which she eagerly read, and then carried to her mother.

The letter contained something that was destined to be of great importance in accomplishing their cherished purpose. Nadia's opportunity to be of service to her father was close at hand, and, like many other opportunities in this world, it was a matter of accident.

CHAPTER XXXIV.

AN INFLUENTIAL FRIEND.

Alexei's letter was principally devoted to the account of an excursion down the Neva to Cronstadt on the occasion of a naval review. He had accompanied a friend on a steamboat, which was crowded with passengers, after the customary manner of excursion steamers the world over.

Everything went well until the return to St. Petersburg. A mile or more below the city something went wrong with the machinery, and the boat was driven against the bank with a shock that made the timbers creak. There was a temporary panic among the passengers and, in the rush that ensued, several persons were pushed or thrown overbroad; men shouted and women screamed, contradictory orders were given, and in the general excitement there seemed to be danger that those who had fallen into the river would be drowned for lack of aid.

Among them were two women, one a middle-aged personage and the other a young woman of not more than eighteen or twenty years. Alexei had previously observed her as she chatted gaily with her companions, a woman somewhat older than herself and an old gentleman and lady, whom he took for her grandparents, as in fact they proved to be.

As the boat struck the bank the young woman was leaning carelessly on the rail of the upper deck, and the suddenness of the shock, combined with her slight hold, caused her to fall overboard. Alexei was standing near her at the time of the occurrence; he was a good swimmer, so good in fact that he had won several prizes at the competitions in the swimming-school, and when he saw the bright young woman fall overboard, he felt that here was an opportunity to put his ability in swimming to practical use.

Throwing off his coat he sprang into the water and dived where she had disappeared. Clutching her clothing he brought her to the surface, and very quickly, too; she had swallowed some water, but not much, and in a few moments he had her close to the steamer's side, whence a rope was lowered by a few of the passengers who had not joined in the general panic. The young man passed the rope beneath the woman's arms and she was quickly hoisted to the lower deck. By the time she reached it, her friends had descended, and they hurried her into a cabin, where she fell into a complete faint, from which she was restored with no great difficulty.

Alexei was helped to the deck of the steamer; a boat was lowered to look after the other involuntary bathers, and it was assisted by a steam-launch that happened in the vicinity. The other woman who fell overboard was one of the first that the steam-launch rescued, and there was no occasion for Alexei to jump into the water again.

The young man resumed his coat, his only dry garment, and was the centre of a group that testified its admiration of his courage and his ability as a swim-

mer, in no stinted terms. In a little while the old gentleman rushed out of the cabin, and as he neared the group he exclaimed :

"Where's the man that saved my grand-daughter?"

"Here he is," half a dozen voices responded at once. As the propounder of the question came nearer the crowd opened and made way for him, so that he had no difficulty in reaching the object of his search. The water that dripped from Alexei's garments showed very plainly that he was the rescuer.

"I can't thank you enough," said the old gentleman, taking the youth by both hands. "Had it not been for you the poor girl might have drowned. Did you know who she was?"

"Not at all," replied Alexei. "I only saw it was a woman that had fallen overboard, and her life was in danger. I acted upon the impulse that every good swimmer should have, and does have, under such circumstances, and you know the rest."

"You perilled your own life," said the other, "as you might have been dragged under by some of those in the water, or even by the woman you saved. Many a good swimmer would not have been as ready to jump overboard for a total stranger as you were. And so you don't know who it was you saved," he continued, in a paternal air. "What is your name?"

"Alexei Hartmann."

"Where do you live?"

"Number — Alexandroffski Ulitza. That is where my rooms are in St. Petersburg, but my home is in Province Tambov."

"Ah! Alexei Hartmann, of Province Tambov," said the old gentleman, as though talking to himself and fixing the name in his memory. Then, turning to Alexei, he said :

"I am General Kolaskoff, retired from active service, but not out of use altogether. Here is my card. An old general may be of service, perhaps, to a young man like you; if he can't do anything more he can give him advice. Come and see me to-morrow, and meanwhile, think if I can repay you in any way for the great service you have done to me. That girl you saved is my grand-daughter, and she's a precious darling if ever there was one. I want to see you at my house, and she'll want to tell you how much she appreciates your action."

Alexei took the card and thanked the donor, who went away to see how his grand-daughter was getting along. The disability to the steamer was such that she was unable to proceed, and the passengers were transferred to other boats that were returning from the excursion and had room for a few extras. Alexei managed to get on the first boat that stopped, and in a little while he was at home and had exchanged his wet garments for dry ones.

He slept late, and before he was dressed on the following morning there was a rap at the door of his room. The caller proved to be a tailor, who said he had come to take the gentleman's measure for a suit of clothes.

"But I haven't ordered any clothes," said Alexei; "it must be some other tenant in the building. You've made a mistake."

"Your High Nobility's pardon," said the tailor, bowing. "I came to measure Alexei Hartmann, of Province Tambov, now living here in this house."

"I am Alexei Hartmann, of Province Tambov, but

I've not ordered a tailor to come here and, moreover, I'm not a High Nobility."

"I am the tailor of General Kolaskoff," said the other, as he drew himself up proudly, "and the general sent me to measure you for a suit of clothes to replace the one ruined by the river yesterday. I am to take away the old suit and carry it to the general, who wants to keep it as a souvenir."

The young man's impulse was to close the door in the tailor's face, but a moment's reflection taught him that he would act unwisely by so doing. He had determined to apply to the general for aid in the matter that brought him to the capital; evidently, the veteran had his own way of doing things, and it would be best to humor him even at the sacrifice of a little pride. Besides, the old fellow wanted the ruined clothes. What he would do with them it was difficult to guess, as a set of masculine garments is not a picturesque article to frame and hang in one's parlor, and altogether too large to be set as a brooch or a watch-charm. His demand for them was a "saving clause," and so Alexei admitted the tailor and told him to go on with his measurement.

The tailor wished to make something in the highest style of his art, and hinted that here was an opportunity for the youth to be the owner of the most gorgeous raiment known to the great city. But he was disappointed, when, in spite of repeated urging and the assurance that the general was rich beyond computation, Alexei ordered a suit of clothing of no better quality than the one in which he rescued the maiden from the engulfing river.

Verily Alexei builded wiser than he knew. General

Kolaskoff had instructed the tailor to urge a liberal draft on his purse, and to take any orders the young man chose to give. He was also to go straight from Alexei to the general and report the result of his interview; when the latter heard the story, he smiled satisfactorily, and said to himself:

"That's an honest young fellow, and if I can help him in any way, I will."

At the proper hour for making his call, Alexei was at the door of the general's house, and promptly admitted. He was cordially received by the general, who presented him to the ladies of the family, and to others who were in the parlors at the time he arrived. The young woman for whom he had leaped into the water was not in the parlors, but she was sent for and soon appeared. She added her thanks to those of the old gentleman, and had evidently made up a pretty speech, which she delivered with the ease for which Russian ladies are famed. She said she was not fully recovered from the effects of her sudden immersion, but hoped to be so in a day or two. They chatted for a few minutes, and then her attention was drawn towards several visitors, who had heard of her mishap, and came to congratulate her on her escape from drowning.

Then the general turned to Alexei and asked him to step into his 'bureau,' which was on the side of the hall opposite the parlors. Alexei followed, and when they were seated, the old officer came to the point at once.

"You are a young man here in St. Petersburg, but not a resident. Are you here for any purpose in which I can be of assistance? I like you; I want to show that I appreciate what you did yesterday, and you may talk with me just as freely as with your own father."

At the last words, 'your own father,' the color came into Alexei's face, and then quickly faded out. The sharp eye of the general observed the change ; he smiled and nodded as an encouragement to the youth to proceed.

"Thank you, very much indeed," replied Alexei. "I will be frank with you, frank as with my own father, and it concerns him that I am in St. Petersburg."

Then he told the story of which we already know, of the arrest and exile to Kara of Carl Pushkin, the arrest of Hartmann and Ivan Pushkin, and the subsequent banishment as sylni, the arrest, imprisonment and subsequent release of mother and daughter, told how he was engaged to Nadia, and that he had come to St. Petersburg in the hope that he might ascertain in some way the cause of the calamities that had fallen upon the houses of Pushkin and Hartmann. That none of the banished persons had done aught to justify their fate he was as certain as of his own existence ; he had tried to obtain employment in the office of the Minister of the Interior, so that he might ascertain in the proper way the nature of the charges under which they had been arrested and exiled. Thus far he had not succeeded, though he had partial promise of admission to a vacancy before a great while.

"I can help you in this matter," said the general, grasping Alexei's hand. "But don't be too sure of the future, as it may reveal something more than you expect."

"Whatever it reveals I will accept without complaint," was the reply. "I am as sure as I am that we are here, that there has been a great mistake somewhere, and that it will be shown by the records to whoever can reach them."

"I can and will reach them," said the general, as he rose and thereby intimated that the interview was ended. "Come to-morrow, an hour later than to-day."

Alexei went away feeling lighter at heart than for months. The object for which he had come to the capital was about to be realized. Until late at night he wrote in his room, sending letters to his mother, to Nadia, and to the lawyer at Tambov.

He was in his room on the following morning when a servant came from General Kolaskoff, bearing a large parcel packed for shipment by railway. With the parcel was a note, which said that Mademoiselle —— had learned from her grandfather that Mr. Hartmann was engaged to Miss Nadia Pushkin, of Province Tambov. Mademoiselle had asked and obtained her grandfather's and her mother's assent to send the accompanying dressing-case to Mr. Hartmann, with the request that he send it to his betrothed, with the expression of Mademoiselle ——'s wish that it would be accepted as a token of the gratitude of one who felt that she owed her life to Mr. Hartmann's courage and ability.

Such a delicate offer could not possibly be declined. Alexei despatched the box immediately, without opening it to look at is contents, and wrote to Nadia concerning it. He inclosed in his letter the note that came to him with the box, as the best possible explanation he could give of the circumstance, and then went out to call on some friends, before getting ready for his visit to the general. And the first of these was Mr. Lodoff, whom the reader will remember as the wealthy contractor, to whom Alexei brought a letter of introduction.

Alexei told him all that had occurred. When his story was ended, Mr. Lodoff said :

"I congratulate you most heartily on the new friend you have made. General Kolaskoff is a man of great influence with the Interior Department, and can obtain anything within reason that he asks for. When you see him, refer to me, as I know him very well. Stop, I will write a letter which you can hand him, and that will be better than any verbal message."

Mr. Lodoff wrote a warm letter, commending the young man as honorable and truthful in every way, and he added, that it was his firm belief that none of the three exiles, on whose behalf he was acting, had ever done anything to merit the treatment they had received. He judged from his general knowledge of their character, that they were not at all likely to indulge in any revolutionary measures, or take any action unfriendly to the government.

When Alexei delivered the letter, the general read it carefully and then tore it into many fragments before consigning it to his waste-basket. He gave a nod of approval and remarked that he was glad his favorable opinion of his new acquaintance was so heartily confirmed by an old one.

Then he came to the subject of the exiles. "I find there is nothing against your father and young Pushkin," said he, "except that your father is an intimate friend of Carl Pushkin and Ivan is his son. Those were the reasons for the arrest and banishment."

"But is there anything wrong about Ivan's father?" Alexei asked.

"I am sorry to say there is," replied the general in a kindly tone. "He seems to have been a troublesome revolutionist; he was concerned in plots against the life of His Majesty the Emperor, he was an active member of the terrorist party, and the murder of

Colonel Metsovitch was traced to him. He did not fire the shot, but he supplied the weapon with which the colonel was killed, and he assisted the murderer to escape. That is the record against him."

"Impossible!" exclaimed the young man, "I'm sure there is a great mistake somewhere."

"It does honor to your friendship for the father of the girl to whom you are engaged that you believe so, but I am afraid there is no mistake. The record against him is very clear."

Alexei's face fell and tears welled from his eyes.

The general assumed not to see the tears, but calmly continued:

"It will take a day or two for the formalities, and I cannot say exactly when the papers will be ready. The department is making further inquiries about your father and young Pushkin, and if nothing is found against them, beyond what I have told you, orders will be issued for their release."

"Thank you, thank you, a thousand times," said Alexei, his voice choking with emotion as he grasped the old gentleman's hand. After a pause, he asked:

"And can you cause further inquiries to be made about Carl Pushkin, and what he has done? Oh! I beg and implore that you will."

"Yes, I certainly will do so. Come here day after to-morrow, unless I send for you sooner. Come at the same time as to-day. But don't expect favorable news, as the case against Carl Pushkin is certainly very bad."

Alexei rose to go. He was near the door, when he suddenly recalled a part of his mission, and turned back.

"Please present to your grand-daughter my thanks for her kind remembrance of my *fiancée*, from whom she will certainly hear as soon as her handsome present reaches Tambov and the time has elapsed for a reply. The box and the letter that came with it are already on their way."

The general smiled, and said he would do as requested, and then the visitor departed.

Let us follow the box, and see what came of it.

CHAPTER XXXV.

THE MYSTERY REVEALED.

Alexei's letter arrived several hours in advance of the box ; the excitement in Nadia's mind over the contents of the former was at fever-heat when the latter was brought to the house.

No time was lost in opening it. As the cover was torn off and the wrappings were removed, a dressing-case of polished rosewood was brought to light The contents of the case were such as would delight a princess, how much more then were they pleasing to the eye of a Russian maiden who had never lived the life of a princess, or aspired to anything of the kind The entire household was assembled to look at the wonderful gift that had come from the capital city, and the air resounded with expressions of astonishment and admiration.

Lying inside the case was a note in the handwriting of the donor, asking the recipient to accept the token of friendship from a stranger, and receive the stranger's congratulations at her possession of the love of a young man who had shown himself a hero. Nadia laughed, and danced, and cried with delight, as she read the note, and wondered what she would say in reply.

The box containing the dressing-case was about to be sent to the receptacle for rubbish, the papers that had been wrapped around the case and stuffed into the box to wedge everything tightly, were gathered up and heaped together, and already a servant had taken the bundle in his arms to remove it, when Nadia espied several newspapers along with the brown paper. Newspapers did not come often to the house, and as these might prove interesting, she ordered them saved. They were carefully taken out and placed on the table where the dressing-case stood.

It was several hours before Nadia could leave her new treasure long enough to look at the newspapers. When she did so, she found some copies of the leading journals of St. Petersburg of a recent date, and half a dozen French and Swiss publications. She had never seen a newspaper from Switzerland, and her girlish curiosity was at once drawn to the *Journal de Genève*.

She glanced over its columns carelessly, reading a few lines here and there, paying more attention to the advertisements than to anything else, and was about to lay the paper aside for another, when her eye caught an item of local news, which she read intently. She rubbed her eyes and read again, and then sprang from her chair and ran to her mother's room.

"Oh! mother," she almost screamed, as she dashed through the door. "See what I have found in the *Journal de Genève*."

Then she read the following, which she rendered into Russian from the French in which the newspaper was printed:

"The man who was drowned in the boating accident near Hermance two days ago will be buried to-day, this afternoon, at three o'clock, from the Russian chapel in the Rue Sturm. His body was recovered last evening. He was a native of Rostov, where he was identified with the revolutionary party, with which he is said to have been very active. He fled from Russia two years ago to escape arrest upon charges which would have exiled him to Siberia for life. He has lived here very quietly under the assumed name of Feodor Domorski, and his identity was known to but few persons, even among his compatriots. His real name was Carl Pushkin."

"What do you think of that, mother?" said Nadia as she drew breath after reading the paragraph and sank into a chair.

The mother was so excited that for a minute or more she was unable to speak. When her words came, she said:

"Heaven has heard our prayers at last, let us hope. The Carl Pushkin who was drowned at Hermance may be the one for whom your dear father is now in the mines of Kara."

Then she sprang to her feet and summoned a servant.

"Order the tarantass and horses ready to go at once to Tambov," she commanded. "Nadia, dress for a ride to the city; I shall go with you, and we will have Joseph on the box with the driver. Take the paper with you, and be careful not to lose it. Your father's return to us may depend upon it."

The mother's precautionary advice concerning the paper was entirely unnecessary. Nadia would have preserved the paper as carefully as though it represented the wealth of a principality or the ransom of a king, yes, it was to her the ransom of a king, for what king could be more precious to her than the father she loved?

By the time the women were dressed for their journey the horses with the tarantass stood at the door. Joseph saw that his charges were properly bestowed in their respective corners of the vehicle, and then he sprang upon the box at the side of the driver and gave the order to start.

Away went the steeds. Joseph knew that speed was an object; he had caused a troika (three horses abreast), to be harnessed, and they were the best horses in the stables. Off they went at their best speed, but in spite of their rapidity Joseph repeatedly shouted '*Poshol* (Faster)' to the driver, whose arm obtained active exercise through free use of the whip.

As they neared Tambov, Joseph turned to the occupants of the tarantass and asked where they wished to go.

"Domu Kosavitch," was the reply. And so they went straight to the house of the lawyer, who has figured so prominently in the case. As the panting and sweating horses were brought to a halt, Joseph rapped at the door and asked for that gentleman.

Fortunately the lawyer was at home. It was his usual evening for going to the club, but something had detained him, and now he was very glad of the detention.

The ladies descended from the carriage and entered the house. The horses were sent to a stable and the men were to find lodgings wherever it suited them. It was the intention of the ladies to spend the night at the hotel, but the Kosavitch family would listen to nothing of the sort.

"We'll talk of that later," said Madame Pushkin; "here's something more important than whether we sleep here or at the hotel."

Then she briefly told about the present for Nadia, from the young woman whom Alexei had rescued, the finding of the newspaper, and the important paragraph it contained. Nadia unfolded the paper and read the translation as it has already been given.

"That is certainly very important," said the lawyer. "It was a fortunate thing that the box was packed in the general's house, and not at the shop where the dressing-case was bought."

"Why so?"

"Because the paper would have been mutilated if it had been addressed to a shopkeeper; the censor would have obliterated a paragraph referring to a revolutionist, lest it might give information to his friends, or for some other reason best known to himself. But papers may go to a high official, like General Kolaskoff, without being opened, and so I say it was very fortunate."

Then he looked at the clock in the room, and asked his wife to bring him the time-table of the railway. She brought it at once, and he was immediately absorbed in studying it.

It was quickly arranged that he would take the night train for Moscow and St. Petersburg, and in the morning his wife would send a telegram to Alexei, telling him to meet Mr. Kosavitch at the station on his arrival. The lawyer pinned the precious newspaper in his most inner pocket, along with some other documents which he took from his desk. His travelling bag was hastily packed, and then he jumped into a droshky that had been called to the door, and was whirled away to the station just in time to catch the train.

From Moscow he telegraphed to Lodoff to meet him at the station in St. Petersburg. That gentleman was promptly on hand, nearly half an hour before the train was due. He was somewhat surprised to find Alexei impatiently walking the platform, but the mystery was partially explained when Alexei showed the telegram he had received.

"It has something to do with the business between you and the general," said Mr. Lodoff. "He did not have time to receive your last letter, and I can't imagine what has brought him. Perhaps there have been some important discoveries at Tambov, that we know nothing about."

His surmise was certainly correct, as we have reason to know.

It was about eight o'clock in the morning when the train from Moscow rolled into the great station at St. Petersburg and Mr. Kosavitch alighted. The three men immediately entered Mr. Lodoff's carriage and were driven to that gentleman's house, where a substantial breakfast awaited them. On the way from the station the lawyer told about the finding of the newspaper, and what it contained, and before they reached the house it was arranged that Alexei should send a note to General Kolaskoff soliciting the favor of an early interview on a matter of great importance, and permission to bring with him the two gentlemen whom he named.

The note was sent, and in due time the messenger returned with a letter from the general. It bore a large seal and the crest of that dignitary. Alexei's hand trembled as he opened the portentous document, and he was greatly relieved to find that his request had been granted. The general's missive had all the brevity of a telegram. It read as follows :

"Certainly—come at 11.30 and bring your friends.
KOLASKOFF."

Promptly, at the time named, they were at the general's door and were taken at once to his office, where the veteran received them cordially. The story was briefly told, the paper was produced, and as the general looked at it, he remarked that he had a faint recollection of seeing the paragraph, but very naturally he did not regard it as of any consequence at the time. His only regret was that all the Russian refugees in Geneva had not been with the victim of that boating accident and shared his fate.

"Leave this paper with me," said he, "and go yourself to Mr. Lodoff's house and wait there till I send for you. I may not send for you to-day, and yet I may do so. If you don't hear from me by to morrow at eleven, come here without waiting any longer."

They thanked him and made their adieux. As they were leaving the house, they heard him give an order to his secretary to call his carriage at once.

While they are waiting, we will follow him and see what he does.

He went straight to the office of the Minister of the Interior and asked for the papers in the case of Carl Pushkin. Then he telegraphed to the Russian consul at Geneva, and to the governor of Rostov, asking for information about the individual in question, and requesting a reply by telegraph at the earliest possible moment. The governor replied in the course of the day, but the consul's telegram did not come until the following morning, about ten o'clock. Immediately on receiving it, the general ordered his carriage and went again to the ministry, leaving word for the three gentlemen who called the day before to wait for him in case he had not returned when they arrived.

They waited nearly an hour, as the general did not return until a few minutes before noon. He came in with his face all aglow, as though he had been undergoing violent exercise, and with a smile playing all over his features. He shook hands with his visitors cordially, and motioning them to be seated, dropped into a chair at his desk.

"I have done the heaviest morning's work I've known for a long time," said he, "and it isn't over yet. I'm going again this afternoon for some documents that are being prepared, and when they are signed, I shall have the pleasure of handing them to you.

"But never mind the documents," he continued with scarcely a pause. "Everything is being pushed forward as rapidly as possible, and a telegram has gone to Kara from the Minister of the Interior, telling Carl Pushkin that he is a free man. Unless there has been some delay in the working of the lines, he knows it now. Telegrams have also gone ordering the release of your father," said he, turning to Alexei, "and of Ivan Pushkin, and they will be sent back to their homes at once."

Alexei tried to speak, but there was a lump in his throat that held back the words. The general saved him from embarrassment by continuing:

"Carl Pavloff, surnamed Pushkin, of Rostov, who was drowned near Geneva, was the man for whose misdeeds Carl Pavloff, surnamed Pushkin, of Tambov, was sent to Siberia. He disappeared after the assassination of Colonel Metsovitch, and no trace of him was found for some time; then it was learned that he was living near Tambov, and orders were sent for his arrest. You know the rest. I know what you are probably thinking, but don't say it ; we won't have any discussions on that subject. Let bygones be bygones."

They could have said a great deal about the injustice of sending a man into exile for life without trial, and without even allowing him or his family to know the charges against him. Mr. Kosavitch had a very emphatic speech on this subject ready in his mind, and doubtless he would have spoken had he not been forestalled by General Kolaskoff.

"Your friends will be allowed to return immediately," the general continued. "They will be supplied with money for their expenses, and will have *paderoshnias* (road-passes) of the highest class, so that they can travel at courier speed. And now, is there anything more that can be done in their behalf?"

There was a moment's pause, and then Mr. Kosavitch spoke.

" Carl Pavloff has mentioned a friend and companion, named Dubayeff, to whom he is greatly attached. May we ask for his release, so that he can accompany our friend on his way home?"

" Dubayeff, let me see," said the general, musingly. "Ah! yes, I think I remember the name. A troublesome subject, unless I'm mistaken."

Then he paused and thought while the others maintained a respectful silence. The room was as still as though it had been unoccupied.

" Well, yes, Dubayeff may be released and have a safe conduct to accompany Pushkin to Tambov, where he must report to the governor. In the meantime, his case shall be carefully examined ; he may receive a full pardon, he may be returned to Siberia, or he may be conducted to the frontier and forbidden to return to or remain in Russia. If he is returned to Siberia, he will be escorted by an officer and treated as a high-class misdemeanant until he reaches the place where his sentence is to be completed. All will depend upon the history of his case. Mind, I don't promise anything absolutely, but that's what I'll urge the minister to grant."

All the listeners saw the justice of this decision, and at once assented to it. They were profuse in their thanks, but the general insisted that he was still their debtor, as he would always be under great obligations to Alexei for his conduct at the steamboat accident.

In a few minutes they took their leave. Alexei telegraphed the state of affairs to the parties at and near Tambov most interested in them, and Mr. Kosavitch took the evening train for home. He was followed two days later by Alexei, who carried the pardons of the three exiles, which he had received from the old general's hands. The young man wondered how it was possible to grant a pardon to one who has done no wrong, but he prudently refrained from propounding this conundrum to his benefactor, lest he might give offense.

Thenceforward, there was great joy, mingled with feverish anxiety, in two households near Tambov. Hartmann reached Tomsk a few days in advance of Ivan, who had to be sent for at the Yakut village, where we last saw him. Anxious as he was to reach home, he decided to wait for Ivan, and did so; then the two of them waited for Pushkin and Dubayeff, so that all returned together. What a contrast was this journey to the one that took them to Siberia! Words fail to describe it, and we will not make the attempt.

Neither will we try to tell what occurred in the houses of Pushkin and Hartmann when the victims of Russian injustice reached their old homes. That the meeting was joyous, and the greetings most affectionate, it is needless to say.

Dubayeff reported to the governor of Tambov according to stipulation. The investigation of his case showed that he had been an active enemy of the government, and he frankly admitted that he had done all in his power against it. He was given the choice of returning to Siberia, expatriating himself from Russia, or taking the oath of allegiance to the Czar.

"How much time can I have for deciding?" Dubayeff asked.

"I will give you a week, yes, two weeks," was the reply, "and in the meantime, Pushkin and his counsel must be responsible for you."

"Thank you," said the prisoner, for such we must still consider him. "Pushkin has urged me to stay with him, and I'll go there for a fortnight. At the end of that time I'll report here and say what I have determined."

On the expiration of the allotted time, Dubayeff reported that he could not conscientiously take the oath of allegiance. Of the other alternatives he preferred, as would any sensible man, a residence in a foreign country, to exile at hard labor in Siberia. He was accordingly conducted to the frontier by two soldiers, and a few days later he appeared among the Russian refugees in Geneva, where he was at last accounts.

A few months later there was a wedding which united the houses of Hartmann and Pushkin. General Kolaskoff sent a present for the bride, and so did his granddaughter and Mr. Lodoff. Dubayeff did not forget the child of his former companion in sorrow, and from far away Geneva, he sent, in a registered letter, a pretty souvenir.

"But you haven't told us of the contents of the letter Pushkin received from his wife the day after he was arrested," some one remarks.

"Yes," says another, "nor about what Pushkin surmised to be the cause of all his trouble. Nor why the husband and wife had a previous understanding about letters in the seams of overcoats."

The contents of the letter, My Dear Readers, and the surmises which proved to be wrong, are family matters, about which it would be impertinent for me to inquire. And granting the existence of those family matters, it was but natural that husband and wife should have a way of communication agreed upon against emergencies. Emergencies may occur in any part of the world—especially in Russia.

THE END.

www.ingramcontent.com/pod-product-compliance
Lightning Source LLC
Chambersburg PA
CBHW020304240426
43673CB00039B/699